100 years

of European cinema

Entertainment or ideology?

EDITED BY

DIANA HOLMES & ALISON SMITH

Manchester University Press

MANCHESTER AND NEW YORK

distributed exclusively in the USA by St. Martin's Press

Published by Manchester University Press
Oxford Road, Manchester M13 9NR, UK
and Room 400, 175 Fifth Avenue, New York, NY 10010, USA
http://www.manchesteruniversitypress.co.uk

Distributed exclusively in the USA by
St. Martin's Press, Inc., 175 Fifth Avenue, New York, NY 10010, USA

Distributed exclusively in Canada by
UBC Press, University of British Columbia, 2029 West Mall,
Vancouver, BC, Canada V6T 1Z2

British Library Cataloguing-in-Publication Data
A catalogue record for this book is avalaible from the British Library

Library of Congress Cataloging-in-Publication Data applied for

ISBN 0 7190 5871 6 *hardback*
0 7190 5872 4 *paperback*

First published 2000

07   06   05   04   03   02   01   00   10 9 8 7 6 5 4 3 2 1

Typeset in Scala with Meta display
by Koinonia, Manchester
Printed in Great Britain
by Biddles Ltd, Guildford and King's Lynn

100 years of European cinema

MANCHESTER
UNIVERSITY PRESS

Contents

List of illustrations

1–3 are from Richard Taylor's private collection,
4 is copyright Icestorm International and 5 is courtesy of Peter Hames

List of tables

Notes on contributors

DANIELA BERGHAHN is Principal Lecturer in German Studies at Oxford Brookes University. She is the author of *Raumdarstellung im englischen Roman der Moderne* (1989) and co-author of *German Studies in Transition* (1997). She has published essays in the area of German cinema, in particular on the theory and practice of cinematic adaptations of literature, Wim Wenders, and East German cinema. She is presently working on a book of East German cinema and co-editing a book on *Unity and Diversity in the New Europe*.

STEVE CANNON is Senior Lecturer in French Studies at the University of Sunderland. Following a doctoral thesis on Jean-Luc Godard, he has published on Godard in special issues of *Nottingham French Studies* and *French Cultural Studies*. He has also published on hip-hop in France, and on its uses in film soundtracks. He is currently co-authoring a book on Godard for the Manchester University Press *French Film Directors* series.

JULIA DOBSON is Research Fellow in French at the University of Wolverhampton. She works primarily on contemporary French theatre and cinema and recent articles have appeared in *Theatre Research International* and *Forum for Modern Languages*. She is currently working on the cinema of Kieslowski.

PETER WILLIAM EVANS is Professor of Hispanic Studies at Queen Mary and Westfield College, University of London. He is the author of *The Films of Luis Buñuel: Subjectivity and Desire* (1995), and *Women on the Verge of a Nervous Breakdown* (1996), and has written widely on other aspects of Spanish cinema, as well as on Hollywood and British cinema.

WENDY EVERETT is Lecturer in French and Film at the University of Bath. She is the author of *European Identity in Cinema* (1996), and has published essays in *Screen*, *Europa* and the *Literature/Film Review*, as well as in several edited collections. She is currently a member of the editorial board of the *Literature/Film Review*.

DAVID GILLESPIE is Reader in Russian Studies at the University of Bath. He has published widely in the UK, Europe, USA and Russia on modern Russian literature and cinema, and is currently completing a book, *The Poetics of Russian Film*.

PETER HAMES is Honorary Research Associate and former Subject Leader in Film and Media Studies, Staffordshire University. He is author of *The Czechoslovak New Wave* (1985, 1999) and contributing editor of *Dark Alchemy: The Films of Jan Svankmajer* (1989). He has also contributed to *Post New Wave Cinema in the Soviet Union and Eastern Europe* (1989), *Five Filmmakers: Tarkovsky, Forman, Polanski, Szabo, Makavejev* (1994), *Encyclopaedia of European Cinema (1995)*, and the forthcoming *Cinema in Transition* and *Censorship: An International Encyclopaedia*.

DIANA HOLMES is Professor of French at the University of Leeds, and was previously Professor of French at Keele University, where the project that led to this volume began. She is co-editor of the Manchester University Press series *French Film Directors* and co-author of the volume on *François Truffaut* in that series. She has published extensively on French women writers, including the books *Colette* (1991) and *French Women's Writing 1848–1994* (1996), and is co-editor of the interdisciplinary journal *Modern and Contemporary France*.

PETER KRAMER is Lecturer in Film Studies at the University of East Anglia. His essays on Buster Keaton, early cinema and contemporary Hollywood have appeared in *Screen*, *Velvet Light Trap*, *Theatre History Studies*, the *Historical Journal of Film, Radio and Television* and *History Today*, as well as numerous edited collections, including the *Oxford Guide to Film Studies*.

ELIANE MEYER is Senior Lecturer in French Studies at the University of Sunderland. Her main research interests focus on women and film, and she has published on feminism and popular film in the *Journal of Literature and Film*, Poitiers University Press. She is currently co-authoring a book on Godard for the Manchester University Press's *French Film Directors* series.

PARVATI NAIR is Lecturer in Hispanic Studies at Queen Mary and Westfield College, University of London. She is currently completing a doctorate in Spanish Cultural Studies and has several articles in press on Spanish cinema, music and photography.

ANDREA RINKE is Senior Lecturer in German at Kingston University and has researched widely in the field of cinema in the former GDR. Her recent publications include articles on the role of screen heroines in GDR cinema, on women in recent German cinema, and on Evelyn Schmidt's film *The Bicycle*.

ALISON SMITH is Lecturer in European Cinema at Liverpool University, and was formerly at Keele University. She has published several articles on French cinema in the 1970s, and her monograph on Agnès Varda for the Manchester University Press *French Film Directors* series appeared in 1998. She is currently working on the inter-relation between theatrical practice and cinema and specifically on Patrice Chereau.

ROSEMARY STOTT is a Senior Lecturer in German at London Guildhall University. She specialises in Film Studies and has carried out extensive research on cinema in the GDR, an interest she developed during study periods in the GDR during the 1980s.

RICHARD TAYLOR is Professor of Politics at the University of Wales Swansea. He edited the four-volume English-language edition of Eisenstein's *Selected Works* for the British Film Institute, and his two most recent books are *The Eisenstein Reader* and a revised edition of *Film Propaganda: Soviet Russia and Nazi Germany*. He has published widely on various aspects of Russian and Soviet cinema and edits the *KINO: Russian Cinema Series* for I. B. Tauris, London.

STEFAN WOLFF is Lecturer in German at Bath University. Research interests include contemporary German politics and society and the history of, and transformation process in, East Germany. Among his more recent publications are articles on elite transformation in eastern Germany between 1989 and 1991, on East German political identity, and on minorities and minority rights.

DIANA HOLMES & ALISON SMITH

Introduction

What is the cinema for? From the earliest days of the medium, this question has lain behind the production of film. Several potential answers have been offered, and the aim of this book is to explore in particular the often stormy relationship between two of them, the two which have been both the most important and the most controversial functions of film since its invention. On the one hand, there is the prime aim of cinema: to attract and hold an audience, and to give that audience pleasure for the duration of the film. On the other, there is the undoubted ability, and some would say the inevitable fate, of cinema to carry, and to communicate to large numbers of people, a set of values and priorities, a certain way of imagining society. Such concepts of cultural relations, which underlie a social system and, according to the Althusserian Marxists who brought the issue to the fore in the 1970s, thus help to sustain it, may be referred to as the field of ideology.

Born as a medium of entertainment, the moving pictures were from the first immensely successful in this field – and at their very outset probably envisioned no other, except perhaps the specialist function of scientific investigation. They outclassed all previous optical curiosities: not only could they recreate recognisable life, but they could inspire the thrill of fear, provoke laughter, bring to a wondering audience impossible sights which seemed to make magic into reality (such was the speciality of the conjuror Méliès, one of the first European directors), and finally tell simple stories where the audience was kept guessing as to the next turn of dramatic events. For the pioneers, the pictures became a licence to print money. They were ever-new, they were relatively cheap, and the audiences kept coming.

As they came, so the potential of the new medium to achieve other goals began to be obvious. Should the cinema, perhaps, be used to educate the masses by exposing them to 'high' culture (and if so, what constituted high culture)? Should formal experiment take priority and the cinema become a new art-form? And should – or rather, could – this superbly efficient means of communication be used to spread the values, goals and ways of reading the world which were officially considered desirable? Clearly, it could, and soon it was. Political leaders anxious to change societies by changing mentalities leapt on the cinema as a means of support.

Lenin considered the cinema as the most important of all the arts, and (as Daniela Berghahn describes in chapter 3 of this volume) in 1919 the new Soviet government sent film-trains around the country to inculcate the virtues of public hygiene and Communist society. If some films were straightforwardly educational, the majority took care to attract and hold their audience using the cinema's power to thrill, to jerk tears, or to exploit pure broad humour. The Soviet cinema, incidentally, also exploited audiences' potential pleasure in seeing themselves on screen, with experiments in local production as well as exhibition. In Hitler's Germany Goebbels, equally aware of the penetrative power of cinema, sponsored many films which incorporated Nazi values in eye-catching historical epics and dramas heart-rending or breathtaking – humour being apparently the only inaccessible seam.

The experience of the 1920s and 1930s, as well as that of the war years, made it quite clear that propaganda could enter the cinema disguised as entertainment. As the hot war froze into the Cold, the question which gradually came to the fore in Europe – caught between the great powers and faced with the messy conflicts of decolonisation – was this: could cinema ever escape the condition of propaganda for *something*? To the extent that a film incorporated some sort of value-system, it would tend to assume in an audience to whom it gave pleasure a similar set of priorities. Therefore, could not the most avowedly apolitical of films be imbued with 'ideological' propaganda? If this was the case, then the idea of 'innocent' entertainment vanished – and as the theory gained ground, so the very concept of entertainment as a desirable goal became discredited. The commercial success of entertainment cinema continued to guarantee its survival, but politically aware critics and makers of films on both sides of the 'iron curtain' increasingly shared the view that a film which simply amused its audience was likely to confirm not only that audience's value-system, but probably its prejudices and narrow-mindedness as well. Simple amusement was inimical to thinking, and a society in need of change required a thinking population. To the neo-Marxist critics and film-makers of the 1960s and 1970s, who articulated this position with particular clarity, film's first duty was to encourage its audience to think and to question, and not to forget themselves in the spectacle.

The problem was that the majority of audiences were not attracted to picture-shows which appealed to their rational but not their emotional selves. Those who were interested in the issues saw the films; those who were not stayed away or rushed to whatever lighter relief was available. Clearly, ideology, however new and exciting, *without* the old mechanisms of entertainment was a recipe for disaster. The only way forward – as a substantial minority of European film-makers realised – was to make films which *did* set out to entertain, but remained aware of their responsibilities and of the social messages that they were inevitably sending out. This truth imposed itself upon socially conscious film-makers in both Western and Eastern Europe. It had a relevance to those responsible for state film industries, too, particularly in countries which still overtly used cinema to propagate official ideologies: as several chapters in part I suggest (Stott's chapter 2, Berghahn's chapter 3, Hames's chapter 5), puritanically ideological régimes had to contend with the large market which existed for light relief among the population, and with the risk that if they did not supply that market themselves, other sources – notably American – would.

It is from such an apparently balanced position that this book starts out. Clearly, this position requires constant questioning. In recent years the concept of ideology has fallen into critical disrepute to an extent similar to or even greater than that of entertainment in the 1970s. The idea of purposely inculcating values through the entertainment media has become such a bugbear that it sometimes seem virtually unmentionable – the issue has been perceived as outdated, the problems gone away. And yet it is hard to escape the lasting logic of the contention that films must incorporate cultural and social values, that value-systems will tend to be shared among a large number of films from the same or similar sources, and that the cinema draws large numbers of people who must react in some way or another to the values which the films which they enjoy assume them to have. The co-presence in the most watched cinema of mechanisms to spark in the audience the desire to watch, and to partake in, the film, and of elements of the cultural and social assumptions of its makers which are rarely brought explicitly to the audience's attention, is still a hot issue and one which the European cinema occasionally shows itself able and willing to address.

The chapters in this volume examine the relationship between these two elements, and the importance given to each, at different times and places in the 100-year history of European cinema. Collectively the chapters form a fascinating overview of the ways in which relations between state and public at large have at various times been mediated through cinema, in all parts of Europe. The mediation has not always been one of messages from the top – in several countries films have been presented, with greater or less justification, as articulating the citizen's response to the state and publicising criticism from the public. The extent to which such criticism may be accessible to a mass audience, and the question of whether it really represents a commonly held position, is central to the papers in the second section of part I. The chapters throughout the book have in common a concern with the way in which filmgoers have been and are implicated in the experience of film; throughout the controversies of the century the spectators had often been paradoxically taken for granted, their awareness of the processes acting on them underestimated. We hope not to fall into that trap.

The chapters are grouped in two parts. Part I, 'Ideologies and cinematic pleasure', addresses the relation between cinema and the highly codified ideologies of this century. This part considers films, or indeed whole national cinemas, which were conceived with their ideological function as paramount, and the chapters discuss the ways in which such cinema addressed the problems of holding its audience.

The first group of chapters in part I considers official, state ideologies and their relationship to the films which appeared, more or less under their auspices, as entertainment for the population.

Richard Taylor (chapter 1) analyses the ways in which musical comedy was used in the USSR under Stalinism to encourage a utopian vision of the new Soviet society, through classic tropes of the entertainment cinema such as romantic stories and memorable melodies. Rosemary Stott, Daniela Berghahn and Andrea Rinke (chapters 2, 3 and 4) all concentrate on the film industry of the German Democratic Republic, where the cultural policy was one of the most strictly ideological of all the Communist bloc. Stott shows that despite the rigid control, Western films were officially accepted to a surprising extent in the GDR, and were very popular. She advances as explanations a certain degree of ideological blindness on the part of the authorities – coupled with an apparent preference, if heresy is to be propagated, for it to come from abroad rather than be home-produced – together with the need to draw audiences to finance the national industry. Berghahn examines that national industry at a moment of particular crisis: the Eleventh Plenum of 1965, at which a period of relative openness to home-grown cinematic criticism was brought to an abrupt end, with devastating consequences for those involved in film production. Rinke concentrates on one very popular GDR 'entertainment' film of the early 1970s, and shows that despite the authorities' eventual acceptance of it it does in fact contain many subversive elements, some of which stem directly from its status as entertainment, appealing to the emotions rather than the intellect.

In Peter Hames's study of Czech film comedy (chapter 5), the issue of national identity comes to the fore as in some measure an alternative to a dominant ideology fostered outside Czechoslovakia. He argues that the figure of the 'little Czech' as an unspectacular, independent-minded anti-hero constituted a traditional antidote to any régime which took itself too seriously, and that this originally literary archetype takes on a new significance in the films of directors such as Jiří Menzel, which had considerable resonance outside Czechoslovakia.

Turning to Western Europe, Peter Evans and Parvati Nair (chapters 6 and 7) investigate the content of popular comedy in Franco's Spain. Both studies focus on films that represent the individual in a social and family context. Evans's centre of interest is a trilogy which largely reinforces the family values of the period; he shows how, despite its apparent conservatism, the development of the trilogy reflects the ideological tensions and changes in Spanish culture from 1962 to 1979, including the rapid erosion of Franco-era values after the dictator's death. Nair examines the work of a more oppositional director, Luis García Berlanga, and the ways in which his films reflect an ambivalent experience of masculinity that undercuts the patriarchal/heroic stereotype which the Falangist ideology favoured, privileging instead a pragmatic, fallible anti-hero in an easily recognisable environment. Such subversion by an appeal to the values of the 'common man' bears analogy to Hames's analysis.

In the second section of part I is grouped a number of analyses of films consciously questioning the ideological assumptions of liberal régimes. Steve Cannon and Eliane Meyer (chapters 8 and 9) offer readings of the work of the French director Jean-Luc Godard, one of the best-known exponents of critical analysis of liberal capitalism. Both Cannon and Meyer set out to question Godard's reputation as an effective subversive, Meyer through an investigation of his approach to femininity (often heralded as indubitably progressive on an arguably superficial basis), Cannon in an analysis of Godard's most overtly critical and least-viewed films, the 'underground' productions of the Dziga Vertov Group of the early 1970s. Stefan Wolff (chapter 10) examines the ways in which the cinema of the Federal Republic of Germany reacted to the phenomenon of terrorism in the 1970s, 1980s, and 1990s, and even more to the paranoia which often characterised the official response to the phenomenon. Although not claiming that the cinema offered a fully satisfactory alternative position, Wolff shows that directors were able through fiction to question the reaction of the authorities and to open the possibility of ambivalent responses.

Part II of this book, 'Entertainment and its ideologies', concentrates on the mechanisms and functions of entertainment under liberal capitalist régimes which openly prioritise it, and suggests some ways in which such entertainment may have social relevance either by reinforcing or by seeking to influence the dominant values of society.

David Gillespie (chapter 11) offers an analysis of how post-Soviet Russian cinema approaches the difficulties inherent in the breaking down of a highly structured society, and shows that the strategies it uses have a long tradition in Russia, appealing for example to concepts of masculinity and of Russian fellowship which were in use in nineteenth-century literature.

Diana Holmes and Alison Smith (chapters 12 and 13) both concentrate on the functions of entertainment in the French cinema with reference to directors more or less associated with the *Nouvelle Vague*. Holmes approaches the late films of François Truffaut, a director usually associated with uncontentious entertainment and a certain ideological conservatism, in order to show that, if not subversive, he is certainly far from reactionary, and that much of the pleasure to be derived from his films springs precisely from his tendency to self-criticism and to a broad-minded acceptance of many differing world-views. Smith's study of the films of Agnès Varda looks at the way in which this director represents entertainers and the process of entertainment in her films, and what can be deduced from this regarding her perception of the function of her own practice; the conclusion being that entertainment to be effective must have genuine roots in the lived experience and environment of both author and audience.

Wendy Everett (chapter 14) takes a broader, pan-European perspective. She considers the ways in which popular song has recently become a central vehicle of memory in films made in several European countries. Her analysis of this phenomenon shows the profound implications of this apparently most unpretentious of entertainment genres; the multiple layers of psychological response which are involved in our pleasure in consuming popular song and in the ways in which it can be related to the moving image are a powerful means for constructing a collective memory.

The last two chapters in this section examine the relationship between Europe and the USA. Starting from French cinema, Julia Dobson (chapter 15) examines the ideological implications of the transference of film-plots from France to the USA – the phenomenon of the Hollywood remake. She argues that, contrary to a frequent and rather hasty assumption, such transference implies not any drastic ideological realignment, but rather more subtle variations in the mechanisms through which essentially similar values are reproduced.

Finally, Peter Krämer (chapter 16) illustrates how a Hollywood film of the immediate post-war period, *Roman Holiday*, seeks direct implication in European affairs. The film is shown as 'European' by reason of its assumed market and even its personnel; more profoundly, it presents a complex and sophisticated Hollywood-mediated vision of Europe, designed to construct a European identity recognisable and acceptable to a pan(Western)-European audience. Thus the book closes with the complex and crucial question of the relationship between Hollywood and European film industries, and the relevance of this both for the nature of entertainment and for the ideological climate of the new Europe.

Ideologies and cinematic pleasure

RICHARD TAYLOR

But eastward, look, the land is brighter: towards a topography of utopia in the Stalinist musical

1

Why *not* Stalinist musicals?

A recent article was entitled: 'Why Stalinist musicals?' (Anderson 1995).[1] The manner in which the question was posed is itself significant and reflects the distorting lens through which both Western and 'Soviet' scholars have historically viewed Soviet cinema, even though Anderson's article did much to refocus that lens. We nowadays take for granted that audiences in Western countries look for escapist entertainment in times of collective stress. As the British director David Lean once remarked, 'Films are not real. They are dramatised reality,' and, 'A shop girl earning three pounds a week doesn't pay to see an exact replica of herself on the screen – she pays to see what she would *like* to be, in looks, dress and mode of living' (Lean 1947: 31, 29). For some years we have accepted that musicals were the most popular form of entertainment in the United States and much of Europe during the Great Depression, and even that during the Third Reich German audiences preferred to see musicals like *Wunschkonzert* (*Request Concert*, 1940) rather than the more obvious products of Nazi propaganda such as *Triumph des Willens* (*Triumph of the Will*, 1935) or *Der ewige Jude* (*The Eternal Jew*, 1940) (Taylor 1998). Why then should we not accept that, in the midst of the forced industrialisation and collectivisation programmes of the early Five-Year Plans, in the maelstrom of the massive economic and social dislocation that these caused, in the thick of the purges and the Great Patriotic War, the Soviet peoples might also have wanted something to alleviate their mass suffering and give them hope in a better future? So the question that I want to ask first of all is: why *not* Stalinist musicals?

The distorting lens through which Western and Soviet scholars have viewed the construct known as 'Soviet cinema' has been analysed by Ian Christie (Taylor and Christie 1988). There is a growing literature on Soviet popular culture, and especially on popular cinema, to which a number of scholars have contributed, most notably Denise Youngblood, Richard Stites and James von Geldern, to name only those writing in English. This literature emphasises the continuities in Russian cultural history between the pre- and post-Revolutionary periods on the one hand, and between the 1920s and the 1930s on the other, while acknowledging the very serious discontinuities and ruptures that have traditionally been the focus of research.

I have argued elsewhere that a crucial role in the establishment of a Soviet *mass* cinema was played by Boris Shumyatsky, who in October 1930 was charged with creating 'a cinema that is intelligible to the millions' (Taylor 1991). He argued that a 'cinema for the millions' required the establishment of new entertainment genres such as the musical comedy: 'Neither the Revolution nor the defence of the socialist fatherland is a tragedy for the proletariat. We have always gone, and in future we shall still go, into battle singing and laughing' (Shumyatsky 1935: 239–40).[2]

As James von Geldern has argued (von Geldern 1992: 62), 'In the mid-1930s, Soviet society struck a balance that would carry it through the turmoil of the purges, the Great War and reconstruction. The coercive policies of the Cultural Revolution were replaced or supplemented by the use of inducements.' The *exclusive* cultural policies of the first Five-Year Plan period (1928–32) were replaced by the inducements of *inclusive* cultural policies, following the dissolution of the self-styled *proletarian* cultural institutions in April 1932 and their replacement by all-embracing *Soviet* institutions like the new Union of Soviet Writers. The doctrine proclaimed by the latter was Socialist Realism, which Andrei Zhdanov, who was effectively Stalin's cultural commissar, claimed meant depicting reality 'not ... in a dead, scholastic way, not simply as "objective reality", but ... as reality in its revolutionary development' (Zhdanov 1934: 4). Anatoli Lunacharsky, in charge of Soviet cultural policy in the 1920s, tellingly remarked that 'The Socialist Realist ... does not accept reality as it really is. He accepts it as it will be ... A Communist who cannot dream is a bad Communist. The Communist dream is not a flight from the earthly but a flight into the future' (Lunacharsky 1933). In official terminology this element was called 'revolutionary romanticism'.

The credibility of revolutionary romanticism, the 'flight into the future', was enhanced by the audience's apparent complicity in the exercise. Political speeches, newspaper articles, poster campaigns, official statistics and above all what Lenin had called 'the most important of all the arts' (Lenin 1922) depicted life not as it actually was but as they hoped it was becoming. The media furnished what Sheila Fitzpatrick has memorably described as 'a preview of the coming attractions of socialism'

(Fitzpatrick 1994: 262). If the Great Terror of the 1930s was to become the stick with which to modernise the Soviet Union, entertainment cinema was to provide the carrot.

Entertainment and utopia

The musical was in many ways the perfect vehicle for the depiction and promulgation of the Socialist Realist utopia. This is especially true if we bear in mind Richard Dyer's argument that the central thrust of entertainment is utopianism and that, while 'Entertainment offers the image of "something better" to escape into, or something we want deeply that our day-to-day lives don't provide', it 'does not, however, present models of utopian worlds ... Rather the utopianism is contained in the feelings it embodies' (Dyer 1977: 3). In fact the Stalinist musical did both: it presented models of utopian worlds (in the case of the *kolkhoz* (collective-farm) musical the 'Potemkin village') while also embodying the utopian feelings that stimulated audience identification. The task of Soviet cinema in the 1930s and 1940s was to convince audiences that, whatever their current hardships, life *could* become as it was depicted on the screen: life not as it is, but as it will be. In this reel utopia, if not in everyday reality as then experienced by cinema audiences, the Stalinist slogan 'Life has become happier, comrades, life has become more joyous' was made real.

The reel realisation of utopia was achieved by both representational and non-representational signs. Dyer's observation that we pay more attention to the former at the expense of the latter is still largely true (Dyer 1977). The non-representational signification in the Stalinist musical lies primarily in three areas: the use of fairy-tale narrative conventions; the music itself; and the topographical conventions of the image of utopia, all of which weakened audience resistance to the reception of the utopian model depicted on screen. This chapter will focus on the work of the two leading directors of 'musical comedies' (the word *'miuzikl'* was officially regarded at the time as too bourgeois), Grigori Alexandrov (1903–84) and Ivan Pyriev (1901–68), while arguing that their films need to be seen in their historical and cultural context, so that the works of other film-makers will also be discussed where relevant. Alexandrov founded the Soviet musical comedy genre with *Veselye rebiata* (*The Happy Guys*, 1934) and went on to make *Tsirk* (*The Circus*, 1936), *Volga-Volga* (1938), and *Svetlyi put'* (*The Radiant Path*, 1940) in the same mould. Pyriev's first musical comedy was *Bogataia nevesta* (*The Rich Bride*, 1938), which established the model for the *kolkhoz* musical. This was followed by *Traktoristy* (*Tractor-Drivers*, 1939), *Svinarka i pastukh* (*The Swineherdess and the*

Shepherd, 1940) and *Kubanskie kazaki* (*The Kuban Cossacks,* 1949), the apotheosis of what Khrushchev was later to call the 'varnishing of reality' that characterised Soviet cinema's depiction of the Potemkin village of the Stalin period (Khrushchev 1956).

The path to utopia: the fairy tale

Maya Turovskaya has brilliantly analysed the way in which Pyriev in particular used the conventions of the Russian fairy tale to project his 'folklorised' (cf. Miller 1990) vision of the Potemkin village, and Masha Enzensberger has extended this analysis to Alexandrov's *Radiant Path* (Enzensberger 1993). The use of these conventions enabled the Soviet musicals to act, in Turovskaya's own words, 'not so much as the reflection of their time's objective reality, but rather as the reflection of the reality of its image of itself' (Turovskaya 1988: 132).

The plots of these films almost invariably centre on what the Russians call a 'love intrigue': but it is not 'tainted' by sexual or erotic impulses; rather it is a 'pure' romantic love based on its object's labour proficiency. In the conventions of the Soviet musical – as indeed of its Hollywood equivalent – it is clear from the beginning when 'boy meets girl'. But the resolution of this 'inevitable' liaison is retarded by a misunderstanding and/or by competition between two male 'suitors', one of whom is in terms of his own labour productivity 'worthy' of the heroine, one of whom is not. The plot develops around the heroine's journey towards an understanding of which is which. Sometimes, as in *Circus,* this is obvious from the beginning and the plot therefore revolves around the heroine's discovery of the true path – the Soviet path – towards that understanding. The exceptions to this rule are the last two films by each director listed above. In *Radiant Path,* based very closely on the Cinderella story, the heroine has to prove to *herself* that *she* is worthy of *her* suitor by successfully emancipating herself through a Party-sponsored training programme. In *Kuban Cossacks* the hero has no rival in love: his battle is with his own Cossack male chauvinist pride.

In almost all these films, and in all the *kolkhoz* musicals, the central character, who eventually resolves the difficulties, is a woman. There are no fundamentally weak or evil women characters in these films. The only evil characters are foreigners, such as the Hitler lookalike von Kneischitz in *Circus* (Mamatova 1995: 65), or those forces threatening the frontiers of the USSR in *Tractor-Drivers.* The weak Soviet characters are either marginalised (the bourgeois women in *Happy Guys,* or Kuzma and his associates in *Swineherdess*) or won over to the work ethic (Alexei the bookkeeper – a truly bourgeois because 'unproductive' profession – in *Rich Bride* and Nazar the idler in *Tractor-Drivers*). In utopia, weakness is therefore redeemable: evil is not, but it is externalised.

The main characters are depersonalised and universalised as in a fairy tale; they are symbolic figures, and the frequent use of choral singing helps this process of generalisation: in both *Rich Bride* and *Kuban Cossacks*, for instance, the 'battle of the sexes' is fought out in choral form. The Soviet version of the star system helped in this: all Alexandrov's films starred his wife Lyubov Orlova, the 'prima donna' of Stalinist cinema (Nikolaevich 1992), and all Pyriev's starred his wife Marina Ladynina. Their appearance in a series of films with similar plot structures but different settings in different parts of the Soviet Union and with different casts helped audiences all over the country to identify with them more directly on the one hand, while broadening the appeal of the films and their message on the other. It must also be said that neither Orlova nor Ladynina conformed to the traditional stereotype of 'femininity'. While Ladynina in the *kolkhoz* musicals sometimes appeared in folk costume, both she and Orlova also appeared in 'masculine' clothing (Ladynina in *Rich Bride* and *Tractor-Drivers*, Orlova in *Circus*, *Volga-Volga* and *Radiant Path*), which desexualised them (*pace* Enzensberger 1993). For Soviet

1 Moscow as magic space: Luybov Orlova's moment of understanding as she marches through Red Square during the May Day parade in Alexandrov's *The Circus* (1936)

women caught in the 'double bind' of housework and motherhood on the one hand and collective labour on the other this must have represented truly utopian wish fulfilment. The heroine is always depicted in the workplace, be it *kolkhoz*, circus or spinning mill, and only in the home *as a workplace*, like the Cinderella heroine of *Radiant Path*. Some critics have argued that the Soviet musical heroine is a mother figure, but this is not true in the conventional sense: domesticity is absent and there is no family but the collective as workplace in microcosm or the collective as country in macrocosm. This elision between the two is effected partly by the use of folklore and partly through the music, to which I shall return.

The characters are introduced to one another 'accidentally', sometimes through the fairy-tale medium of a picture, updated as a photograph (*Tractor-Drivers*, *Swineherdess*). The accident of their initial encounter reinforces the sense of the inevitability of their romance, as if it has been ordained from 'on high'. Often this is reinforced by a direct or indirect 'blessing' from that same source. In Alexander Medvedkin's *Chudesnitsa* (*The Miracle Girl*, 1936) (set on a *kolkhoz* but not a musical), the Stakhanovite heroine is summoned to Moscow, where she sees and hears Stalin speak, as a *reward* for her labour achievements. In *Circus* the heroine 'understands' her situation when she joins the May Day parade in Red Square and sees Stalin, here signified as God by the icon-like image carried at the head of the procession in the immediately preceding shot. In *Tractor-Drivers* the wedding feast finale is accompanied by toasts and oaths of allegiance to Stalin. In *Radiant Path* the heroine is summoned to a fairy-tale Kremlin to receive the Order of Lenin from someone whose aura reflects light upon her face: this must be Stalin, because in a Soviet film in 1940 it could hardly be anybody else.[3] These 'unforgettable encounters' occur in numerous other Soviet films, posters, paintings and newspaper articles of the period: they form a central thread in the fairy tale of Stalin as father of his people, the genius who has time for everyone, who can solve everybody's problems, even when Stalin's divinity is mediated through another Party or state official such as the Soviet President Kalinin or the local Party secretary (*Radiant Path* or *Kuban Cossacks*). Stalin is the omniscient and implicitly omnipresent father of the collective Soviet family, the avuncular patriarch of the peoples (Günther 1997a). Participation in this larger family sublimates the need for the heroines, and indeed the heroes, to participate in nuclear domesticity: sex is absent, and even the kissing is 'innocent' (*Happy Guys*, *Volga-Volga*). The family is the country itself (Günther 1997b) in which all are equal, or at least all have equal opportunity.

A central part of the fairy tale in Alexandrov's films, though not in Pyriev's, is the idea that any Soviet citizen, however humble, timid or wretched at the beginning of the film, can make a success of life and rise to the heights that socialist society has to offer. In *Volga-Volga* the heroine, a local letter carrier, overcomes numerous obstacles to win the All-Union Olympiad of Song. In *Radiant Path* the heroine receives the Order of Lenin and later becomes a deputy to the Supreme Soviet, a sure sign that she has 'arrived'. These closures are in fact also apertures allowing the audience to participate in the action (Anderson 1995). *Radiant Path* has perhaps the most interesting, and certainly the most bizarre, ending of any Stalinist musical. Following the award of the Order of Lenin the heroine finds herself in a Kremlin ante-room decorated only with chandeliers and mirror. Scarcely able to believe that what is happening to her is real, she checks in the mirror. She sees her reflection and therefore 'knows' that it is real. Then she turns her face back to the camera and sings a duet with mirror images of her earlier selves. The image in the mirror then turns into her late mother (also played by Orlova) as fairy godmother, complete with tiara, who opens the frame of the mirror and invites her into the world of mirror (reel?) reality. The two are seated in a car that then takes off, flying over the Kremlin, then Moscow, then high mountains, and then back to Moscow to the showpiece All-Union Agricultural Exhibition, landing at the foot of the famous statue by Vera Mukhina of 'The Worker and the Collective Farm Woman'. The final

2 The four incarnations of Tanya in the magic mirror of the Kremlin Palace in Moscow in Alexandrov's *Radiant Path* (1940): Cinderella, the shock-worker, the fairy godmother and the deputy to the Supreme Soviet

scene of the film takes place in the Exhibition itself and the one-time Cinderella figure, now crowned with success, re-encounters her Prince Charming against a magic background of fountains and other symbols of abundance. Implicitly, now that they have both established their equality in successful careers, they *may* have time for domesticity, but this is by no means made explicit.

Other films use festivals or mass scenes to draw the audience into the action and, above all, the emotional uplift: the 'storming' of the Bolshoi Theatre against all obstacles by the hero and heroine of *Happy Guys*, the Olympiad of Song at the end of *Volga-Volga*, the wedding feast at the end of *Tractor-Drivers*, the implied weddings that conclude both *Swineherdess* and *Kuban Cossacks*. But the device that really involves the emotions of the audience is the use of popular music in its various forms.

The path to utopia: the music

The music for all the Alexandrov and the first and last of the Pyriev musicals was written by the most prolific composer of Soviet popular music, Isaak Dunayevsky (1900–55). He was awarded his first Stalin Prize in 1941 for the music to Alexandrov's *Circus* and *Volga-Volga* and his second ten years later for the score to Pyriev's *Kuban Cossacks*. One of the songs from *Circus*, the 'Song of the Motherland', became the call sign for Moscow radio and the unofficial state anthem of the Soviet Union until an official anthem was introduced in 1943.

The music played a crucial part because it played to the emotions of the audience and helped to weaken any intellectual resistance they may have had to the message of the films (Anderson 1995). As already indicated, the scores made widespread use of choral singing, which helped to universalise the characters and the situations in which they found themselves. Furthermore, the combination of catchy tunes and ideologically loaded texts (mostly by Vasili Lebedev-Kumach, 1898–1949) meant that, when the audience left the cinema humming the tune, it also carried with it the message of reel reality into the real world outside. This helped make audiences feel that they were part of the world depicted on the screen: it elided the actual with the utopian ideal, collapsing the 'fourth wall' in the auditorium (Anderson 1995).

In *Happy Guys* the first verse of the theme song extolled the uplifting popularity of song, while the refrain made clear the use to which this uplift was to be put:

A song helps us build and live,
Like a friend, it calls and leads us forth.

And those who stride through life in song
Will never ever fall behind. (cf. von Geldern and Stites 1995: 234–5)

Further verses enjoined the audience 'When our country commands that
we be heroes, / Then anyone can become a hero' and finally warned that
any enemy threatening 'to take away our living joy' would be resound-
ingly rejected with 'a battle song, staunchly defending our Motherland'.
The idea of song as a central and necessary part of life is echoed in 'Three
Tank Drivers', by Boris Laskin and the Pokrass brothers, written for
Tractor-Drivers: 'There they live – and singing guarantees it – As a tight,
unbroken family.' That family was not the nuclear family, but the Motherland: the word *rodina* – deriving from the Russian verb *rodit'*, to give birth
to – was resurrected to reinforce this metaphor (Günther 1997a, 1997b).
This was the Motherland of 'Socialism in one country', a land whose vast
size and variety was constantly extolled (*Circus, Volga-Volga, Tractor-Drivers,
Swineherdess*), a land that was largely hermetically sealed against apparently hostile outside forces (*Circus, Tractor-Drivers*).

Dunayevsky's music carefully reflected the setting of each film. For
Pyriev's *kolkhoz* musicals he wrote scores that were heavily influenced by
folk music, Ukrainian or Russian as appropriate. The Alexandrov musicals,
on the other hand, were urban-oriented and the scores drew upon urban
musical forms such as jazz, music hall and military marches, however
unlikely that combination may appear. All three are evident in *Happy
Guys* and *Circus*. *Volga-Volga* centres on a musical civil war (the device
used here for narrative retardation) between the heroine, who has written
the 'Song of the Volga', which eventually wins the Olympiad of Song, and
the hero, who prefers to rehearse classical music with his brass band. For
him the music of Wagner is a sign of culture and civilisation: in 1938 this
was a clear indication of 'false consciousness'. In these three musicals
popular or 'low' culture triumphs over 'high' culture. In *Happy Guys* the
respectable buffet party literally becomes a 'carnival of the animals', while
later on the jazz band ends the film taking the Bolshoi Theatre audience
by storm; in *Circus* the action largely takes place within the confines of a
'low' cultural form; in *Volga-Volga* it is the popular *amateur* song that
triumphs over *professional* classical music, and a child maestro who out-
conducts the adults. Similarly in *Radiant Path*, the least musical of the
Stalinist musicals, it is Cinderella who outstrips her 'ugly sisters'. These
films provided confirmation that 'When our country commands that we
be heroes, / Then anyone can become a hero' – 'and singing guarantees
it'!

The texts of the songs in the Stalinist musicals tell us a great deal about
the topography of utopia and clarify some of the confusions and errors
committed by those critics and scholars who have ignored them.

On arrival: the topography of utopia

The Stalinist utopia is hermetically sealed against the outside world: the only depiction of 'abroad' (the lynch mob at the start of *Circus*) is unflattering, and other references are boldly defensive (*Tractor-Drivers*). It has been argued that in this utopia gender construction was quite straightforward: the man was identified with the city, with industry, defence, modernity, the rational and therefore progress; the woman, by contrast, was identified with the countryside and the land, with agriculture, nurture, nature, the emotional and therefore also with backwardness. This construction reaches its apotheosis in Vera Mukhina's statue, designed to top the Soviet pavilion at the 1937 Paris Exhibition, of 'The Worker and the Collective Farm Woman', 'a syntactically symmetrical pair but with the man wielding the mace of modernity: the industrial hammer' (Stites 1992: 84). This characterisation is, however, an oversimplification and each musical explored different parts of the Stalinist utopia, *pars pro toto*. We must therefore construct our topography of that utopia by pulling together those parts into a coherent whole.

Utopia exists in these films at two levels which may be broadly characterised as the periphery and the centre. Alexandrov's musicals are geographically centripetal, Moscow-oriented; Pyriev's are not, but they are not, as Evgeni Dobrenko has claimed, centrifugal films in which the movement is *away* from the capital (Dobrenko 1996: 109). Pyriev's forms merely explore the periphery and validate it as part of utopia.

Exploring the periphery

The Alexandrov musicals begin at the periphery: in *Happy Guys* it is a resort in the Crimea; in *Circus*, for once, it is overseas, the USA; in *Volga-Volga* it is the small provincial town of Melkovodsk (meaning literally 'little waters'); and in *Radiant Path* it is a small town in the Moscow region. In the course of the film the action moves to Moscow, where it ends: in the Bolshoi Theatre, in Red Square by the Kremlin, in the Olympiad of Song, and in the All-Union Agricultural Exhibition respectively. The ties that link the periphery to the centre vary: the translation of the main characters from the one to the other is the principal one of these links, but boats provide the principal method of interurban transport in *Happy Guys* (although a train is also mentioned but not seen) and in *Volga-Volga*, where the postal system is also crucial, as it is in Pyriev's *Tractor-Drivers*, where the postman sings a song encapsulating the variety and breadth of his vast country. In *Circus* trains offer a means of arrival and (interrupted) departure from and to abroad, but not within the USSR itself. Telegrams act as catalysts in both *Volga-Volga* and *Radiant Path*, while in the latter the first link between Melkovodsk and the capital occurs when the radio announces 'Moscow calling' and the last is effected through the fairy-tale mirror device discussed above. The use of radio is familiar from other films of the period, including the Kozintsev and Trauberg *Alone* (1931) and the documentaries of Dziga Vertov and Esfir Shub, but the virtual absence of aircraft and trains as means of *internal* communication and linkage, when they featured so strikingly elsewhere, is curious.

It is almost as if the periphery is in some ways 'living in the past', which would have been present reality for most audiences of the time. The presence of the bourgeois ladies early in *Happy Guys* strengthens this interpretation. There is surely a visual reference to the women in *October* (1926) who stab the Bolshevik workman to death with their parasols when the women in Alexandrov's film 'spike' the 'wrong' artiste with theirs. In *Radiant Path* the heroine Tanya is employed as a domestic servant, as is Anyuta in *Happy Guys* – a most un-Soviet occupation even if still widespread in the 1930s: both liberate themselves from this drudgery as the plot develops. Similarly Melkovodsk in *Volga-Volga* is initially depicted in a very unflattering light: the ferry breaks down, the telephones do not work, the telegram from Moscow 'slows down' when it arrives in the provinces, and the population of the town seems to spend its time either petitioning the local bureaucrat Byvalov (meaning 'nothing new', hilariously played by the leading comic actor Igor Ilyinsky), or practising their music (Turovskaya 1998). Yet this is itself depicted as a caricature: whereas Byvalov, who regards his recent posting to Melkovodsk as a mere staging post on his long career track to journey's end in Moscow, claims that 'There can be no talent in such a dump', Strelka ('little arrow') the letter carrier insists there is 'no lack of talented people' and goes on to prove her point by singing Tchaikovsky and reciting Lermontov. It is, however, the retarded telegram from Moscow announcing the 'socialist competition' of the Olympiad of Song that breaks the logjam of stagnation and, in a deliberate irony, it is through Strelka's efforts that Byvalov, despite his own efforts to obstruct her, eventually arrives with the entire local musical talent in Moscow.

In Pyriev's films the *kolkhoz* is largely a self-sufficient microcosm, a closed world of 'social claustrophobia', to use Dobrenko's term (Dobrenko 1996). In *Tractor-Drivers* the hero does, it is true, enter from outside, but he comes from the fighting in the Far East, which is therefore no longer peripheral but strategically significant (cf. films like Dovzhenko's *Aerograd* (1935)). Furthermore, while in transit to Moscow, this time by train, he has chosen to travel to the Ukrainian *kolkhoz rather than to the capital*. In *Kuban Cossacks* the outside world hardly intrudes either, although it is referred to obliquely, as is the war, fought less than a decade previously on this very terrain. The plot in all three films is characterised by what became known as 'conflictlessness [*beskonfliktnost*]': in other words it is confined to microcosmic personal rivalries expressed in differing personal labour contributions rather than to macrocosmic forces like class conflict or war, which were all too evident in other Soviet films of the period.

The leading characters in the periphery are almost invariably women. It is they who organise and produce, they who resolve the love intrigue by recognising, albeit somewhat belatedly, the production achievements of the hero and therefore his suitability as partner in labour and love. The exceptions are in Alexandrov's *Happy Guys*, where it is the hero who effects the resolution through his talent for improvising in the most adverse circumstances; and in Pyriev's *Swineherdess*, where the heroine weakly accepts her fate at the hands of the deceitful locals while the hero has to ride like a knight on horseback to rescue her at the eleventh hour. One reason for the privileging of women in the countryside was the need to encourage them to play a greater part in collective, as opposed to domestic, labour in the light of male migration to the cities and the consequent labour shortage in rural areas. Another resulted from the context in which these musicals were made: by male directors to showcase the acting, singing and dancing talents of their wives. Yet another was to emphasise that women were equal and thus to underline the superiority of the Soviet way of life. For these reasons women were never villains: the villainous characters were always men, but they could be cured of their villainy by the intervention of women, unless they were foreigners, like von Kneischitz in *Circus*.

Exploring the centre: Moscow

Moscow constituted the fairyland at the heart of the Stalinist utopia. It was where unusual, even magic, things happened: the triumph of the jazz band in *Happy Guys*; the journey to understanding of the heroine in *Circus*; the victory in the singing competition in *Volga-Volga*; the translation of Cinderella into the Fairy Princess in *Radiant Path*; and the labour of love/love of labour that blossoms in *Swineherdess*.

It was to Moscow that characters went to improve their lives and to be rewarded with recognition for their achievements. Within Moscow the Kremlin and the newly opened Exhibition of Agricultural Achievements played significant and separate roles. The Kremlin was the seat of government and can be seen as a synonym for Party–state power and thus for Stalin. Sometimes this is explicit (*Circus* or *Radiant Path*; cf. *Miracle Girl*), although the general context of contemporary propaganda images rendered such explicitness unnecessary. The role of the Exhibition is more complex: it features prominently in both *Swineherdess* and *Radiant Path*. Dobrenko argues that in the first of these 'the Exhibition represents not Moscow but the "Country"' (Dobrenko 1996: 112). This is an over-simplification. In both films the Exhibition offers a dual representation: to the periphery it represents Moscow, while in Moscow it represents the country in all its diversity. In *Swineherdess* the hero and heroine sing the 'Song of Moscow', which opens:

> Everything's fine in spacious Moscow,
> The Kremlin stars shine against the blue sky,
> And, just as rivers meet in the sea,
> So people meet here in Moscow.

3 Girl from the north meets boy from the south in the magic space of Moscow's All-Union Agricultural Exhibition, the microcosm of the Soviet macrocosm in Ivan Pyriev's *The Swineherdess and the Shepherd* (1940)

The refrain includes the lines: 'I shall never forget a friend, / Whom I have met in Moscow.' Moscow is therefore *special*. We must remember that most Soviet citizens had never visited Moscow: internal passport controls and sheer cost made the journey impossible except as a special, officially sponsored reward. Most people 'knew' Moscow only from screen images, and for propaganda reasons only parts of the 'great stone city'⁴ were shown: the Kremlin and/or Red Square, because of their historical and political associations; the Exhibition, because it was very much a 'preview of the coming attractions of socialism'; and the new construction projects, such as the Hotel Moskva (*Circus*), the river station (*Volga-Volga*) or the showcase metro (*Circus*). As Oksana Bulgakova has pointed out, 'Even more frequently real Moscow was replaced by a painted backdrop, a set' (Bulgakova 1996: 57): this applies to *Happy Guys*, *Circus* and Medvedkin's *Novaia Moskva* (*New Moscow*, 1937), and it increased the air of unreality for those familiar with the city from personal experience. But most of the audience had nothing real to compare to this reel image, and that enhanced its magic power.

Conclusion

The purpose of this chapter has been to sketch the basic outlines of the topography of the Stalinist musical, focusing on four films each by the fathers of the genre, Alexandrov and Pyriev. Since these are preliminary remarks, the conclusions can be only tentative. These films were popular and the image of the country that they created, while not 'real' in any objective sense, became real in the minds of contemporary audiences. The 'Potemkin village', the small town, the capital city of this reel reality created a powerful Soviet equivalent of the 'Russia of the mind' (Figes 1998). By entertaining the mass audience with glimpses of utopia, the Stalinist musical promoted the illusion encapsulated in popular songs not only that 'Life has become better, comrades, life has become happier' but further that 'We were born to make a fairy tale come true' (von Geldern and Stites 1995: 237–8, 257–8). As Stalin, who as 'Kremlin censor' was in a unique position to know, once remarked, 'Cinema is an illusion, but it dictates its own laws to life itself' (Volkogonov 1988).

Notes

I am indebted to Emma Widdis, Cambridge, whose as yet unpublished PhD thesis first alerted me to the literature on this subject, and to Julian Graffy, London, for reading an earlier draft of this chapter and for supplying numerous relevant materials.

1 I have here reversed the concluding line of the poem 'Say not the struggle naught availeth' by Arthur Hugh Clough (1819–61). The second stanza, even though written in the middle of the nineteenth century, could stand as a summary of the message of the Stalinist musical and of much Socialist Realist art in general:

If hopes were dupes, fears may be liars;
It may be, in yon smoke concealed,
Your comrades chase e'en now the fliers,
And, but for you, possess the field.

2 All translations are the author's.

3 These analyses are based almost entirely on the versions now available, either from Polart and Facets in the USA or on off-air recordings from Russian television. These are the versions restored and de-Stalinised in the 1960s and 1970s. A tantalising sequence from the original version of *Tractor- Drivers* was included in Dana Ranga's film *East Side Story* (1997).

4 Much was made in the 1930s of the reconstruction of Moscow as a symbol of the modernisation of the country as a whole. The capital is presented as 'the great stone city' in Vertov's *Three Songs of Lenin* (1934).

References

Altman, R. (ed.) (1981), *Genre: The Musical. A Reader*, London, British Film Institute.
Anderson, T. (1995), 'Why Stalinist Musicals?', *Discourse*, 17:3, 38–48.
Bulgakova, O. (1996), 'Prostranstvennye figury sovetskogo kino 30-kh godov', *Kinovedcheskie zapiski*, 29, 49–62.
Dobrenko, E. (1996), '"Iazyk prostranstva, szhatogo do tochki", ili estetika sotsial'noi klaustrofobii', *Iskusstvo kino*, 9, 108–17, and 11, 120–9.
Dyer, R. (1977), 'Entertainment and Utopia', *Movie*, 24, 2–13; reprinted in Altman (1981), 175–94.
Enzensberger, M. (1993), 'We Were Born to Turn a Fairy Tale into Reality', in Taylor and Spring (1993), 97–108.
Figes, O. (1998), 'The Russia of the Mind', *Times Literary Supplement*, 5 June 1968, 14–16.
Fitzpatrick, S. (1994), *Stalin's Peasants: Resistance and Survival in the Russian Village after Collectivization*, New York and Oxford, Oxford University Press.
Günther, H. (1997a), 'Wise Father Stalin and his Family in Soviet Cinema', in Lahusen and Dobrenko (1997), 178–90.
Günther, H. [Kh. Giunter] (1997b), 'Poiushchaia rodina. Sovetskaia massovaia pesnia kak vyrazhenie arkhetipa materi', *Voprosy literatury*, 4, 46–61.
Horton, A. (ed.) (1993), *Inside Soviet Film Satire: Laughter with a Lash*, Cambridge and New York, Cambridge University Press.
Khrushchev, N. S. (1956), Speech to the delegates of the 20th Party Congress in February 1956, trans. in *The Secret Speech*, Nottingham, Spokesman Books, 1976.
Lahusen, T. and E. Dobrenko (eds) (1997), *Socialist Realism without Shores*, Durham NC and London, Duke University Press.
Lean, D. (1947), 'Brief Encounter', *Penguin Film Review 4*, London and New York, Penguin.
Lenin, V. I. (1922), 'Of All the Arts ...', in Taylor and Christie (1988), 57.
Lunacharsky, A. (1933), 'Synopsis of a Report in the Tasks of Dramaturgy' (Extract), in Taylor and Christie (1988), 237.

Mamatova, L. (1995), 'Model' kinomifov 30-kh godov', in *Kino: politika i liudi (30-e gody)*, Moscow, Materik, 52–78.

Miller, F. J. (1990), *Folklore for Stalin: Russian Folklore and Pseudofolklore of the Stalin Era*, Armonk NY, Sharpe.

Nikolaevich, S. (1992), 'Poslednii seans, ili Sud'ba beloi zhenshchiny v SSSR', *Ogonek*, 4, 23.

Shumyatsky, B. (1935), *Kinematografiia millionov*, Moscow, Kinofotoizdat.

Stites, R. (1992), *Russian Popular Culture: Entertainment & Society since 1900*, Cambridge, Cambridge University Press.

Taylor, R. (1991), 'Ideology as Mass Entertainment: Boris Shumyatsky and Soviet Cinema in the 1930s', in Taylor and Christie (1991), 193–216.

Taylor, R. (1998), *Film Propaganda: Soviet Russia and Nazi Germany*, second edn, London and New York, I. B. Tauris.

Taylor, R. and I. Christie (eds) (1988), *The Film Factory: Russian & Soviet Cinema in Documents, 1896–1939*, London, Routledge and Kegan Paul, Cambridge MA, Harvard University Press; paperback edn, London and New York, Routledge, 1994.

Taylor, R. and I. Christie (eds) (1991), *Inside the Film Factory: New Approaches to Russian & Soviet Cinema*, London and New York, Routledge.

Taylor, R. and D. Spring (eds) (1993), *Stalinism and Soviet Cinema*, London and New York, Routledge.

Turovskaya, M. (1988), 'I. A. Pyr'ev i ego muzykal'nye komedii. K probleme zhanra', *Kinovedcheskie zapiski*, 1, 111–46.

Turovskaya, M. (1998), 'Volga-Volga i ego vremia', *Iskusstvo kino*, 3, 59–64.

Volkogonov, D. (1988), 'Stalin', *Oktiabr'*, 11.

von Geldern, J. (1992), 'The Centre and the Periphery: Cultural and Social Geography in the Mass Culture of the 1930s', in White (1992), 62–80.

von Geldern, J. and R. Stites (eds) (1995), *Mass Culture in Soviet Russia*, Bloomington IN, Indiana University Press.

White, S. (ed.) (1992), *New Directions in Soviet History*, Cambridge, Cambridge University Press.

Youngblood, D. J. (1991), *Soviet Cinema in the Silent Era, 1918–1935*, Austin TX, Texas University Press.

Youngblood, D. J. (1992), *Movies for the Masses: Popular Cinema and Soviet Society in the 1920s*, Cambridge, Cambridge University Press.

Zhdanov, A. (1934), Speech to the First Congress of Soviet Writers, in *Pervyi Vsesoiuznyi s"ezd sovetskikh pisatelei 1934: Stenografischeskii otchet*, Moscow, Khudozhestvennaia literatura.

ROSEMARY STOTT

Entertained by the class enemy: cinema programming policy in the German Democratic Republic

2

On the 23 September 1961, the union members of the film theatres in the Borough of Lichtenberg in Berlin issued the following statement:

> We thank our government under the leadership of the Party of the Working Class for the measures they have taken. Since 13 August it has no longer been possible to infect people from our Workers and Farmers State via the cinema in West Berlin with the evil spirit of imperialist ideology. The miasma of gangster, military and horror films is being held back by a solid wall. (*Landesarchiv Berlin*, Rep. 121 Kultur, Bd 19)

The undesirable excesses of the commercial entertainment film, referred to in the polemic above, were no longer accessible to the citizens of the German Democratic Republic (GDR) following the closure of the border between their country and the Federal Republic of Germany (FRG) in August 1961, and this was to remain the case until the collapse of the wall twenty-eight years later. A significant number of films produced in capitalist countries still, however, continued to play an important role for those responsible for the selection of films at the Hauptverwaltung Film (HV Film; the Film Authority within the Ministry for Culture). These films were selected to broaden the appeal of the cinema programmes and to provide genre films which were not sufficiently catered for by socialist film production. For audiences, films from the West represented a source of information about the life and culture of countries they had little prospect of visiting.

The main principles and problems related to cinema programming which preoccupied the film functionaries at the HV Film remained fairly constant throughout the history of the GDR. They will be summarised here on the basis of a document entitled 'Die Lage im Filmwesen der DDR und seine Hauptaufgaben bis 1970' ('The Situation in the GDR Film Industry and its principal aims until 1970'), issued by the HV Film for presentation to the Central Committee of the SED (Socialist Unity

Party of Germany) and dated 9 February 1965 (Bentzien 1965). This was a significant year for the history of cinema in the GDR, being the year of the Eleventh Plenum, which resulted in a withdrawal of the ideological freedoms which had immediately preceded it. The effects were most devastating for the GDR's own national cinema (DEFA), since a whole year's production was withdrawn in the aftermath, but there was also sweeping criticism of the dissemination of bourgeois popular culture as a whole, including the Western entertainment film (Wiedemann 1998). The open manner in which the document discussed the problems facing the cinema industry can be seen against the background of the relatively liberal phase in cultural policy in the early 1960s. However, the document also expressed the will to improve the distribution and exhibition of films from socialist countries and to reduce the influence of bourgeois entertainment films, and this presaged the resolutions passed following the Eleventh Plenum.

The document stated that two-thirds of the annually imported films were produced in socialist countries. This figure did not change radically during the following years and, together with a reliable yearly national production of between twelve and fifteen films, formed the cornerstone of the stated strong orientation towards a socialist cinema. The 'Verleihkonzeptionen' (film distribution plans) published annually by Progress (Progress Film Distribution), for instance, were based on this strict division between films from socialist and capitalist countries and always filled a given quota for each. For example, in 1983, the total number of new licences acquired was 125, fifteen produced by DEFA (including three children's films), eighty imports from socialist countries and thirty imports from capitalist countries (Klemm 1983:7).

One of the difficulties for the HV Film was to meet the required quota for films from socialist countries with high-quality films which could attract a large audience. As the document from 1965 made clear, the reputation of films from socialist countries was suffering as a result of compromises with respect to theme and genre made in order to fill the quotas. The choice was further curtailed by the fact that some films produced in other socialist countries were not ideologically acceptable to the HV Film.

> The political and ideological tendencies of a selection of films from some of the socialist countries do not meet the cultural and political aims of the cinema programmes in our Republic. (They negate the successes during the establishment of socialism and they display nationalistic, existential and pessimistic tendencies, Modernist influences etc.) (Bentzien 1965: 8)

The political upheavals and ensuing cultural liberalisation in a number of Eastern-bloc countries affected the cinema programmes. The Prague

Spring in the mid to late 1960s had a significant effect on Czech imports. Polish imports were compromised in the early 1980s following the establishment of Solidarnosc, and Soviet imports were affected in the mid to late 1980s as a result of glasnost and perestroika.

The document claimed that the tendency to fill the gaps in the cinema programme with Western entertainment films, such as comedies or musicals, promoting petty bourgeois values had largely been overcome and that films imported from capitalist countries were mainly of high artistic quality, with 'bourgeois-humanist and socially critical tendencies' (Bentzien 1965: 8). However, the HV Film stated here that the need amongst audiences for light entertainment films was significant and this need could not be fulfilled by the relatively limited range of entertainment films produced nationally or in the other socialist countries. Thus it was considered necessary to revert to importing western entertainment films. From the mid-1960s onwards, a proportion (usually the greater) of these imports therefore consisted of pure entertainment films promoting the values of the 'Western imperialists' the East German ideologists theorised as antipathetic to their own.

If one were to consider only the number of the imports – as the annual film distribution plans published by Progress did – the impression gained is that the bourgeois entertainment film played a relatively minor role. As has already been stated, the total number of Western imports accounted for less than a quarter of the annual number of new film licences acquired. The degree of influence the films from capitalist countries exerted cannot, however, be judged solely on the number of films imported. A more complete picture is established if one also considers other aspects of the films' exhibition and reception. The number of prints acquired, the volume of screenings and the audience statistics for films released in the GDR demonstrate that the cinema's most important function was to distract and entertain rather than to serve as an instrument for the promotion of socialist ideology.[1]

The detailed analysis of the distribution, exhibition and reception of the Western import offered here will be restricted to the last decade of the country's history. This is because the reliance on Western imports grew during this period (Stieher and Wiedemann 1990: 418; Wiedemann 1998: 128). Statistics relating to film exhibition and reception are also more readily available for this last decade. The study is focused on films from the FRG and the United States of America and is limited to the exhibition of films on the 'standard' cinema circuit; that is, cinemas operating on a basis comparable to that of the commercial cinema in the West and not including the numerous cinema screenings which took place within factories, schools, cultural centres etc.

The percentage share of Western imports remained constant (1970s – 22.8 per cent of total film imports, 1980s – 23.2 per cent of total film imports), although there were fluctuations with regard to the number of films imported from individual countries. These fluctuations were sometimes an indication of changes in political relations with the country concerned. In the 1950s, for instance, the East German cinema was heavily reliant on film imports from the FRG, but following the closure of the border between the two countries in 1961, there were hardly any films imported from the Federal Republic. Fluctuations were also, however, the result of more arbitrary factors, such as the quality and number of films produced in individual countries or whether the licence for the film in question could be purchased at a reasonable price. Because of the GDR's chronic lack of 'Devisen' (Western currency), financial factors frequently outweighed ideological ones in the selection of Western imports.

The FRG was one of the countries from which the number of film imports increased during the 1970s and 1980s, although, as has already been mentioned, there were fluctuations from year to year. Disregarding coproductions, only one West German film production was imported in 1975, four in 1976 and one in 1977. In 1984, there were five West German imports; in both 1985 and 1986 there were eight. In the 1970s, there was a total of twenty-two imports, in the 1980s, thirty-nine.[2] In terms of number of films imported there is, therefore, a significant increase.

With respect to the category of films imported from the FRG, there is also a decisive development. The greater proportion of the few films imported in the 1970s were politically engaged critiques of the Federal Republic, emanating for the most part from exponents of the 'New German Cinema'. In 1976, for example, Lina Braake (Bernhard Sinkel, 1975)[3] and Die verlorene Ehre der Katharina Blum (The Lost Honour of Katharina Blum, Volker Schlöndorff and Margarete von Trotta, 1975) were shown. Films of this type still represented a proportion of the imports from the FRG in the 1980s. In 1981, Trotta's Schwestern oder die Balance des Glücks (Sisters, or the Balance of Happiness, 1979) was released in the GDR and in 1982 Die bleierne Zeit (The German Sisters, 1981) by the same director. In 1987, Günter Walraff's documentary Ganz Unten (At the Bottom of the Heap, 1986) was imported, and in 1988, 40m² Deutschland (40m² Germany, Tevfik Basar, 1986), both of which portrayed a lamentable picture of the situation for immigrant workers in the Federal Republic. Films such as these supported the dominant ideology in the East that capitalist work practices resulted in the exploitation of employees. In the 1980s, however, a significant number of films imported from West Germany presented their critique in the form of more light-hearted comedy – as, for example, Männer (Men, Doris Dörie, 1985) – or could be classified as pure entertainment films – as, for example, the 'Otto' films – the first of which, *Otto – der Film* (*Otto – the Film*, Xaver Schwarzenberger, Otto Waalkes, 1985) was shown in the GDR in 1986. Notably absent were the formally more experimental films of the New German Cinema, such as most of the films of Fassbinder and Wim Wenders.

A further development regarding Western imports during this last decade is the extent to which genres previously represented only by films from socialist countries were introduced, often with a significant time lapse following their original date of production and their release in the West. The 'Indianerfilme', Westerns which focused on the native American Indians and which aimed to present a historically accurate picture of nineteenth-century America, were, from the mid-1960s onwards, a successful home-produced genre. They were the socialist response to the conventional Western, of which there were only rare examples amongst the Western imports. In the 1980s, East German productions of the genre became less frequent, and the last ones were produced in 1982 (*Der Scout*, *The Scout*, Konrad Petzold) and 1985 (*Atkins*, Helge Trimpert). In the mid-1980s, a number of classic West German versions of the genre from the 1960s (which were mainly coproductions with Yugoslavia) were imported for the first time; for example, *Der Schatz im Silbersee* and *Winnetou 1* (*Treasure of Silver Lake*, *Winnetou the Warrior/Apache Gold*, both directed by Harald Reinl in 1963) were released in 1985. These West German 'Indianerfilme' were mainly adaptions of the Karl May stories, which were highly popular in West Germany but which were not published in the East until the 1980s. It would seem to be no coincidence that the demise of the home-produced genre was accompanied by a flurry of imports of the same genre emanating from the FRG.

An analysis of the films imported from the US during the 1970s and 1980s reveals a trend towards the entertainment film analogous to that described with respect to films imported from West Germany. Hollywood box-office hits, in the form of thrillers such as *Papillon* (Franklin J. Schaffner, 1973), which was imported in 1975, melodramas such as *The Way We Were* (Sydney Pollack, 1973), imported in 1975, and comedies such as *The Return of the Pink Panther* (Blake Edwards, 1975), shown in 1977, established their place in East German cinemas from the mid-1960s. In the 1980s, there were more examples of the 'blockbuster' commercial entertainment film, ones in which the ideological tenor of the film is one of reinforcement and endorsement of the American way of life, the 'feel-good' movies, which succeed in finding a large international audience. *The Woman in Red* (Gene Wilder, 1984) shown in the GDR in 1986, *Out of Africa* (Sydney Pollack, 1985), released in 1987, *Prince – Sign O' the Times*

(Prince), and *Dirty Dancing* (Emile Ardolino), both of which were produced in 1987 and shown in 1989, are all examples of these. Certain American genres which were popular in the West, such as the horror film, were never shown in the GDR. Also absent were some contemporary, independently produced films from the United States which had found success in the West, such as the films of Jim Jarmusch and some of the older American classics like the Sirk melodramas, which would have attracted audiences to art-house ('Studio')[4] or film archive ('Camera')[5] screenings.

A relatively or occasionally very long time lapse (at least eighteen months, sometimes ten years) between the release of films in the West and their screening in the GDR was a significant aspect of American and West German imports throughout the period, although in the latter half of the 1980s, there is a slight increase in the number of films which were released no more than two years after their date of production. In 1989, for example, of the ten American films imported, eight were less than two years old. In 1981, of the seven American films imported, only one was less than two years old. This demonstrated an increasing trend towards releasing American commercial hits at approximately the same time as in Western Europe.

The number of Western imports and the speed with which they were released are, as I have already argued, only one aspect under consideration in assessing their role for the cinema industry and for audiences. The next factor one should bear in mind is their exhibition: the nature of the cinemas in which they were exhibited, the number of screenings they were given, the number of prints which were circulated and the time of year when the individual films were released. To consider the first point: most of the Western imports, in particular the box-office hits from the US and the FRG, were premiered in the large 'Erst- und Uraufführungstheatern' (first-screening and premiere cinemas), which guaranteed them a high profile and large audiences. The films from the developing countries, socially committed features, documentary films such as *Ganz Unten* or films from the national film archive were limited to the art-house or film archive screens (see notes 4 and 5).

The second factor relating to exhibition which one needs to consider is the number of screenings. A study of the cinema programmes for six months in two premiere cinemas (the International and the Kosmos) and five suburban cinemas (the Tivoli, the Forum, the Astra, the Vorwärts and the Sojus in Marzahn) in East Berlin (Klemm 1983: 8), which took into account the main evening programmes and worked out the percentage of screenings for films from socialist and non-socialist countries respectively, produced the statistics shown in table 1:

Table 1 Screenings of socialist and non-socialist films

CINEMA	SOCIALIST PRODUCTIONS (%)	NON-SOCIALIST PRODUCTIONS (%)
Kosmos	28.8	71.2
International	28.8	71.2
Tivoli	30.8	69.2
Forum	23.1	76.9
Astra	23.1	76.9
Vorwärts	32.7	67.3
Sojus – Marzahn	28.8	71.2

Source: Klemm 1983.

The statistics show that national films and films produced in the Eastern bloc were given fewer than half the number of screenings of Western imports in all the cinemas in the study. The number of Western imports as a percentage of the total (23.2 per cent in the 1980s) suggested that they were of less significance than the films produced in socialist countries. These figures relating to the screenings demonstrate the converse; that is, that it was the films from the non-socialist countries which determined the cinema landscape in the GDR.

To examine the other factors related to exhibition (number of prints circulated and timing of release), we should glance at the figures for distribution and exhibition over one year. The statistics are those issued by Progress for 1987, which were analysed in an unpublished study by Peter Glaß in 1988. The study was prepared for the Congress of the Verband der Film und Fernsehschaffenden (Association of Film and Television Employees) in 1987. This year was significant because it was the 750th anniversary of Berlin, the capital of the GDR. The ruling party was anxious to be able to present a capital city, which was, in terms of its architecture and social amenities, including culture, of a standard comparable to that of capital cities throughout the world. This may well have contributed to the particularly impressive list of internationally successful releases, although the focus on blockbuster hits was certainly established prior to 1987. In that year, there were new film releases from fifteen countries: the GDR itself, the Soviet Union, Poland, Hungary, Bulgaria, Romania, Czechoslovakia, Cuba, Yugoslavia, Korea, China, the FRG, including West Berlin, the US, France, Italy, Great Britain, Spain, Switzerland, Indonesia, Japan and Australia.

The most striking aspect of the statistics is the large number of prints of Western imports that were available, although it must be said that the number circulated for individual films was subject to external factors, such as conditions imposed by Western distributors. Therefore it would be wrong to consider the number of prints distributed as the sole indicator of a particular film programming policy. A comparison of the number for East German films with that for films produced in the US reveals that the same number of films, that is six, from each country were available with more than twenty-six prints. However, there were two more East German films than American films released that year in total, which means that a higher proportion of American films than East German films had the potential to reach large audiences. Although there were a larger number of films from the Soviet Union than from the US, the number of prints in circulation for Soviet films was far lower. The highest number of prints for any one film from the Soviet Union was twenty-two, whereas the American film *Beverly Hills Cop* (Martin Brest, 1984) was circulated with forty-eight prints, the highest number for any film released that year.

An analysis of the films which were circulated with a large number of prints reveals that for all the countries concerned, whether socialist or capitalist, these were films which belonged to popular entertainment genres, such as comedies, thrillers or detective films. The film *Tschuchije sdes ne Chodjat* (*No Entry for Strangers*, Anatoli Wechotko, Roman Jerschow, 1985), a detective film with plenty of action from the Len film studio in the Soviet Union, was circulated with twenty-two prints. *Trois hommes et un couffin* (*Three Men and a Cradle*, Coline Serreau, 1985) and *Astérix et la surprise de César* (*Asterix Versus Caesar*, Paul and Gaeten Brizzi, 1985), both produced in France, were circulated with thirty-three prints each. By contrast, the politically committed film *Ganz Unten*, the ideology of which was a far better match for the professed politics of the GDR, was circulated with only three prints. Documentary films of this type were expected to attract only small audiences and were therefore given only limited circulation. Films from socialist countries outside Europe were also considered to be of minority interest and were circulated with only small numbers of prints. The three films from Cuba were released with eight, eight and five prints respectively.

The timing of a film's release was also significant, since a large proportion of takings was concentrated in the summer months. Because of the restrictions on travel abroad and the large number of workers who took holidays arranged by their local trade union, many citizens spent their annual summer holiday in the GDR. Temporary open-air cinemas were set up in the resorts, such as those on the Baltic coast, to cater for the large influx of tourists who had high expectations of the films released under the much promoted title 'Kinosommer' (cinema summer).

Table 2   Top 10 new releases[a] of 1987

COUNTRY OF ORIGIN	FILM TITLE	DATE	PRINTS OF RELEASE	AUDIENCE CIRCULATED
USA	*Beverly Hills Cop*	24 July	48	2,210,298
FRG	*Seitenstechen*	13 March	33	1,322,157
USA	*Out of Africa*	4 Sept	33	1,246,786
USA	*Amadeus*	29 May	19	876,886
Yugoslavia	*Lepota poroka*	12 June	26	866,474
France	*Asterix et la surprise de César*	9 Oct	33	712,844
France	*Trois hommes et un couffin*	27 Feb	33	612,356
Japan	*Legend of Eight Samurai*	2 Jan	33	577,048
GDR	*Johann Strauß*	29 May	33	534,052
GDR	*Vernehmung der Zeugen*	27 March	26	424,907

Source: constructed on the basis of Glass 1988: 41–2 and Dieter Wiedermann, private archive, unpublished.

[a] The popularity of the films judged here solely on the number of tickets sold.

'Kinosommer 1987' accounted for 21.9 million of the yearly 69.2 million cinema screenings, which is almost a third (31.6 per cent) of the yearly total in three months. The statistics for 1987 show that the release of the American films was timed to coincide with the summer months. Five of the nine American films imported that year were released between the end of June and the beginning of September. These five were: *Amadeus* (Miloš Forman, 1984), premiered in Berlin on the 29 May and opening the Kinosommer on 26 June (nineteen prints); *A Breed Apart* (Philippe Mora, 1984), released on 17 July (thirty-three prints); *Beverly Hills Cop* (Martin Brest, 1984), released on 24 July (forty-eight prints); *Prizzi's Honour* (John Huston, 1985), released on 14 August (twenty-six prints) and *Out of Africa* (Sydney Pollack, 1985), released on 4 September (thirty-three prints). By contrast only two of the Soviet films were released in the premiere cinemas during the same period.

The final aspect to be considered is the reception of the films. There was a close correspondence between the number of prints distributed and the audience figures, as table 2 demonstrates. Those films which were distributed with a large number of prints were successful in drawing a substantial audience. The audience figures for the same year, 1987, serve to confirm the dominance of Western imports highlighted during the analysis of film distribution and exhibition.

Only one film in the top ten new releases of 1987 is an import from the

Table 3   Most popular films in the GDR, 1983–7 (cumulative figures)

COUNTRY OF ORIGIN	FILM TITLE	DATE OF RELEASE	AUDIENCE
FRG	*Otto – der Film*	25 July 86	5,033,230
USA	*Blue Thunder*	20 July 84	3,786,718
France/Belgium	*Les douze travaux d' Asterix*	21 Dec 84	3,231,330
FRG	*Ach du lieber Harry*	9 Nov 84	2,932,836
France	*Le gendarme et les gendarmettes*	17 Feb 84	2,554,259
USA	*Tootsie*	15 June 84	2,314,981
USA	*Beat Street*	14 June 85	2,042,912
Italy	*Il bisbetico domato*	16 Sept 83	1,994,018

Source: Glass 1988: 30.

Eastern bloc. National cinema is represented by two films, but the remainder are Western imports. Table 3 reveals that there was a clear trend towards a small number of imported commercial entertainment films drawing huge audiences over a relatively long period of time. This is in contrast to distribution practice in the West, where commercial films are distributed with hundreds of prints but are swiftly replaced by the next blockbuster hit. The most popular film in the 1980s in the GDR, for example, was *Otto – der Film*. By 1988, this film had attracted 5,033,230 spectators, who represented almost a third of the total population, a staggering figure by any standards.

Out of a total figure of 69.2 million cinema visits in 1987, 10 million were to one of the ten most popular Western film imports. The ten most popular films from socialist countries attracted approximately 3.5 million visitors, and none of the individual films managed to reach an audience over a million. In other years some films from socialist countries did succeed in competing with Western imports with respect to box-office takings, but they were exceptions. What is more, some of these were films which eschewed overt ideology and favoured escapist, populist narratives. *Ärztinnen* (*Doctors*, Horst Seemann, GDR, 1984), for example, which reached an audience of 1,644,240, was a hospital suspense drama which was set in West Germany, and *Sexmission* (Juliusz Machulski, Poland, 1983), which reached an audience of 1,049,500, was a science-fiction fantasy with numerous sex scenes.

Although films such as *Ärztinnen* proved that the national film industry could compete with Western imports in terms of ticket sales, films such as this were the exception. Most of the East German films which achieved box-office success were the 'Gegenwartsfilme' (contemporary realist dramas), which dealt with socialist realities at home. Although the exhibition practice already discussed (high number of prints, focus on 'Kinosommer' etc.) seemed to favour the commercial entertainment film from capitalist countries, individual East German films of this type did compete with Western imports at the box office. The national film output had a poor reputation overall, but still it represented one of the relatively few outlets for uniquely national concerns and problems which were close to the hearts of all East German citizens. Films which addressed these issues in an open manner and which were successful cinematically did attract large audiences. *Einer trage des anderen Last ... (Bear Ye One Another's Burdens*, Lothar Warneke, 1987), a film about a hitherto taboo subject (relations between the church and the state), reached an audience of 1,300,000 in 1988, for example. Some home-produced films could potentially have reached large audiences and could have sparked off debate if their production and/or subsequent release had not been delayed, compromised or even abandoned altogether by officials from the HV Film. *Insel der Schwäne (Island of the Swans*, Hermann Zschoche, 1982), for instance, raised the controversial issue of the social problems caused by the new high-rise estates and delinquency amongst the youth who lived there. The film's success was prevented by its partial withdrawal from cinemas after it had been heavily criticised in the party press (Wiedemann, 1998: 132–3). Thus East German films with social and political messages did have a place alongside the entertainment films from the West, but the quality was not consistently high enough to compete with what was, after all, a selection of Western import films, the popularity of which had already been tried and tested on Western audiences.

The central question is why the functionaries at the HV Film seemingly had fewer ideological scruples in the selection of Western entertainment films than in the selection of films from the national studios or from the other socialist countries. There are a number of reasons why this was the case. First, these films were valued for their economic efficiency and their capacity to prop up the cinema industry.[6] Although strictly speaking the motives which shaped cinema distribution and exhibition were ideological rather than profit-seeking, the cinema industry found itself under pressure to increase economic efficiency and milk the most from a small number of popular films. Second, the light-entertainment Hollywood film or Hollywood-style film was perceived, rightly or wrongly, as ideologically benign.[7] In cases where there was concern, appeals were made to trust the critical faculties of the socialist-educated youth.[8] Third, cinema workers were badly paid, but could receive

'Prämien' (extra payments) for tickets sold. Thus films which could draw large audiences were favoured. A feeling of being isolated from cultural as well as social and political developments in the West motivated East German citizens to gain exposure to cultural output from Western countries, and thus it was easier to attract audiences to these films than to those from socialist countries.

Whereas some contemporary film-makers[9] and critics[10] saw the dominance of the bourgeois entertainment film as a contradiction of socialist cultural policy, the officials at the HV Film did not perceive it as such. 'Unterhaltungskunst' (entertainment art) was one of the most important facets of the arts in the GDR and was theorised not in opposition to high culture, but as being of equal status. The paradox in the case of the film industry was that the traditionally low-culture entertainment arts were generally theorised in opposition to the 'vulgar', financially oriented entertainment industries of the capitalist West. The Deputy Minister for Culture and Head of the HV Film defended the release of the Western imports as follows:

> A state which cares for the welfare of its citizens must accept that it has to provide them with the spiritual commodities of life too. That is a part of socialist cultural policy. As a result of the policy of dialogue and the absence of confrontation, business contacts have grown. We deal with partners who respect our achievements and who also have a vested interest in exhibiting their films here. (Pehnert 1988)

Another argument might be that these films functioned as a kind of consolation for the increasingly disillusioned and effectively disenfranchised East German public. Particularly with regard to film imports from the FRG, it would seem that the authorities were trying to placate young people and deter them from leaving for the West (also using other measures such as increased travel opportunities and Western consumer goods). It is well known that in times of political and economic crisis, entertainment films play an increasingly important role for governments and citizens alike. For governments, entertainment films increase morale but keep down political consciousness, and for spectators, they function as an escape from the unpleasant realities of their everyday life.

Notes

1 The term 'cinema' here refers to the equivalent of the commercial cinema in the West and not to the large number of film screenings which were held for social and political purposes.

2 Both figures exclude coproductions.

3 The director and date of production are given in brackets for each film.

4 Most 'art-house' films were imported with only small numbers of prints as they were not expected to appeal to large audiences. From 1982, approximately eighteen films per year were targeted specifically for 'Studio' screenings, which were mostly late-evening, sometimes only single-showing screenings.

5 The archive cinema known as the 'Camera' was established in Berlin in 1963, although the cinema had existed under this name prior to this date. In subsequent years, 'Camera' screenings were established in other large cities too. The programme was mainly composed of non-commercial screenings of films from the state film archive and was designed to inform about the film as an art form. The audience had to pay a small membership fee to gain access to the screenings.

6 Interview with Dr Erhard Kranz, former Head of the Abteilung Zulassung (Department of Film Censorship) at the HV Film, Berlin, 26 May 1998.

7 Interview with Dr Erhard Kranz, 26 May 1998.

8 See, for instance, the defence from the HV Film to a petition by General Horst Toman concerning the film *Star Trek* in Bundesfilmarchiv, File HV5890C.

9 See, for example, an interview with filmmaker Peter Kahane in *Film und Fernsehen*, 16 (1988), no. 8 (August), 13–14.

10 In *Eulenspiegel*, 18, (1971), no. 22 (1 June), 6, Renate Holland-Moritz writes of a 'film exhibition policy which defies all our cultural and political aims' ('An diesem Beispiel wird eine Spielplanpolitik deutlich, die all unseren kulturpolitischen Absichten hohnspricht').

References

Bentzien, H. (1965), 'Die Lage im Filmwesen der DDR und seine Hauptaufgaben bis 1970', *Landesarchiv Berlin, C* Rep. 121 Kultur, Bd 97.

Glaß, P. (1988), 'Der Kinospielfilm 1987 im Progress Film-Verleih', July 1988, unpublished manuscript.

Klemm, H. (1983), 'Trendwende in den Kinos der Republik', *FILM-Korrespondenz*, 28:16, 7–8. *Landesarchiv Berlin*, C Rep. 121 Kultur, Bd 19.

Pehnert, H. (1988), Interview in *Wochenpost*, 8 April 1988.

Stiehler, H. J., and D. Wiedemann (1990), 'Kino und Publikum in der DDR – der kurze Weg in eine neue Identität?', *Media Perspektiven*, 7/90, 417–29.

Wiedemann, D. (1992), 'Der DEFA Spielfilm im Kontext gesellschaftlicher Kommunikations- prozesse in den achtziger Jahren', in P. Hoff and D. Wiedemann (eds), *Der DEFA Spielfilm in den 80er Jahren – Chancen für die 90er?*, Berlin, Vistas Verlag.

Wiedemann, D. (1998), 'Lebenswelten und Alltagswissen: DDR-Jugend als Gegenstand empirischer Sozialforschung', in C. Führ and C. L. Furck (eds), *Handbuch der deutschen Bildungsgeschichte. Band VI: 1945 bis zur Gegenwart, Zweiter Teilband: Deutsche Demo- kratische Republik und neue Bundesländer*, Munich, Verlag C. H. Beck.

DANIELA BERGHAHN

The forbidden films: film censorship in the wake of the Eleventh Plenum

3

The history of European cinema and, in particular, that of German cinema seems to suggest that there is a direct correlation between the degree of freedom and democracy enjoyed by the citizens of a state and the degree to which film and art in general are used as vehicles of propaganda. Though arguably no political regime ever made use of film as a key instrument of propaganda with the same effectiveness as Goebbels and Hitler during the Third Reich, it was in fact Lenin who first employed film, alongside other media and arts, to mobilise an entire nation to join the first organised mass movement and 'to protect the revolution from an unbridled individualism that could threaten the state's *raison d'être*' (Hoffmann 1996: 76). Film, which in the context of a backward and largely illiterate country was regarded by Lenin as the most important of all arts, played a prominent part in the ideological indoctrination of the Russians. In order to achieve total control, Lenin nationalised the film industry in 1919, and sent film-trains round the vast expanse of the sparsely populated country to reach even the most remote parts. He was acutely aware that as a successful propaganda medium, cinema had to entertain as well as persuade, and he therefore suggested a ratio between propaganda and entertainment films, known as the 'Lenin proportion' (Vincendeau 1995: 260). The propagandistic use of art was further refined in the 1930s, when Stalin provided an aesthetic theory – Socialist Realism – which informed all the arts. As the only officially approved aesthetic doctrine within the Communist and socialist empire, it prescribed that 'the depiction of social reality could be used only to emphasise the positive accomplishments of socialism as the supreme principle of the new reality' (Hoffmann 1996: 76). In order for Socialist Realist art to be accessible and intelligible to the masses, it eschewed any form of experimentation, be it in form or content. Any deviations from the tenets of Socialist Realism were denounced as formalism or decadent bourgeois art and were prosecuted by the state accordingly. Where necessary, censorship was used in order to enforce the artists' adherence to state-decreed forms of expression and ideology.

After World War II, the aesthetic and ideological principles of Socialist Realism were 'imposed as a constituent part of the Soviet hegemony over Central and Eastern Europe' (Vincendeau 1995: 394), including the German Democratic Republic (GDR). Consequently art, including film art, was used as a major instrument of ideological indoctrination and was subjugated to an ever-changing political and cultural agenda. Immediately after the war, for instance, the GDR was concerned with its historical and political legitimisation as the only truly democratic and anti-fascist German state. The theme of anti-fascism dominated both film and literature. Soon economic challenges came to the fore: until the mid-1950s art was to motivate GDR citizens for the tasks of building a socialist nation with a state-owned and controlled economy. By the 1960s that goal had been achieved: the nation had 'arrived at socialism' (*Ankunft im Sozialismus*) (Schlenker 1972: 6). Henceforth, one of the prime aims governing all spheres of life, ranging from politics to economics and even culture, was to increase the rate of productivity. At the Fourth Party Congress of the Socialist Unity Party (SED) in 1963, Kurt Hager, Secretary of the Central Committee of the SED and responsible for culture, education and science, declared that 'it is necessary to make culture subservient to the comprehensive task of building the socialist state and, in particular, to make it subservient to the attainment of economic tasks' (Schlenker 1972: 153).

This instrumentalisation of art was bound to result in a loss of entertainment value. This was particularly detrimental to film art, which as a mass medium is strongly reliant on spectacle and, arguably more so than other art forms, needs to offer some form of escapism. However, overburdened with an educational mission, East German films during the late 1950s and early 1960s failed to offer this kind of relaxation, and consequently audience numbers rapidly declined. The DEFA, the East German state-owned film production company, and the HV Film, the division of the Ministry of Culture in control of national film production, realised that they had to counteract the decline of the national film industry by offering films with greater popular appeal which, none the less, did not relinquish their educational role. However, instead of trying to draw audiences back through entertainment, the strategy was to show films which dared to examine socialist society in a more critical and controversial manner. In a repressed society, a certain degree of openness and criticism promised to have nearly as much appeal as sheer escapist entertainment: a new type of critical *Gegenwartsfilm* (film about contemporary society) emerged.

One event in particular made possible the new *Gegenwartsfilm*, which came to the fore in the early 1960s: the erection of the Berlin Wall in 1961, which literally closed off East Berlin from the Western Sectors and thus barred the last escape route from East Germany to the West. With the GDR populace practically imprisoned in their own country, a more liberal atmosphere began to prevail, which lasted until winter 1965. Kurt Maetzig, one of DEFA's most prominent directors, describes the spirit of hope that reigned after the erection of the Wall as follows:

> After 1961, we had high hopes that we could take a more critical look at ourselves. We were fully aware that a lot of things were not right and had to be changed ... After the erection of the Wall, the situation in the country stabilised and became calmer. We thought the time had come to tackle the problems in our country more relentlessly, more critically and outspokenly. (Maetzig 1990)

For several years, the optimism of artists and intellectuals was well founded. The early 1960s heralded a number of measures of democratisation, which culminated in three significant events in the year 1963. A milestone of liberalisation was the Criminal Justice Edict, which abolished the dogmatism of Stalinist jurisdiction and allowed for a more immediate involvement of the populace in criminal cases. While until then it was possible to exclude the public from court trials, after the legal reform many cases were dealt with by tribunals, where representatives of workers' collectives and other public bodies assumed responsibility in the dispensation of justice (Zimmermann 1985: II, 1340–1). In parallel with the democratisation of the legal system, the GDR opened up to Western cultural influences: the Politburo Communiqué on Youth problems, March 1963, states that henceforth a more open-minded attitude would be taken towards Western pop music and a youth culture that had hitherto been regarded as decadent. A major reform of the economic sector led to the introduction of the so-called New Economic System which aimed to combine the advantages of Western capitalist economies with the centralised Eastern planned economy.

In the light of such all-embracing reforms, the DEFA film-makers mustered the courage to contemplate the creation of many of those critical *Gegenwartsfilme* which were subsequently censored at or in the wake of the Eleventh Plenum in December 1965. However, it had not been their intention to make subversive films. On the contrary, they felt that they were supporting the socialist cause by endeavouring 'to liberate Socialism from the horrible deformations which were inflicted upon it by Stalinism' (Steinborn and von Eichel-Streiber 1990: 22), which, despite de-Stalinisation under Khrushchev, was still deep rooted in the GDR.

Unfortunately, before the crippling effects of Stalinism could be fully overcome in the GDR, the period of thaw in the Soviet Union came to a sudden end, when Khrushchev was ousted from power in October 1964 and Brezhnev took over. This resulted in a massive political backlash in the GDR. Already at the Seventh Plenum of the Central Committee of the SED in November 1964, SED hardliners were calling for stricter Party control, a tougher line with the West, and restrengthening allegiance with the socialist bloc. The ratification of a new trade agreement between Brezhnev and Ulbricht in November 1965 indicated that the New Economic System had been superseded by the political changes in the Eastern bloc. Moreover, it had failed to resolve the persistent economic problems in the GDR. It has been argued that the Eleventh Plenum of the Central Committee of the SED, convened between 15 and 18 December 1965, put cultural and ideological issues on the agenda in order to divert attention from the unresolvable economic problems and political controversies of the time.

The constantly shifting political and cultural agenda made the devastating censorship imposed at the Eleventh Plenum, which affected both literature and film, unpredictable. In his keynote address at the Eleventh Plenum, 'A clean state with unshakeable principles', Erich Honecker leaves no doubt that the relative ideological latitude which had encouraged writers and film-makers to take a critical look at socialist society and depict the existing contradictions and tensions was abandoned at that Plenum. Biermann's poems, Heiner Müller's play *Der Bau* (*The Building Site*), Werner Bräuning's novel *Rummelplatz* (*Fairground*), Kurt Maetzig's film *Das Kaninchen bin ich* (*The Rabbit is me*) and Frank Vogel's film *Denk bloß nicht, ich heule* (*Don't Think I'm Crying*) were suddenly regarded as manifestations of Western ideological subversiveness: through infusing socialist society with a sense of pessimism, through weakening its moral substance with pornography, trash literature and decadent beat music, the class enemy was trying to undermine the unshakeable principles and convictions of the socialist state. This resulted, as Honecker declared at the Eleventh Plenum, in a generalised scepticism and nihilism, in particular among artists and intellectuals (Honecker 1965: 21).

The '*Kahlschlag*' (clearing the ground), as the Plenum is usually referred to, caused permanent and crippling damage to the nation's film culture. Almost the entire year's film production disappeared in the archives for some twenty-five years. No fewer than eleven leading figures in the East German film industry lost their jobs. Among them were one of the DEFA's best-known directors, Frank Beyer, head of the DEFA studios, Jochen Mückenberger, and even the Minister and Deputy Minister of Culture, Hans Bentzien and Günter Witt (Mückenberger 1990: 355–6).

The decisions of the Eleventh Plenum took film directors and cultural functionaries by surprise, for they had acted in good faith.

Since in the GDR art was perceived as a weapon of class struggle, its power was grossly overestimated. Film, which according to Lenin's much-cited dictum was the most important of all art forms, was hardest hit by censorship in the wake of the Eleventh Plenum. As though they were highly explosive weapons, nearly a dozen films were put under lock and key in a high security depot, the state film archives. Even the film-makers were denied access to their own films. Yet taking them out of circulation did not mean they were ever forgotten.

It was not until the *Wende* (reunification of East and West) that the forbidden films were retrieved from the archives. Shortly after 7 October 1989, a number of film-makers, critics and film historians put pressure on the cultural functionaries to admit that the censorship of some twenty-five years earlier had been wrong. The film historian Ralf Richter founded a Commission of the Association of Film and Television Makers of the GDR, whose aim it was to make the forbidden films accessible to the public. The Commission together with the film-makers retrieved the banned films from the cellars and raised the funds necessary to reconstruct or, where necessary, complete them. With the exception of three films which remained unfinished, and two which had been released earlier, the forbidden films of 1965–6 were eventually shown in February 1990 at the Academy of Arts and shortly afterwards at the Berlinale.[1] When they were eventually released nationwide, they were box-office hits. Yet soon GDR citizens were too caught up in the massive changes brought about by the *Wende* to take much notice of something that had already become history. Only Frank Beyer's *Spur der Steine* (*Trace of the Stones*) stayed a box-office hit in both East and West Germany, and it became the most successful German film of the year.

Of the twelve films which were banned only two had actually been discussed at the Eleventh Plenum. These were Frank Vogel's *Denk bloß nicht, ich heule* and Kurt Maetzig's *Das Kaninchen bin ich*. *Der Frühling braucht Zeit* (*Spring Takes Time*) by Günter Stahnke had been screened once, on 25 November 1965, just a few weeks before the Plenum, and was then taken off the programme in Berlin the same day. Beyer's *Spur der Steine* was already finished prior to the *Kahlschlag*, while the other films were still in production at the time of the Plenum and banned or withdrawn in the course of the following year. Some of them were never completed, since the HV Film, the chief body responsible for film censorship, found fault with them prior to their completion,[2] or because Franz Bruk, who became DEFA studio director after Jochen Mücken-berger's dismissal, pre-empted censorship by not applying to the HV

Film for permission to release these films.[3]

While the individual censorship history of each of the twelve forbidden films is different and the alleged subversiveness varies from film to film, they have a number of things in common: with the exception of Ralf Kirsten's *Der verlorene Engel*, which is set in 1937, all forbidden films are *Gegenwartsfilme*, thus falling within the genre which was assigned the greatest importance in the GDR's film production because it was meant to support the state's political and economic objectives. Not surprisingly, therefore, the portrayal of working life, and scenes set in factories and on construction sites, abound. As indicated in the Youth Communiqué of 1963, youth played a crucial role in society and the education of young people was of paramount importance: since the majority of cinema audiences were adolescents, nearly all of the forbidden films portray the lives and conflicts of the young. Also featuring prominently in the forbidden films were the institutions of the GDR, such as the Party, the legal and educational systems and their representatives.

These elements combined do not provide the stuff that dreams on celluloid are made of – and DEFA film-makers were fully aware of it. As Balla, the jovial and likeable foreman in Frank Beyer's *Spur der Steine* says rather tongue-in-cheek to Kati Klee, the woman he woos: 'I'd even go and see a DEFA film in your company.' The last thing people who worked in a factory all day wanted to see at night in the cinema was more industrial plants and factory floors. But this was the domain of the *Gegenwartsfilm* and DEFA film-makers had to make the most of it.

Klein and Kohlhaase's film *Berlin um die Ecke* touches upon two taboo topics: the inefficiency of the planned economy and the generation conflict. The film makes repeated references to a shortage of materials which impedes efficiency at a metal-processing plant. Moreover, the two adolescent heroes, Olaf and Horst, who work in a youth brigade, exceed the productivity goals by 250 per cent, which is a barely disguised reference to the general inefficiency of the centralised economy. Finally, the atmosphere at the plant bears little resemblance to the kind of socialist work ethos which DEFA film-makers were expected to render in their films. When tensions come to a head, Horst writes on the wall in the locker-room: 'We are all slaves.' Conflict, even physical violence, erupts between the old Communist Hütte and Olaf. The very suggestion of a generation conflict was a highly sensitive issue, since it belied the official view that such a thing could not exist in the socialist society of the GDR, where old and young agreed upon all the fundamental issues in life and were united in the pursuit of socialist goals. This was one of the main reasons for the ban on *Berlin um die Ecke*. In a statement dated 29 September 1966, Dr Jahrow of HV Film writes that Klein and Kohlhaase's film assumes precisely those ideological positions criticised at the Eleventh Plenum. The older generation is portrayed as stupid and arrogant and is blamed for the existing tensions between young and old: 'capitalist immorality, isolating individualism, no sense of collectivism, superficiality of emotions, anarchism in the workplace, incompetence of management, selfishness ..., greed, dishonesty, fraud, hypocrisy and similar "human qualities" dominate this film, which pretends to depict the reality of Socialism' (Stellungsnahme ... 1996).

According to HV Film's final verdict, *Berlin um die Ecke* was dishonest and anti-socialist in its attitude, pessimistic, highly subjective and not in keeping with the Party line. Worse still, the makers of this harmful film had not availed themselves of the opportunity to make significant changes, which had been recommended by Bruk in the light of decisions reached at the Plenum and the censorship of Beyer's *Spur der Steine*, a film very much in the same league as Klein and Kohlhaase's Berlin film. As a result, the film was not completed and consigned to the archives until 1987, when it was shown in its rough-cut version during the celebrations marking the 750th anniversary of the founding of the city of Berlin.

More so than any other of the forbidden films, Frank Beyer's *Spur der Steine* documents the ideological volatility which prevailed in the mid-1960s, and was equally confusing for film-makers and cultural functionaries. Unlike Klein and Kohlhaase, Beyer decided to re-edit parts of the film and reshoot a number of scenes to make the political message more acceptable in this highly charged atmosphere. In May 1966, Bruk applied to HV Film for approval to release the film, stating that 'in our [the DEFA's] view, this film is one of the most important and effective *Gegenwartsfilme* the DEFA has ever made and we are convinced that its political commitment will inspire a wide audience' (Bruk 1966). Initially, it seemed as though Beyer's film was made to order for the cultural officials. It had all the ingredients of success: set on a large construction site, the film is about the working class and production in a nationally owned enterprise. Moreover, the film promised to have great popular appeal, with Manfred Krug, one of the GDR's most popular actors, in the lead, and a witty, comic screenplay that none the less had significant political import. When *Spur der Steine* was first shown at the Potsdam Workers' festival on 15 June 1966, there was a full house for an entire week. In addition, it was earmarked for the film Festival in Karlovy Vary, the East European equivalent of Cannes, and fifty-six copies – by GDR standards a very high number – were released in cinemas across the country on 30 June. Two days before the film's official premiere, the Politburo convened and reconsidered Beyer's film. The next day, the Central Committee devised a strategy to get *Spur der Steine* removed from the cinema programmes at short notice. At the official premiere in Berlin on 1 July 1966 gangs of youths, planted in the cinema by SED hard-liners, disrupted the performance entirely unexpectedly, expressing their indignation at the film's portrayal of society. The only review it received was in *Neues Deutschland*, and this was essentially an extract from the Politburo's directives – a fake review published under a pseudonym (Schenk 1995: 114–18). In most cinemas *Spur der Steine* was instantly taken off the programmes and then – alongside those films already banned at the Eleventh Plenum – sent to the state film archives.

Set before 1961, on a large construction site in Schkona, the film focuses on three protagonists: Party secretary Werner Horrath, foreman Hannes Balla, a hard-working, hard-drinking carpenter with little interest in socialism, and Kati Klee, a young engineer with whom both men fall in love. Kati starts an adulterous liaison with Horrath, a married family man, and falls pregnant. Horrath is too much of a coward to own up to his fatherhood, leaving Kati expecting an illegitimate child and ostracised by the men on site. Balla is supportive and protective. But not only on the personal level does Balla take the moral high ground; professionally too he is more competent than Horrath. Intuitively he chooses what is right or wrong for his workmen and for the efficient running of the site. The very fact that he is not committed to toe the Party line makes him a better judge of what is required, and he is free to speak his mind when he feels that projections and targets are wrong. Horrath, by contrast, fails on all counts: the film begins and ends with Party disciplinary proceedings against Horrath, who is charged with 'immoral behavior, careerism and political and ideological failure'.

Unlike in other forbidden films where the controversy often revolved around specific scenes, in *Spur der Steine* the harmful tendencies were perceived to be virtually ubiquitous. According to HV Film, the representation of the Party is entirely biased and negative. In the character portrayal of Party members and non-members, the latter invariably fare better. Moreover, the leading functionaries at Schkona are portrayed as incompetent and autocratic in their decision-making processes. Chief site supervisor Truthmann is responsible for a number of plans and projections which turn out to be flawed. When Horrath arrives on site, the first thing he witnesses is the foundation and pillars of a building being blown up. This is a not altogether subtle reference to the mismanagement and economic inefficiency prevalent at Schkona. To make things worse, HV Film even detected ideological tendencies echoing the convictions of Havemann and other dissidents and critics of the GDR. The verdict was clear: *Spur der Steine* was a dangerous film and had to be banned. Frank Beyer did little to defend himself. Unlike his colleague Kurt Maetzig, who had distanced himself from his film, *Das Kaninchen bin ich,* in an open letter to Ulbricht in *Neues Deutschland,* Beyer did not avail himself of the opportunity of self-censorship. He stuck to his guns, lost his job with the DEFA studios and was exiled from Berlin for several years.

Yet self-criticism, a very common practice in the GDR, did not necessarily prevent state-imposed punishment: witness the case of Günter Witt, the Deputy Minister of Culture and head of HV Film at the time of the Eleventh Plenum. He was present at the Eleventh Plenum and was invited to explain why he had actually passed the two films shown there, *Denk bloß nicht, ich heule* and *Das Kaninchen bin ich.* Maetzig's film *Das Kaninchen,* in particular, raised a number of questions, since it is based on a novel by Manfred Bieler, *Maria Morzeck oder Das Kaninchen bin ich,* which had already been censored and was never published in the GDR.

Maria, the heroine of book and film, is a nineteen-year-old Berlin girl who is denied access to university because her brother Dieter has recently been charged with openly provocative behaviour against the state, for which he has been imprisoned for three years. When Maria falls in love with Paul Deister, a married man much older than herself, she soon finds out that he is the judge who passed the sentence on Dieter. Initially, she tries to separate her love for Paul from his involvement in her brother's case. During the course of their liaison, the penal code is reformed and significant steps towards democratisation are introduced. When Maria gets involved in a tribunal against fisherman Grambow, who, like her brother is charged with slander against the state, she is amazed to see that Grambow gets only three months' probation. She begins to surmise that justice is a relative thing and questions the harshness of Paul Deister's verdict. At the same time, the legal reforms afford her the opportunity to plead for mitigation in her brother's case. For Deister the legal reforms are disadvantageous because they make his verdict now appear too dogmatic. He realises that he can use Dieter's case – for the second time – to advance his career, if he, instead of Maria, suggests that the judgement be reviewed. But Maria, realising her lover's motivations are exploitative, leaves him. Paul is now unmasked as an opportunist and ruthless careerist.

The portrayal of judge Deister was seen as provocative by the censors. However, Maetzig and Witt had argued that the film script differs from the novel in so far as it does not merely dwell on the apparent shortcomings of the legal system in the GDR, but clearly shows how these were amended when the dogmatic principles of Stalinist jurisdiction were overcome. In particular the tribunal involving fisherman Grambow is an alibi scene, not based on any corresponding scene in the novel, and clearly intended to placate the HV Film. But the censors were not satisfied. Maetzig's representation of the justice system was considered to distort reality, since it equated the penal code prior to the legal reform of 1963 with the dogmatism of a careerist judge. This implied that the Criminal Justice Edict was a reform necessary in order to correct certain errors within the legal system. The Party, by contrast, stated that these legal reforms had gradually evolved in synchrony with the overall progression of socialist society (SAPMO-BArch ... 1965: 7). This misrepresentation, as well as the portrayal of one of the elite of socialist society as an opportunist and adulterer, was regarded as an attack upon the state.

The film was shown to the Members of the Central Committee at the Eleventh Plenum in a private screening. The verdict was that it was poison to the people. Günter Witt, Deputy Minister of Culture and head of HV Film, was asked to explain why he had given permission to make a film based on a forbidden novel. While justifying his decision by pointing out that the political thrust of the film differs significantly from that of Bieler's novel, he eventually conceded having committed a serious error of judgement:

> A correct view of the developing political maturity of the population, that is to say our audience, led to the false conclusion that the audience would be able to solve the contradictions and conflicts shown in the film by themselves. As a result the film abandons its educational mission which consists in disseminating the ideas of socialism amongst the masses through art. Consequently, any ideational development is left to spontaneity and the crucial element of Socialist Realism, Party doctrine, is ignored. (Witt 1965: 24)

The self-criticism which Witt exercised at the Eleventh Plenum could not save him. He was dismissed. Maetzig learnt of the banning of his film from the press and was invited by Kurt Hager to discuss the film with him. During a four-hour conversation, Hager suggested that Maetzig, one of DEFA's most honoured directors, five times awarded the National Prize, should write an open letter to Ulbricht, the Council of State Chairman, recanting the critical point of view and nihilistic propaganda expressed in *Das Kaninchen bin ich*. On 5 January 1966, an article appeared in *Neues Deutschland* entitled 'The artist does not stand outside the class struggle', in which Maetzig admits to having made a detrimental film and to having perpetrated a political error (Maetzig 1966).

A few days later, Walter Ulbricht wrote a letter of reply to Maetzig which also appeared in *Neues Deutschland*. While reiterating Maetzig's self-accusation – 'your film was a mistake, as you openly declared' (Ulbricht 1966) – Ulbricht refers to the film itself only in passing. Primarily, the letter is a treatise on the role of art in socialist society, dwelling on the political commitment expected of artists. It is an exhortation not to trespass beyond the confines of Party ideology or to adopt the dangerous attitudes of scepticism and nihilism:

> Writers and artists must close rank more tightly around the Party. They must fight ideological diversion, the poison of scepticism, the negation of any heroism and of great emotions. In other words, freedom for everything that benefits our State but no freedom for filth and pornography, no freedom for an ideological pact with the enemies of Socialism, no freedom to sully our state. (Ulbricht 1966)

The Eleventh Plenum was never forgotten amongst DEFA film-makers, not only because the *Kahlschlag* had such a devastating effect on the state-owned film industry but also because the complex relationship between *Geist und Macht* – between intellect and power – continued to affect intellectuals and artists until the demise of the socialist system in the GDR in 1989. While it was apparent to everyone in the GDR that the relationship between art and power – that is to say, between intellectuals, artists and writers on the one hand and SED hard-liners and high-ranking officials on the other – was ridden with conflicts, Ulbricht states the very opposite in the letter to Maetzig, claiming 'that the GDR is the only German state which fulfils all the necessary conditions for the relationship between power and intellect to be free from conflict' (Ulbricht 1966).

Notes

1 The following films were never completed or shown after the *Wende*: *Fräulein Schmetterling* (*Miss Butterfly*), *Ritter des Regens* (*Knights of the Rain*) and *Hände hoch – oder ich schieße!* (*Hands Up – or I'll Shoot!*), while *Der verlorene Engel* (*The Lost Angel*) and *Berlin um die Ecke* (*Berlin Around the Corner*) were released earlier. Ralf Kirsten's film *Die verlorene Engel* benefited from the 'no taboo' ethos which prevailed around the time when Honecker came to power in 1971. Kohlhaase's and Klein's Berlin film premiered in 1987 at the festival marking the 750th anniversary of the city of Berlin.

2 This was the case with Kurt Barthel's *Fräulein Schmetterling*; likewise Egon Schlegel's and Dieter Roth's debut film, *Ritter des Regens*, and Hans-Joachim Kaprzik's *Hände hoch – oder ich schieße!*.

3 This was the case with Hermann Zschoche's *Karla* and Jûrgen Böttcher's *Jahrgang '45* (*Born in '45*).

References

Bruk, F. (1966), BArch HV Film 52, *Spur der Steine*, VEB DEFA Studio für Spielfilme, 16. Mai 1966, Einschätzung zum Film *Spur der Steine*.

Hoffmann, H. (1996), *The Triumph of Propaganda: Film and National Socialism, 1933–1945*, trans. J. A. Broadwin and V. R. Berghahn, Providence RI and Oxford, Berghahn Books.

Honecker, E. (1965), SAPMO-BArch, DY30 IV/2/1/338 *Tagungen des Zentralkomitees: Protokoll der 11. Tagung des Zentralkomitees 15.–18. Dezember 1965*, JIV 2/1–126 No. 2051 I, 1–23.

Maetzig, K. (1966), 'Der Künstler steht nicht außerhalb des Kampfes', *Neues Deutschland*, 5 January.

Maetzig, K. (1990), 'Es war, als wenn ein Damoklesschwert auf die gesamte Kultur unseres Landes herunterfiel: Gespräch mit Kurt Maetzig, Regisseur von *Das Kaninchen bin ich*', 20. Internationales Forum des Jungen Films Berlin 1990, No. 16, unpaginated.

Mückenberger, C. (1990), *Prädikat: Besonders schädlich*, Berlin, Henschel Verlag.

SAPMO-BArch DY 30 IV/A2/9.06/124 Bestand SED, ZK Abteilung Kultur, Zwei Standpunkte in der Beurteilung des Films *Das Kaninchen bin ich*, 15 October 1965, 1–9.

Schenk, R. (1995), *Regie: Frank Beyer*, Berlin, Edition Hentrich.

Schlenker, W. (1972), *Das 'kulturelle Erbe' in der DDR: Gesellschaftliche Entwicklungen und Kulturpolitik 1945–1965*, Stuttgart, Metzler.

Steinborn, B. and C. von Eichel-Streiber (1990), 'Verbotene Filme: *Filmfaust*-Gespräche mit DDR-Filmemachern', *Filmfaust*, 77.

Stellungnahme der HV Film zu *Berlin um die Ecke*, 29 September 1966 (1996), *Film und Fernsehen*, 1–2, 30–1.

Ulbricht, W. (1966), Brief des Genossen Walter Ulbricht an Genossen Prof. Kurt Maetzig, *Neues Deutschland*, 23 January.

Vincendeau, G. (ed.) (1995), *Encyclopaedia of European Cinema*, London, British Film Institute.

Witt, G. (1965), SAPMO-BArch, DY30 IV/2/1/338, *Tagungen des Zentralkomitees: Protokoll der 11. Tagung des Zentralkomitees 15.-18. Dezember 1965*, JIV 2/1–126 Nffl 2051 I, 23–6.

Zimmermann, H. (1985), *DDR-Handbuch*, ed. Bundesministerium für innerdeutsche Beziehungen, Cologne, Verlag Wissenschaft und Politik.

ANDREA RINKE

Sex and subversion in German Democratic Republic cinema: *The Legend of Paul and Paula* (1973)

4

During the forty years of the existence of two separate German states, the Federal Republic of Germany (FRG) in the West and the German Democratic Republic (GDR) in the East, Western media have sometimes tended to stigmatise GDR cinema as part of the regime's propaganda machine, with films merely illustrating political doctrines and evoking the socialist new *Mensch*. And indeed, the film production company in the GDR (the DEFA) was financed and controlled by the state, and was thus affected – often in very subtle ways, such as through the film-makers' self-censorship – by the regime's cultural policies. However, the extent to which individual film-makers actually followed ideological directives, and the extent to which specific film projects were subjected to censorship, varied considerably, depending on the political climate and on the individual officials in power at any given time.

The film discussed here, *Die Legende von Paul und Paula* (*The Legend of Paul and Paula*) by Heiner Carow (1973), is a particularly interesting example of the complex relation between entertainment and ideology in GDR cinema. Whilst presenting itself as aiming merely to divert and move its audience by a – part comical, part melodramatic – love story, it was, in fact, covertly subverting the values and priorities proclaimed by the GDR regime. *Die Legende von Paul und Paula* was to become the most successful GDR film ever, seen by over three million viewers during its first year, with cinemas sold out for months. Its heroine, the popular actress Angelica Domröse, was showered with flowers by the viewers when she appeared after screenings, and newborn children were christened Paula or Paul (Carow 1995: 39).

In an interview conducted recently – that is, a few years after the demise of the GDR – director Heiner Carow stressed that, at the time of the film's conception, he had been acutely aware of the public having become disgruntled with DEFA films incorporating the officially propagated doctrine of socialist realism. Together with the scriptwriter Ulrich

Plenzdorf, he had therefore deliberately set out to make a film which deviated from this value-system by appealing to the audience's emotions rather than their intellect, trying to entertain rather than educate them: 'You know, the funny thing is, that Ulli and I said to ourselves: Why don't we just try to make a film for once which people will really *want* to go and see?' (Gehler and Kasten 1996). As a result, *Die Legende von Paul und Paula* caused some concern amongst the film authorities in the Ministry of Culture before and after its release, and there were even rumours of a ban. In my analysis I shall aim to determine the reasons for both the concern it caused the chief ideologues in the ministry and the pleasure it gave GDR audiences.

The film tells the love story of two young people who, having known each other as neighbours for years, each go through disappointing relationships before they become lovers. By this time, Paul is unhappily married and Paula struggling to raise her two children on her own. Paul hesitates to commit himself to Paula and to leave his wife, as a divorce may jeopardise his career in the Ministry of Foreign Trade. It is not until Paula has lost her son in a car accident and withdraws from Paul with feelings of grief and guilt that he realises how much he loves her. After persistently pursuing her and eventually overcoming her resistance, he moves in with her. Paula dies giving birth to Paul's child, a risk she has taken deliberately against the doctor's advice. The film ends with a scene set years later, in which Paul is sleeping in Paula's bed, cuddled up with their two children.

At the official morning preview prior to the film's release, one of the chief officers of the State Administration and head of the National Workers Union left under protest and banned it throughout the region under his jurisdiction, having failed to persuade Honecker to ban it nationwide (Gehler and Kasten 1996). Newly appointed head of state Erich Honecker resolved to let the film pass, a decision which was in tune with the benevolent mood of his first few years in office towards artists and intellectuals. Newspaper editors were, however, asked to review the film critically, and Party secretaries were instructed to 'guide' the audience through discussions which typically took place after screenings.

But how do we account for the concern this love story – which to Western viewers seems harmlessly conventional – caused in official quarters on the one hand, and the spectacular success it enjoyed with GDR audiences on the other hand? Years after the demise of the GDR, director Heiner Carow commented on the reasons for the phenomenal success of his film: 'Well, it must have been ... the fact that it was contradictory to the maxims of the times which were constantly imposed from outside, from the top, in the press and elsewhere' (Gehler and

Kasten 1996). What then were these 'maxims of the times' Carow is referring to? In the years following the devastating Eleventh Plenum of the Central Committee of the Party in 1965 (see chapter 3 of this volume), and prior to Honecker's taking office, film protagonists had been expected and had tended to conform to the ideal of the positive socialist hero, a person fighting for the advancement of socialism. The main characteristic of a positive hero in socialist literature and art is his capacity to influence historical processes by his actions, his ability to be the subject rather than the object of social processes and struggles: 'The new image of a hero [i.e. in socialist realist art and literature] is created by depictions of an active, creative person who strives to develop socialist society and to help accomplish the scientific-technical revolution' (Merkel 1978: 266).

The officially proclaimed ideal of a positive socialist heroine was the emancipated working woman, highly qualified and actively participating in social or political causes. The SED had from the outset adopted the traditional Marxist-Leninist idea that the emancipation of women was exclusively the result of the emancipation of labour from capital and therefore only possible in a socialist society. At the same time, the guarantee of equal rights to women was perceived as an essential prerequisite for the construction of a socialist order. The basis for a woman's true emancipation was her economic independence from man, which she could achieve through participation in the process of industrial production (Einhorn 1993: 20). On the basis of these premises, a number of GDR films produced during the years immediately preceding *Die Legende von Paul und Paula* presented their female protagonists' work as the most important aspect of their lives. Heroines in these films enjoyed happiness only as a result of their involvement at work and their socialist consciousness. A particularly wooden example, the film *Netzwerk (Network)* by Ralf Kirsten (1970), illustrates the way in which cinemagoers were lectured about the 'right' way of achieving happiness in a love relationship. The Party secretary's wife, a highly qualified university lecturer in mathematics, chooses to live in a different town from her husband. When asked whether she has experienced any problems reconciling her career with her commitment to her marriage, she replies:

> There is something which helps to cope with all the difficulties of daily life and living apart. Certainly, he could leave his job there. I could give up my job here and move in with him. Some people, however, love each other precisely because they respect in each other the right to develop their personality in as rich and wide a way as possible.

Personal development was perceived as being identical with professional development. It is not surprising, therefore, that many of the heroines in films produced before 1972 were intellectuals and/or occupied an elevated, highly qualified position at work – often in male domains, as surgeons, scientists and engineers, for example – their stories presenting models of progressive gender relations under socialism. Love in those films was dealt with mainly as a phenomenon conflicting with the heroines' work commitments and career ambitions.

The film-makers of *Die Legende von Paul und Paula* wanted to break away from these well-intended but unrealistic role model images of positive socialist heroes and heroines. Carow and Plenzdorf broke new ground by choosing a type of protagonist who was different from her predecessors and in her outlook on life in two respects. First, the heroine Paula, as a single mother struggling to make ends meet, seems to have been portrayed as a deliberate contrast to some of the ideologically idealised working mothers in previous DEFA films, who happily managed to reconcile their family commitments, child-raising and work duties. Second, the film-makers chose to portray not only an unskilled worker, hence someone who does not belong to the category of 'professionally highly qualified and politically active members of society' (Richter 1976: 122), but someone who shows neither professional ambitions nor any interest in further qualification or involvement in political causes. On the contrary, the heroine in *Die Legende von Paul und Paula* pursues her individual quest for happiness on her own, doing it 'her way' against all odds, without needing or wanting any help or advice from people around her, such as her work collective. The focus on a woman who does not wish to share her personal life and to try to solve relationship problems with the help of the work collective was a radical reversal of the depiction of love relationships in earlier films, which seemed to have incorporated the official view of love under socialism:

> Love ... is never solely the private affair of those involved. The socialist society has the legitimate right to influence its citizen's attitudes and relations towards the other sex, including the intimate sphere, according to the needs of their own personalities as well as the needs and demands of society. (Merkel 1978: 455)

Paula is a twenty-three-year-old single mother who lives in an old, run-down Berlin block of flats facing a dark courtyard and works at the bottle deposit counter of a large state-owned supermarket, sometimes helping out at the checkout. In a scene showing her serving a group of grumpy builders, her job is shown as far from a meaningful and fulfilling activity, but rather as physically exhausting and emotionally draining work. Her struggle to cope as a single mother of two small children is conveyed in a moving scene which became famous with GDR audiences: a long shot shows Paula kneeling alone by a huge pile of coal in her courtyard, endlessly lifting and carrying it into her house in heavy buckets until her face is sooty and sweaty and she is exhausted.

Carow attributed much of the controversy as well as the enthusiasm his film triggered to this kind of openly realistic depiction of some of the less endearing features of GDR daily life, which was a novelty at the time:

> The main controversies which the film caused were due to the fact that we ... told a story about people in such a way, with relentless honesty and left everything out which we found hypocritical. That hit a nerve, well, when Paula carried her coals indoors on her own, that was something really important! And that was also a point, for example, which was attacked incredibly viciously. (Gehler and Kasten 1996)

In the coal scene, the lonely figure of Paula in the dark and dirty courtyard is contrasted with shots of happy couples passing by and photographs of screen lovers pinned up in her house: shots of the French adventure film *Angélique* showing the heroine in a luxurious and romantic setting. This montage not only contrasts images of clichéd Western-style glamour with some of the hardships experienced in GDR daily life, but also highlights another aspect of Paula's life as a single working mother: her loneliness and sexual frustration. Paula's feelings of despair at the monotonous drudgery of her life are expressed explicitly in a scene showing her alone on her bed at night, drinking liqueur brandy. Addressing the viewers directly, facing the camera, she asks them: 'Surely, there must be more to life than just sleeping, working, sleeping and then again working? At the age of twenty-three!', and then promptly decides to have some fun in a nearby disco bar. Despite the fact that Paula's life is not easy, she is portrayed as remarkably optimistic and resilient, displaying the wry humour and fighting spirit of a typical 'Berliner Göre', a cheeky little miss who gives as good as she gets in a brash Berlin dialect.

Paula occupies a position in the social hierarchy much inferior to her married lover Paul, who pursues a promising career as a government official, having moved up the ladder in the physical as well as metaphorical sense; that is, having moved into the new high-rise flats, located on the opposite side of the street to Paula's derelict old building. However, he is painted in a much less positive light than Paula, living the lie of the respectable family man for the sake of his career while desperately unhappy in his marriage. The disrespectful portrayal of a top official as a person whose human shortcomings are directly related to his high social and political position was a first for the DEFA, and one of many breaks with taboos constituting a 'conspiratorial understanding' between the film-makers and their audience (Blunk 1990: 114).

The film-makers' positive portrayal of Paula, an uneducated, unmarried, working-class woman – a child of the people – as morally superior in her humanity to Paul, who represents the ministry, was an indirect blow to the ruling classes in the GDR, and made her an ideal figure of identification for the viewers. The film's two-fold function was matched by the two diametrically opposed reactions it provoked when it was viewed for the first time. As Carow recalls, the film's official test screening ended with 800 functionaries sitting in icy silence, while at the same time, 400 invited viewers from the general public applauded for nearly twenty minutes (Gehler and Kasten 1996). In the light of contemporary GDR audiences' viewing expectations based on socialist realist DEFA films, it is less surprising perhaps that a simple love story was perceived as a scandal on the one hand and a liberating experience on the other. At the time of the release of *Die Legende von Paul und Paula*, Carow points out, it was a sensation 'that Paula openly admits that love is the most important thing in her life and not self-realisation through socialist labour or anything like that' (Gehler and Kasten 1996).

It is not surprising, then, that GDR critics writing for the Party's newspapers focused on the depiction of love in *Die Legende*, deploring the heroine's single-minded defiance of her social environment and 'the absoluteness of a purely personal desire which defies all the contradictions, obstacles, rules of proper conduct and conventions of society, and, in the case of Paula, which aims at personal happiness isolated from the greater good of society' (Koch 1973). On the other hand, it was precisely the irrational, passionate quality of Paula's love, and her open expression of sexual desire and pleasure, which won the hearts of GDR audiences, who had become tired of love stories on screen based on rational considerations and socialist consciousness. Paula's belief in obtaining happiness through her great love becomes the force which gives her life a purpose for which she fights and dies, not unlike the saints in traditional legends. It is the driving force behind her *joie de vivre*, her vitality and sensuality, glowing with the enjoyment of self-expression. The film shows how, through the power of Paula's love, her grey daily routine is transformed into a joyous celebration of life, putting everyone present under its spell. For instance, in a scene after her first night with Paul, her enraptured state is so infectious that she changes the mood of the stressed, complaining crowd of customers at her store's checkout: in the style of a musical they join her in singing well-known saucy German folksongs. These 'miracle' sequences in the legend style are a means of entertaining the audience with fairy-tale elements but also of empowering them – through identification with Paula – to transgress the limitations and constraints of their 'real-life' experiences. Or as Carow put it:

I was tempted to tell a story about the ways in which many people would like to behave but can't, due to their personal circumstances, their fears. By showing it to them, letting them share the experience – in this case by means of a legend – I am tuning into the longings, the emotions and thus the potential experiences of the audience. (Lohmann and Sylvester 1973: 3)

The film also shows how, through the power of Paula's love, Paul undergoes a major transformation: from the cold and repressed materialistic careerist to a more human person, liberated lover and caring father. There is thus a shift in the focus of the classic narrative of the male hero transformed by the love of a 'good woman'. The female protagonist is now used as a vehicle to express the film-makers' vision of alternative values to those of the dominant order.

Die Legende von Paul und Paula was the first DEFA film which focused on love without relating it to conflicts at work, claiming that love and sex are legitimate and important needs of the individual in themselves. Moreover, it was the first film to address a woman's emotional and sexual needs not just verbally and in a rational fashion but also by openly depicting passion through erotic scenes – including some nudity. Displays of eroticism, let alone of the sexual act, had been taboo in GDR cinema until then (Schenk 1993). Not surprisingly, the chief editor of the Party's paper *Neues Deutschland*, Horst Knietzsch, frowned at the – relatively – explicit depiction of Paula's craving for and enjoyment of sex: 'The film contains impressive scenes which give us a glimpse of the rich inner beauty of Paula. However, it is biological interests that are predominant' (Knietzsch 1973).

In a tongue-in cheek reversal of a cinematic convention which transforms the heroine into an object of male desire and visual pleasure, Carow created a role-reversal scene in which Paula, attending an open-air classical concert with Paul, mentally undresses him. A long sequence of close-up shows how the passionate music brings out her strong feelings of love and arouses an erotic tension within her. Paul is arrested in the passive role of the object of her visual pleasure: in a rapid sequence of stills Paula undresses him down to his bare chest adorned with a medallion containing her photograph, a symbol of his commitment to her. At this point of her fantasy she can no longer stop herself from cuddling up to his 'naked' chest, whereupon Paul pushes her away barking: 'But not here!' After the camera has panned over a few young couples holding hands and sitting close to each other, his disapproval of her spontaneous expression of desire for him – for the man underneath the facade of a government official – seems stiff and repressed. Listening to Beethoven's romantic violin concerto arouses Paula's feelings to such an extent that she does not care about the rules of proper conduct any

4 The kiss. A videocassette of the film *The Legend of Paul and Paula* with English subtitles as well as other East German DEFA films are available. ICESTORM International: info@icestorm-video.com

more, whereas for Paul, attending a classical concert is simply something educated people of his standing ought to be seen to be doing.

Paula's concept of love includes elements of unrestrained passion, chaos and anarchy, which are taken to the extreme in the 'love boat' episode of the film (see below). Again, it is Paula who takes the initiative sexually and who is staging the events of the fantasy. She comes across as a mixture between a noble savage in the style of Gauguin paintings and an Amazon bride who has disarmed the man of her choice and taken him prisoner for the purposes of a mating ritual. Paul enters her bedroom, decorated with flower garlands like a paradise island of love. He has just been on an away-day of the workers' militia branch and is still wearing his military uniform. Paula helps him undress, inviting him to join her in a sensual feast on her bed with offerings of flowers, music, food, wine and sex. After his arrival, having relinquished the martial symbols of someone holding power, Paul turns into a stunned – temporarily intoxicated – child. Not surprisingly perhaps, the scene in which Paula disrespectfully knocks off Paul's military cap was amongst those required to be cut (Jung 1997: 49).

Despite some of the clichéd images in this sequence, it does not come across as kitsch or sentimental, as it is spiced with comical allusions to the less appealing features of contemporary GDR life and with Paula's touchingly obvious seduction strategies. For example, while Paula tries to entice Paul to share the dream of buying a boat with her, he points at the abundance of food, asking drily: 'Where d'you get all that stuff from, then?,' and she replies: 'Well, I'm at the source, aren't I?' These remarks represent a comical clash of moods as well as referring to the notorious shortages of supplies in the GDR.

In a brief surrealistic interlude, Paul has a hallucination which reminds the audience of the omnipresence of social control and surveillance in the GDR: Paul's two colleagues from the Ministry of Trade suddenly pop up in a corner of the room playing dissonant and menacing music on percussion instruments, apparently intent on spying on him. Their appearance serves as a threatening reminder of Paul's position and responsibilities, as well as expressing his fear of losing control over the situation. Meanwhile Paula turns into an omnipotent 'white witch' who is able to perform magic, such as blindfolding the spying colleagues and making them play more harmonious background music for the fantasy sequence to come. Their bed is now floating down a river on an old boat with an erect red sail against a background of phallic factory chimneys to the thumping rhythm of a popular GDR rock song.[1] On the boat, they are suddenly surrounded by Paula's ancestors, the river boat people she has been telling him about, while he is dressed like a gypsy and Paula like a bride, covered with nothing but a long wedding veil and dancing in blissful abandon in the midst of what seems to be a mixture of pagan mating ritual and wedding party. As Paul's colleagues pop up amongst the crowd, there is another tongue-in cheek side-sweep at the regime, this time targeting official prudishness and hypocrisy: when close-ups of Paul and Paula's faces imply that they are making love, one of Paul's spying colleagues protests: 'But that's porn!' The other one advises him not to look, whereupon he covers his face and peeps through his fingers. The imagery of lovers travelling on flowing water removed from the mainland suggests that, in this dream, sex is a liberating force, breaking down the restrictions of time and space. The dream, however, is brought to an abrupt end. Paula's death is visually anticipated when she is chained to the bed next to Paul, her face shown buried under flowers in a symbolic *Liebestod*. One of Paul's colleagues sets fire to their bed, thus violently waking up the lovers; that is, a representative of the authorities destroys the dream, as it cannot be accommodated within this society.

Paul flees the scene of the love feast, withdrawing again into his world of law and order, hiding behind the facade of work commitments, avoiding Paula. Following a desperate impulse, she tries to talk to him at a party hosted by the Ministry of Trade, disguised in a red wig and huge sunglasses, but is humiliated and rejected:

Paul   All or nothing, that's what you want.
Paula   So what!
Paul   Yes, but one has to fulfil one's obligations, no one can always do just as they please. For the time being, that remains so.
Paula   What about just being happy?
Paul   But never at the expense of others.
Paula   And what if?!

Throughout the film Paul represents the guardian of propriety, of socially constructed norms at the expense of individual difference, relying on ritualistic responses. His rigid paternalistic discipline, resulting in entrapment and denial, is repeatedly contrasted with Paula's childlike emotional indulgence and uncompromising demands. The film-makers construct a binary opposition of traditional male and female gender stereotypes, whereby Paul represents the public sphere, external authority, emotional rigidity and discipline, and Paula is identified with the private sphere, emotional excess, spontaneity and warmth. In the case of *Die Legende von Paul und Paula*, this exaggeration of contrasting gender stereotypes can be accounted for by the use of the legend genre, which is characterised by black-and-white judgements, allowing Carow to portray Paula with unquestioned moral superiority from the outset.

After Paula's withdrawal from Paul following the death of her son, Paul responds with a single-minded devotion and radical abandon to love that is of the same order as Paula's love for him: when camping in front of her door, growing a hippy-style beard, drawing a heart on her door, he defies all conventions of sensible, respectable adult behaviour, neglects his duties towards the ministry and risks all for the cause of his love. His one half-hearted attempt to make up with his wife as requested by his superiors fails comically, as she has a lover in the wardrobe yet again. This is the signal Paul needs to break with his former life once and for all. He expresses his feelings of liberation with roaring laughter, and is magically clad in the frilly white shirt of a fairy-tale prince, striding back to Paula's door with renewed courage and determination, accompanied by torero-style march music. Setting the tone for the legendary action to follow, he addresses one of her neighbours in fairy-tale language: 'My good woman, you wouldn't have a hatchet to hand or an axe, would you?' Kissing the axe in courtly fashion – the camera briefly switches to soft focus – he enthusiastically hacks down Paula's door, much to the delight of a crowd of cheering neighbours.

The formal presentation of the whole scene characterises it as a fantasy of overpowering passion which breaks down all barriers, representing in true legend fashion an unheard-of and unbelievable anarchic act. It breaks all rules of the socialist code of proper conduct, such as caution and self-control – being literally a 'breakthrough' victory of strong feelings over rational constraints.

Paul, at the end of the film, undergoes various stages of development: from the carefree, cheeky and rebellious hippy – which incidentally gave the actor Winfried Glazeder the nickname 'DDR-Belmondo' – to the legendary brave White Knight, and finally, in the closing scene of the film which shows Paul in a new home in bed with his two children, to the reformed, caring new man representing the utopia of a more humane socialism.

From the point of view of character development, Paula's decision to 'do it her way', even if she is told that there is only a minimal chance of success and a maximal risk, is consistent with the portrayal of her character throughout the film: to follow her feelings all the way, throwing caution and reason to the wind. Paula's doctor warns her not to insist on her 'all-or-nothing' attitude: 'Ideal and reality never match completely. Something is always left behind.' In this context Paula could be regarded as a revolutionary heroine, albeit fighting for an entirely new kind of cause and choosing to die for it, paving the way for a change for the better. The GDR film scholar Rudolf Jürschik recognises the potentially subversive message Paula's death conveys, commenting that 'the impression remains of a desire for happiness that is not and cannot be fulfilled' (Jürschik 1975: 174).[2]

The realisation of Paula's kind of uncompromising, anarchic love brings with it its own destruction. This can be read, in my view, as an indication of the need for change in GDR society where expressing one's feelings and dreams freely could only take place in the form of a legend. Paula's emotional abandon, losing herself in her love to the point of self-destruction, represents the will to determine her own destiny – that is, not to take the advice of the fatherly doctor – and at the same time, the need for loss of self-control in a regimented society.

In the emphatic focus on an individual's self-interest which signalled a general ideological shift in popular entertainment films in the GDR, love and sexuality played a key role. The depiction of playful irrationality and magical empowerment through love and sex was used to give the audience pleasure as well as to subvert the officially set parameters within which individuals were expected to realise themselves.

Notes

1   The lyrics for all songs in the film are written by the film's scriptwriter, Ulrich Plenzdorf, and sung by the most famous rock group in the GDR, *Die Puhdies*.
2   In the context of the prescribed optimism of the doctrine of socialist realism, death had been a taboo topic in films set in the contemporary GDR, unless it was a heroic death for a great political cause (Knietzsch 1973).

References

Blunk, H. (1990), 'Zur Rezeption von Gegenwartsspielfilmen der DEFA im Westen Deutschlands', in H. Blunk and D. Jungnickel (eds), *Filmland DDR*, Cologne, Verlag für Wissenschaft und Politik, 114–25.

Carow, H. (1995), 'Angelica Domröse', in R. Schenk (ed.), *Vor der Kamera: Fünfzig Schaupieler in Babelsberg*, Berlin, Henschel Verlag, 39–43.

Einhorn, B. (1993), *Cinderella Goes to Market: Citizenship, Gender and Women's Movements in East Central Europe*, London, Verso.

Gehler, F. and Kasten, U. (1996), *Heiner Carow: Legenden und Träume*, a documentary broadcast by the 'Mitteldeutscher Rundfunk 3' , 12 February 1996.

Jung, F. (1997), 'Wir alle lieben Paula, aber uns liegt an Paul: Zur Rezeption des Spielfilms *Die Legende von Paul und Paula*', in R. Waterkamp (ed.), *Frauenbilder in den DDR-Medien*, Bonn, Bundeszentrale für politische Bildung, 41–55.

Jürschik, R. (1981), 'Erkundungen: Filmbilde – Heldentypus – Alltag', *Film und Fernsehen*, 4, 12.

Knietzsch, H. (1973), '*Die Legende von Paul und Paula*', *Neues Deutschland*, 31 March.

Koch, H. (1973), 'Der einzelne und die Gesellschaft', *Neues Deutschland*, 16 June.

Lohmann, H. and R. Sylvester (eds) (1973), *Die Legende von Paul und Paula* im Gespräch: Filmmonographie, Potsdam, unpublished document marked 'confidential', Hochschule für Film und Fernsehen Konrad Wolf.

Merkel, B. (1978), *Kulturpolitisches Wörterbuch*, Pößneck, Karl-Marx-Werk.

Richter, E. (1976), *Alltag und Geschichte in DEFA-Gegenwartsspielfilmen der siebziger Jahre*, Berlin, Hochschule für Film und Fernsehen.

Rüß, G. (ed.) (1976), *Dokumente der SED 1971-1974*, Stuttgart, Seewald Verlag.

Schenk, R. (1993), 'Der erste runtergerutschte Unterrockträger: Wie es die DEFA mit der Erotik hielt. Babelsberger "Sexismus" wurde als "volksschädigend bewertet"', *Tagesspiegel*, 30 May.

The Good Soldier Švejk and after: the comic tradition in Czech film

5

> The Good Soldier Švejk is a bible of the Czech nation, a book that people know by heart ... What the book suggests – namely the effectiveness of irony and satire as a weapon – is something that has been ingrained into the Czech psychology and artistic imagination. (František Daniel, former Dean of the Prague Film School, 1983)

> ... an utterly prosaic element and humour are indeed very important in Bohemian life, and this reached me through Czech literature (Hašek, Čapek, Hostovský, Voskovec and Werich, Žák, Havlíček). (Ernest Gellner, 1995)

Karel Čapek once stated that if anyone wanted to know the true nature of the Czechs, he had only to look in the Prague telephone directory where he would discover forty names that translate as Merry (Veselý), forty as Fun (Kratochvíl) and thirty as Happy (Šťastný), as against only four who were called Sad (Smutný). Joke names such as 'Scratch-head', 'Cabbage-head' and 'Uneatable' abounded, while other names which translate as 'He jumped out' (Vyskočil) or 'He didn't get any supper' (Nevečeřel) were probably the remains of what had once been funny incidents.

The first Czech films, made in 1898 by Jan Kříženecký, were comedies, and one of them, Smích a pláč (Laughter and Tears), consists of the actor, Josef Šváb-Malostranský, miming a mixture of the two emotions. Like the quotations from Daniel and Gellner given above, this suggests that humour and irony may indeed be an important element of Czech self-definition. The same tendency can be seen in international perceptions. If Jaroslav Hašek's Dobrý voják Švejk (The Good Soldier Švejk, 1920–3) is the best-known Czech novel, some of the best-known films include works such as Jiří Menzel's Ostře sledované vlaky (Closely Observed Trains, 1966) and Miloš Forman's Hoří, má panenko (The Firemen's Ball/It's Burning, My Love, 1967). To self-definition, one can reasonably add an international perception of the 'typically Czech'.

The Czech comic tradition relates to ideology in a number of ways. First, the notion that either Czechs or Czech films are preoccupied with humour is an ideological one (it is what people believe, but it may or may not be true). Second, it has manifested itself in a number of different historical periods and under different political and economic systems: the Austro-Hungarian Empire, the inter-war democracy, the Nazi occupation, Communism, and the post-Communist democracy. As a continuing or defining element in national culture, how has it related to differing historical periods, each with its own overt or covert ideology?

While satire and irony are not, of course, inevitable elements of comedy, they are certainly present in the examples quoted above and are arguably key aspects of the Czech tradition. Similarly, the classical definition of comedy as concerned with everyday life and the problems of ordinary people is relevant. Since the aristocracy had been eliminated by the end of the eighteenth century, the Czechs had become 'a thoroughly plebeian nation' (Kusin 1971), hence the stereotype of, 'the little Czech'. As the typical representative of the Czech nation, 'the little Czech' is 'the embodiment of ordinariness and healthy common sense' (Holy 1996: 72).

The existence of a comic tradition as such, although clearly more prominent in some national cinemas, is not in itself unique. The commercial viability of the genre, and the acceptance of a need for laughter even by repressive governments, have, to some extent, rendered it a privileged area. As Miloš Forman once said, he and his colleagues of the Czech 'New Wave' of the 1960s were allowed to get away with a lot because the government did not take comedies seriously (Forman, interviewed in the film *The Kids from Famu,* BBC Television, 1990). The ambiguous nature of comedy means that its effects will always be dependent on context. Palmer (1987: 221–4), for instance, argues that comedy can be both conformist and subversive while Powell (1988: 98–104) suggests that it can function as both resistance and control, and even both at the same time, since reception is never uniform.

Many varieties of comic film were produced in Czechoslovakia, ranging from the slapstick comedies of Vlasta Burian in the inter-war period to the more recent 'Italian-style' comedies of the 1980s such as the *Slunce, seno ... (Sun, Hay, and ...)* series. Many of these could no doubt be placed in Powell's category of being comforting or neutral with respect to the prevailing ideology. In terms of tradition or conscious continuity, the most important films have, however, been linked to similar tendencies in literature and theatre. In this respect, the influence of Hašek and the theatrical double act of Jiří Voskovec and Jan Werich in the pre-war period, and that of the novelists Bohumil Hrabal and Josef Škvorecký in the post-war, have been crucial. However, this should not be seen as a mere capitalisation on literary success since all of them, with the exception of Hašek, who died in 1923, had a direct involvement with cinema. This sense of a continuous and interactive tradition can, perhaps, be related to the creation of the independent state of Czechoslovakia in 1918, and a subsequent clinging to cultural roots under various kinds of political oppression.

While a comic tradition was well established in theatre and film prior to independence, the key text of the inter-war years was clearly *Osudy dobrého vojáka Švejka za světové války* (*The Good Soldier Švejk and his Fortunes in the Great War*), a novel first published in 1921–3, which rapidly became a worldwide success. Piscator's adaptation appeared on the Berlin stage in 1928, and the first English translation of the novel in 1930. Enormously popular in Czechoslovakia, it had gone through no fewer than ten editions by 1936. Initially based on Hašek's experience of the Austrian army in 1915, its anarchistic and apparently idiotic hero was clearly a Czech making fun of his Austrian masters. However, its defence of the little man against tyranny and oppression found a resonance outside Czechoslovakia. Švejk was widely viewed as representing the indestructibility of the human spirit.

Despite its immediate popular success, it was some time before the book acquired literary respectability. The largely improvisatory form did not commend itself to establishment critics and Hašek's style was considered to be illiterate and uncouth. The cinema, however, had few reservations. One of the most popular films of the 1920s was Karel Lamač's *Dobrý voják Švejk* (*The Good Soldier Švejk*, 1926), which was followed by three more Švejk films in the period 1926–7 and the first sound version in 1931. Lamač's 1926 version is normally regarded as the best, although it followed an orthodox narrative form. One of its strengths lay in the use of the original dialogues as intertitles. As a figure familiar from the novel, Josef Lada's later illustrations, Karel Noll's stage and film characterisation, and Jiří Trnka's puppet version of the 1950s, the character of Švejk was to transcend any one medium.

While it is alleged that many Czechs know passages of the novel by heart (Daniel 1983: 54; Holy 1996: 207–8, n. 10), the response to Švejk has by no means been uniform. It is understandable that Czechs might not want to be identified with a halfwit preoccupied only with personal survival. Eva Hoffman has noted that Czechs frequently say 'We are not a nation of Švejks' and, more rarely, the opposite (Hoffman 1994: 131). Writing in the 1980s, the novelist Ludvík Vaculík saw the eyes of Švejk on the face of his police interrogator. 'While Hašek's Švejk is the embodiment of biological idiocy, *our* Švejk represents institutionalised incompetence, ignorance armed with full powers' (Vaculík 1987: 78). These reactions suggest, first, that Hašek has identified a recognisable tendency and, second, that it is an ambiguous one. Švejk's mask of innocence also gives him the privileges of a clown. Here, it is appropriate to recall the subversive role of the clown and the fool in folk traditions. 'Švejkian' characters are rarely absent from Czech film comedy.

A second major influence of the inter-war period was the Osvobozené divadlo (Liberated Theatre) of Voskovec and Werich. Their famous *Vest Pocket Revue* appeared in 1927, and productions followed in regular succession until Nazi pressures forced the closure of the theatre in 1938. Voskovec and Werich were originally brought together by a shared passion for American Westerns and Mack Sennett comedy, and Voskovec spoke of his admiration for the American slapstick comedians, who were 'our Stanislavskys' (Voskovec, quoted in Parrott 1989: 250). The novelist Josef Škvorecký, described their mixture of dadaism, circus, jazz and American vaudeville as 'a new art form ... a kind of intellectual-political musical' (Škvorecký 1971: 23–4).

Voskovec and Werich's first two feature films, *Pudr a benzin* (*Powder and Petrol*, 1931) and *Peníze nebo život* (*Your Money or Your Life*, 1932), both directed by Jindřich Honzl, came closest to their original stage work. In the first, they wove together a number of set pieces from their theatrical productions, in some of which they used the clown make-up from their stage performances. The two films reflect their stage world of absurdist humour, slapstick, and 'semantic clowning' (Jakobson 1937, quoted in Schonberg 1989).

While initially setting out to create a world of 'pure fun', Voskovec and Werich's work was soon to acquire a political dimension. Czechoslovakia had suffered badly in the 1930s economic crisis, with massive unemployment in 1932–3. While this led to increased support for the Communist Party (legal in Czechoslovakia), it was eventually answered by interventionist policies reminiscent of the US New Deal. In *Hej rup!* (*Heave Ho!*, 1934), directed by Martin Frič, Voskovec and Werich dealt with the subject of unemployment. Werich plays the head of a firm that is ruined by a ruthless rival and Voskovec a workers' representative, who loses his job for telling the truth about unemployment on the radio. The two are thrown together, go through a succession of slapstick routines, and eventually form a workers' collective that puts the rival out of business. Enormously successful in Czechoslovakia, the film also enjoyed successful runs in London and New York. *Heave Ho!* formed part of that broader European 'socialist humanist' climate that showed the capacity of the little man to be more than just victim.

The more explicitly political *Svět patří nám* (*The World Belongs to Us*, 1937), also directed by Frič, provides an analysis linking unemployment, capitalism and the rise of Nazism. Voskovec and Werich eventually join with the workers to defeat a fascist plot to overthrow the government. The film was immensely successful when released, but the negative was destroyed during the Nazi occupation. The symbolic importance of Voskovec and Werich remained considerable during the years of Nazi occupation and the Stalinist oppression of the 1950s. 'The Liberated Theatre and the films of Voskovec and Werich remained associated in the consciousness of the Czech people with the highest ideals of liberty and democracy' (Schonberg 1989: 190).

Hašek and Voskovec and Werich were not the only major 'literary' figures to find their place in popular cinema. Another leading comic writer to see his work adapted was the Czech Jewish novelist Karel Poláček, four of whose subjects were adapted in the 1930s. While none of these influences was, of course, present during the Nazi protectorate (1939–45), the Czech film industry was allowed to survive provided, as Goebbels put it, it avoided 'stupid nationalism', positive images of Jews, reference to groups thought to be anti-German, and criticism of the Hapsburg Empire (MacDonald and Kaplan 1995: 154). Frič continued to make comedies and, while production declined, the percentage of artistically ambitious films increased.

It might have been thought that the traditions linked to Hašek and to Voskovec and Werich would have flourished during the Communist period (1948–89). After all, they were anti-war and pro-working class. Despite the fact that *Švejk* had been hailed before the war by such Communist supporters as the novelist Ivan Olbracht and the journalist Julius Fučík, it was only positive evaluations from the Soviet Union and the German Democratic Republic (GDR) that led to a revival of interest in Hašek. The Liberated Theatre had to wait somewhat longer.

Hašek had, of course, been a Bolshevik commissar during the Russian Civil War, but his real political position was closer to anarchism (Parrott 1982: 17). Voskovec, who emigrated to the United States in 1948, argued that if he and Werich championed the cause of the unemployed, it was not because they were Communist but because they were 'human' (Voskovec, quoted in Parrott 1989: 257). Exceptionally, Werich appeared in Frič's *Pekařův císař a Císařův pekař* (*The Baker's Emperor and the Emperor's Baker*) at the height of Stalinism in 1951. Inspired by the Liberated Theatre's 1931 production of *The Golem*, Werich starred in the dual roles of the Emperor Rudolf II and his baker. In 1996, it was still one of the most popular films to be shown on Czech television.

Except in so far as they spoke for the powerless, the comedy of Hašek and of Voskovec and Werich was very different. Yet they were part of a single culture. In the 1930s, when planning a film of *Švejk*, Piscator offered Voskovec the role of Lieutenant Lukáš (Montmarte 1991: 99) and, in 1954, when Jiří Trnka made his puppet film version, Werich provided the commentary, using Hašek's words. Werich established contact with a new generation when he appeared in Vojtěch Jasný's early New Wave satire, *Až přijde kocour* (*That Cat/Cassandra Cat/When the Cat Comes*, 1963), contributing the key idea of the cat for whom people (including Communist bureaucrats) change colour according to their true natures.

The importance of these pre-war traditions was particularly important for the young film-makers of the Czech New Wave, who between 1963 and 1968, produced the most visible manifestation of the reformist forces that finally led to the Prague Spring of 1968. František Daniel, the former Dean of FAMU (the Prague Film School), once said that Miloš Forman felt almost obligated one day to tackle *Švejk*, and nearly all of them expressed their debt to Voskovec and Werich. Forman once said to Voskovec, 'We could not have existed without you two ... we learned how to improvise on the screen, how to speak a living language' (Forman, quoted by Voskovec in Liehm 1975: 4, quoted in Montmarte 1991: 100). However, if the New Wave could not have existed without Voskovec and Werich, it also might not have existed without the work of writers such as Hrabal, Škvorecký and Milan Kundera. Kundera, of course, lectured on literature at FAMU.

The principal literary event of the 1950s centred on the publication of Škvorecký's novel *Zbabělci* (*The Cowards*) in 1958. Originally written in 1949, its portrait of life in his home town at the end of World War II emphasised a teenage world in which resistance and revolution provided a kind of accidental backcloth. Singled out for attack by the government, it was banned and then republished in 1965.

Its significance for the New Wave lay not only in its irreverence towards the sanctity of political events, but in its loose and improvisa-tional style, its links to the vernacular and the life of young people. Connections to the wave were established prior to its breakthrough films of 1963 when Škvorecký wrote *Eine kleine jazzmusik* (*A Little Jazz Music*) for Miloš Forman in 1961. After running into various censorship diffi-culties, it was finally cancelled on the direct orders of the president. Forman's interest in filming *The Cowards* also came to nothing (Škvorecký 1971: 70). In 1968, Škvorecký had planned to reunite Voskovec and Werich in a new film featuring the musical comedy team of Jiří Suchý and Jiří Šlitr, but it was to prove another impossible project.

In parallel with the work of Škvorecký came that of Hrabal. His first collection of stories was prepared in 1949 but never appeared. In 1959, a collection was printed but pulped before publication, finally appearing as *Perličky na dně* (*Pearls of the Deep*) in 1963. In 1965, five of these stories were filmed as *Pearls of the Deep*, with episodes directed by Menzel, Věra Chytilová, Jan Němec, Evald Schorm and Jaromil Jireš. Two additional episodes were directed by Ivan Passer and Juraj Herz and separately released. It was virtually a film manifesto for the new generation.

Pearls of the Deep centred on everyday situations set variously in a pub, a hospital, a motor cycle race meeting, a café and a scrapyard, focusing on the absurdities and eccentricities of ordinary people. Hrabal was closely involved with the film, making guest appearances in the individual episodes, which also provided scope for the rambling conversations and plotless dialogue that characterise his work.

Many Czech films of the 1960s show similar qualities to the novels of Hrabal and Škvorecký. The films of Forman and Passer, for instance, reveal little interest in anything resembling a conventional narrative. In films such as *Černý Petr* (*Black Peter/Peter and Pavla*, 1963), *Lásky jedné plavovlásky* (*A Blonde in Love/Loves of a Blonde*, 1965), *Intimní osvětlení* (*Intimate Lighting*, 1966) and *Hoří, má panenko* (*The Firemen's Ball*, 1967), we find not only an improvisational style but a marvellous gallery of portraits from everyday life, and an acute observation of the absurd and the incongruous.

Hrabal's novella *Ostře sledované vlaky* (*Closely Observed Trains*) was filmed by Menzel in 1966 as his first feature film, and in 1967 it won a Hollywood Oscar as Best Foreign Film. Originally written in 1949, the story began as a far from comic piece, *Legenda o Kainovi* (*The Legend of Cain*), influenced by existentialism, and dwelling on suicide and death. While the novel changes the emphasis from suicide to the hero's search for sexual initiation, it kept much of the original's morbid imagery. Some of this is retained in the film, although the hero's sexual triumph is no longer lit by the fire-bombing of Dresden.

In adapting the novel, Menzel and Hrabal, to some extent, convention-alised the original, but also gave it a more obvious political meaning. The pursuit of the personal is itself shown to have a political significance. Miloš's attempts to lose his virginity; the philandering efforts of Hubička, the station guard; the porter, with his conscientious approach to ignoring minor jobs; even the stationmaster, obsessed with respectability, but even more with keeping pigeons – all assert the values of the everyday. In a key scene towards the end of the film, the Nazi controller of railways summarises the protagonists' responses to the needs of history – one stamps the telegraphist's backside with the station stamps, the other tries to commit suicide in a brothel. His conclusion that the Czechs are nothing but laughing hyenas is answered by the explosion of the German munitions train. The laughter and the stance of legendary indifference are shown to have a political meaning after all.

In *Skřivánci na niti* (*Skylarks on a String*, 1969, released 1990), which won the Golden Bear at the Berlin Festival, Menzel and Hrabal explicitly addressed the problem of Stalinism. This was sufficient in itself to get the film banned for twenty years and to account for the success of the illicit video copies circulating in the 1980s. This time, Menzel opts for a less orthodox narrative and all of the characters are given an equal emphasis.

The setting is a scrap metal yard, where remnants of the bourgeoisie are enjoying the benefits of re-education through enforced labour. The all-male group is soon matched by a group of women prisoners, who have been arrested for trying to escape to the West. The characters include a librarian who refused to destroy books, a prosecuting attorney who insisted on applying the law, a saxophonist who played decadent music, and a hairdresser who refused to work on Saturdays for religious reasons. This array of counter-revolutionaries pays little attention to work since they are on strike against an unauthorised increase in norms. In any case, the setting of Stakhanovite targets is leading to unusable product.

Just as ridicule is reserved for the bureaucratic Nazi railways controller in *Closely Observed Trains*, so Communist bureaucrats are the targets here. The supervisor wears a suit, mouths meaningless platitudes, and carries an empty briefcase. He only comes into his own when lurking proprietorially behind the factory railings as the secret police come to take

5 '... like all my family ... my one desire is to stand on a platform and avoid hard work ...' Václav Neckář as Miloš Hrma, the hero of *Ostře sledované vlaky* (*Closely Observed Trains*). Jiří Menzel (1966)

someone away to a worse fate. The union representative (played by Zdeněk Svěrák, later the writer and star of *Kolja*), arrives by chauffeur-driven car and exchanges his hat for a workers' cap before addressing the men. The Minister of Culture, based on the figure of Zdeněk Nejedlý, is presented as a senile old man interested only in Smetana and Dvořák.

Menzel contrasts his unpleasant realities with the omnipresence of sexual love. Apart from the woman given an additional sentence for copulating under the barbed wire, the approach is romantic: the gypsy girl and the prison guard, the clandestine meetings between the men and the women round the embers of a brazier, the lyrical romance between the hairdresser and one of the girls. However, the hairdresser's eventual marriage is only contracted through surrogates and bureaucrats and remains unconsummated due to his arrest.

In neither film is there a place for the tragic heroes of the Polish and Hungarian cinemas. Ideology is something to be endured; national and cultural identities, whether they be German, Austrian, Czech, Christian or Jewish (or European), are the subject of ironic reflection and obser-vation; heroism is accidental; ordinary people survive. The heroes of *Skylarks on a String*, like those of Forman and Passer, or the anti-heroes of Němec's *O slavnosti a hostech* (*The Party and the Guests*, 1966) or Jasný's *Všichni dobří rodáci* (*All My Good Countrymen*, 1968), also share a group identity. And while *Closely Observed Trains* does have a central character, the film is as much about Miloš's world as his individual problems. If irony is based on the Greek character *eiron*, the clever underdog, they are undoubtedly ironic films. Nor do they lack verbal or dramatic irony.

While it would be quite wrong to argue for any simplistic identification of, say, Hrabal with Hašek, there are some broad similarities in these traditions: the emphasis on the everyday, the values and strengths of those without power, the heretical and ironic attitude towards those that have it, and, of course, in the 1960s films, the rejection of conventional narratives. The subversive effect of this particular tradition of Czech comedy proved almost impossible to curb, and it also played a role in the wider culture of Central and Eastern Europe.

Yvette Biro has divided the history of post-war East European film into two periods. The first, from the 1950s through to the mid-1960s, was dominated by figures such as the Polish Andrzej Wajda and the Hungarian, Miklós Jancsó. If heroism, charismatic sacrifice and faith had been the prime ingredients of Stalinist ideology, these were now examined through the eyes of doubt, despair and frustration. In the second period, the late 1960s through to the 1970s '... the Czech New Wave entered the scene, the best boys like Forman, Menzel, and Passer literally bringing the wind of spring' (Biro 1983: 38).

The so-called 'Czech touch comedies', what Michael Brashinsky des-cribes as 'dramas of Socialist absurdism' (Brashinsky 1993: 60), certainly enjoyed a wider resonance in Eastern Europe. While Péter Bacsó's Hungarian film *A tanú* (*The Witness*, 1969, released 1978) draws fairly obviously on Hašek, it is possible to see the influence of Czech comedies in a number of films from different countries. Prior to glasnost, however, it was not a tradition common in the Soviet cinema (Tolstykh 1993: 18).

Charles Eidsvik has identified the key aspects of East European comedy as comprising the political, the humour of the everyday, allusion to social realities, ambition (or lack of it) and a workplace locale (Eidsvik 1991: 91–4). His examples of 'East European' comedy are, however, nearly all Czech, which suggests that we may be looking at a Czech rather than an East European sensibility. While these elements may differ from 'comedies in the usual American sense' (Eidsvik 1991: 91), and are certainly ingredients of socialist absurdism, they can also be found in other forms of comic cinema. Similar emphases can, for instance, be found in films by Bill Forsyth, Ken Loach, Mike Leigh and other British directors. To cause further confusion, the films of Forman and Menzel may be said to have influenced film-makers in both Western and Eastern Europe.

The years of so-called 'normalisation' that followed the Soviet invasion of Czechoslovakia in 1968 led to a wide-ranging repression of all reform-ist tendencies and, in the case of cinema, the banning of well over 100 feature films (both those already released and others completed in 1968–9). Most leading film-makers were unable to work for six or seven years and some found their careers at an end. Forman, Passer, Němec, Škvorecký and Kundera were among those who left the country. It was some time before Menzel and Hrabal were again able to work together, on *Postřižiny* (*Cutting it Short*, 1980) and *Slavnosti sněženek* (*The Snowdrop Celebration*, 1983), but despite producing sanitised versions of Hrabal's original works, which had been censored before publication, they retain much of the essential flavour of the earlier films. A new comic theatre, the Jára Cimrman theatre of Ladislav Smoljak and Zdeněk Svěrák, with a reputation for black and absurdist humour, found its reflection in a sequence of eight films for which Smoljak and Svěrák wrote the scripts. They demonstrated the continuing power of humour provided it could steer clear of the newly vigilant censor–managers.

After the Velvet Revolution of 1989 and the subsequent reprivatisation of the industry, the work of Hrabal and Škvorecký returned to favour, albeit in rather less impressive films. Two films were adapted from Hrabal, and Škvorecký's banned comic novel about life in the army (written in the 1950s), *Tankový prapor* (*The Tank Battalion*, 1991) was not only the first privately produced film, but a massive box-office success. *Eine kleine jazzmusik* was finally filmed for television in 1996. While younger directors have begun to take the cinema in new directions, the flavour of comic irony is still to be found, not least in the films of Jan Svěrák (*Obecná škola/The Elementary School*, 1990, and *Kolja/Kolya*, 1996) and Petr Zelenka (*Knoflíkáři/Buttoners*, 1997).

There remains a whole range of more 'recognisable' comedies – in the 1960s, parodies of Superman, spy films and science fiction; in the 1980s, crime comedies derived from Conan Doyle, or featuring heroes like the popular tough detective Nick Carter. I have already mentioned the *Sun, Hay and …* series from the 1980s. At the other end of the spectrum, one could note the absurdist humour of Němec in *The Party and the Guests*, the black humour of Juráček and Schmidt in *Postava k podpírání* (*Josef Kilian*, 1964), the black and sarcastic humour of Jan Švankmajer in *Lekce Faust* (*Faust*, 1994), or the mixture of slapstick with the avant garde in Chytilová's *Sedmikrásky* (*Daisies*, 1966).

However, what remains important about the traditions based around Hašek, Voskovec and Werich, Škvorecký, and Hrabal is not only their real influence but also their perceived importance. If Voskovec and Werich were loved for their links to 'liberty and democracy', Hrabal has been described as 'a glorious incarnation of the Czech spirit' (Kundera). It might be argued that one is here talking of national identity, and of a social cement in the face of adversity and repression.

Many varied and contradictory elements have been identified as constituting a Czech national identity, ranging from Herder's influential description of the Slavs as 'quiet, peace loving, hospitable', loving country living, and leading a merry musical life, to self-identification through martyrs (Pynsent 1994: 74). Vladimir Kusin defines the basic traits of the nation as 'nationalism, democracy, and an inclination to heresy' (Kusin 1971: 136). The view of Czech history taken by Masaryk, first president of Czechoslovakia (1918–35), envisaged a continuous evolution, leading to intellectual freedom, equality, brotherhood, justice and democracy. Under Communism, of course, there was a concerted effort to harness notions of nationalism and democracy to the demands of Communist ideology.

In the 1950s and in the 1970s and 1980s, it is interesting to note the cinema turning to biographies of Smetana, Janáček, and Dvořák and to historical films based on the lives of Jan Hus and Comenius. At the height of Stalinism, Otakar Vávra produced his three-part Hussite trilogy, adapted from Alois Jirásek, the principal populariser of Masaryk's view of history. Of course, Hus was now seen as the inspirer of the great Czech medieval bourgeois revolution. Despite their explicit concern with national identity, many of the films can be viewed as at best ambiguous and, regardless of subject, tended to become part of establishment culture.

In contrast, the New Wave films were characterised not only by a rejection of Socialist Realist form but by a penchant for collective heroes and open, non-propagandistic endings. They can certainly be linked to Herder's stereotypes but, unlike in the establishment epics, where Hus and Comenius are joined by a whole range of Communist martyrs, the theme of the martyr takes a different form. In *Closely Observed Trains* there is no deliberate sacrifice. Miloš's death is accidental, his planting of the bomb unintended, a by-product of his membership in a community. In *Skylarks on a String*, the downbeat ending, in which the characters are condemned to life in the uranium mines, scarcely seems to negate the comedy that has preceded it. Yet, in both films, the hero or heroes end up sacrificing themselves for a greater good. That is not what they intend, but the narrative (and history) demands it. It would be an exaggeration to extend these parallels to the heroine of Forman's *A Blonde in Love*, disappointed in love, or Passer's musicians and their mid-life crisis (in *Intimate Lighting*), but they all share a kind of resolution in the face of defeat.

If the more grandiose aspects of national identity are only ambiguously present, others are much more evident. The characters are undoubtedly peace-loving, tolerant (on the whole), heretical, concerned with truth and equality, and plebeian. The 'little Czech' is certainly to be found here, but the negative characteristics of the stereotype (envy, conformity, egoism, laziness) are largely absent or converted to positive ends. In the case of Voskovec and Werich, of course, there is no suggestion of this ambiguity. And in *Skylarks on a String*, the characters in many respects reflect the remains of that more positive of self-images, the democratic, well-educated and highly cultured nation.

The international interest in Czech comedies has tended to overshadow other significant areas (such as the brilliant invention of František Vláčil's historical films and the profound moral studies of Evald Schorm). Yet it would be true to say that the influence of the comedies has been preeminent and, even when censored, represented something more than their surface meanings. Despite their influence on foreign film-makers, their prime significance lies in a kind of national questioning, not only of subjects such as foreign domination, economic depression, Nazism, Stalinism and, by extension, contemporary realities, but of wider notions of tradition and convention. This also suggests that it is as part of a 'national' rather than a 'former Communist' or 'Central East European' cinema that they need to be understood.

References

Biro, Yvette (1983), 'Pathos and Irony in East European Films', in David W. Paul (ed.), *Politics, Art, and Commitment in the East European Cinema*, London, Macmillan.

Brashinsky, Michael (1993), 'Closely Watched Drains: Notes by a Dilettante on the Soviet Absurdist Film', in Andrew Horton (ed.), *Inside Soviet Film Satire: Laughter with a Lash*, Cambridge, Cambridge University Press.

Daniel, František (1983), 'The Czech Difference', in David W. Paul (ed.), *Politics, Art and Commitment in the East European Cinema*, London, Macmillan.

Eidsvik, Charles (1991), 'Mock Realism: The Comedy of Futility in Eastern Europe', in Andrew S. Horton (ed.), *Comedy/Cinema/Theory*, Berkeley, University of California Press.

Hoffman, Eva (1994), *Exit into History: A Journey Through the New Eastern Europe*, London, Minerva.

Holy, Ladislav (1996), *The Little Czech and the Great Czech Nation: National Identity and the Post-Communist Transformation of Society*, Cambridge, Cambridge University Press.

Jakobson, Roman (1937), 'Dopis Romana Jakobsona Jiřímu Voskovcovi a Janu Werichovi o noetice a sémantice švandy', in Josef Träger (ed.), *10 let Osvobozeného divadla*, Prague, Borový, quoted in Michal Schonberg (1989), 'The Theatre and Films of Jiří Voskovec and Jan Werich', in Jaroslav Anděl et al. (curators), *Czech Modernism 1900–1945*, Houston, Museum of Modern Art, and Boston, Bulfinch Press.

Kusin, Vladimir V. (1971), *The Intellectual Origins of the Prague Spring: The Development of Reformist Ideas in Czechoslovakia 1956–1967*, Cambridge, Cambridge University Press.

Liehm, Antonín J. (1975), 'S Jiřím Voskovcem o čemkoli', *Listy*, 5, July (Rome–Munich), quoted in Danièle Montmarte (1991), *Le Théâtre Libéré de Prague: Voskovec et Werich*, Paris, Institut d'études slaves.

MacDonald, Callum and Jan Kaplan (1995), *Prague in the Shadow of the Swastika: A History of the German Occupation 1939–1945*, London, Quartet Books.

Montmarte, Danièle (1991), *Le Théâtre Libéré de Prague: Voskovec et Werich*, Paris, Institut d'études slaves.

Palmer, Jerry (1987), *The Logic of the Absurd: On Film and Television Comedy*, London, British Film Institute.

Parrott, Cecil (1978), *The Bad Bohemian: A Life of Jaroslav Hašek, Creator of The Good Soldier Švejk*, London, Bodley Head.

Parrott, Cecil (1982), *Jaroslav Hašek; A Study of Švejk and the Short Stories*, Cambridge, Cambridge University Press.

Parrott, Cecil, n.d., 'The Liberated Theatre: Voskovec and Werich', in Alan Ross (ed.) (1989), *London Magazine 1961–1985*, London, Paladin/Grafton.

Powell, Chris (1988), 'A Phenomenological Analysis of Humour in Society', in Chris Powell and George E. C. Paton (eds), *Humour in Society: Resistance and Control*, London, Macmillan.

Pynsent, Robert B. (1994), *Questions of Identity: Czech and Slovak Ideas of Nationality and Personality*, London and Budapest, Central European University Press.

Schonberg, Michal (1989), 'The Theatre and Films of Jiří Voskovec and Jan Werich', in Jaroslav Anděl et al. (curators), *Czech Modernism 1900–1945*, Houston, Museum of Modern Art, and Boston, Bulfinch Press.

Škvorecký, Josef (1971), *All the Bright Young Men and Women: A Personal History of the Czech Cinema*, trans. Michael Schonberg, Toronto, Peter Martin.

Tolstykh, Valentin (1993), 'Soviet Film Satire Yesterday and Today', in Andrew Horton (ed.), *Inside Soviet Film Satire: Laughter with a Lash*, Cambridge, Cambridge University Press.

Vaculík, Ludvík (1987), *A Cup of Coffee with My Interrogator*, trans. George Theiner, London, Readers International.

PETER WILLIAM EVANS

6

Cheaper by the dozen: *La gran familia*, Francoism and Spanish family comedy

The trilogy of enormously popular family-centred comedies – *La gran familia* (*The Big Family*, Fernando Palacios, 1962), *La familia y uno más* (*The Family Plus One*, Fernando Palacios, 1965) and *La familia bien, gracias* (*The Family's Fine, Thanks*, Pedro Masó, 1979) – reflects, in addition to the perennial appeal of the genre in Spain, the dramatic changes in social attitudes that took place in the country as it emerged from dictatorship into democracy soon after the death of Franco in 1975. But as the Franco period was itself characterised by subtle shifts and changes in political outlook, so these films mirror as well as partially help formulate in cinematic terms Spain's complicated gradual transition from self-enclosed autarky to tentatively liberalising technocracy to constitutional democracy. From the end of the Civil War (1936–39) until the late 1950s, and as if restaging the reactionary politics of the Counter-Reformation, Spain had in a sense closed its frontiers to outside influence, becoming in effect an isolated nation, suspicious of contact with other cultures, especially in its Hollywoodised forms, attempting as much as possible to survive on its own resources. The Law for the Protection and Development of National Industry (October, 1939) and the Law for the Regulation and Defence of National Industry (November, 1939) were designed to promote economic self-sufficiency, while social legislation, including at first the restoration of the Civil Code of 1889 (which, among other things, legitimated the subordination of women to their husbands), sought to reaffirm the patriarchal values that had been to some extent undermined in the overthrown Second Republic.

However, with the spectacular failure of autarky Spain was obliged to reconsider its relations with the outside world and, in a new spirit of pragmatism, began to tolerate limited doses of liberal reform in exchange for foreign investment and economic stability. In this respect the key piece of legislation, the mechanism that signalled the acknowledged failure of autarky, was the Economic Stabilization Plan of 1959. As Adrian

Shubert puts it: 'The impact of the liberalization measures was felt immediately: a severe recession which made possible a dramatic improvement in the balance of payments. The stage was set for the Spanish "economic miracle" of the 1960s' (Shubert 1990: 207). Economic success had only a limited lifespan as, even more so than many other European countries, Spain soon fell victim to the vicissitudes of international events, including above all the oil crisis in the wake of the Arab–Israeli war (1973). Although Francoism retained much of its authoritarianism well into the 1970s, no real attempt was made to destabilise the regime until the expiry of Franco himself (1975), the signal for serious initiatives to democratise the country. Nevertheless, the history of Spain from 1939 to 1975, as has often been acknowledged, was not one of monolithic surrender to Francoism. Tensions, contradictions, resistances both inside and outside its ideological constraints were its constant prickly companions. Political associations, artistic and intellectual activity, as well as – in a country which even in the more liberal phases of its history had been suspicious of the involvement of women in public life – tentative forms of feminism began to question the social and political orthodoxies of the day. While, as Anny Brooksbank Jones argues, the early days of the regime allowed 'little in the way of alien ideology to unsettle the regime's view of women as repository of the nation's spiritual values' (Brooksbank Jones 1997: 2), the economic demands of the country, as well as the private household, the reform of the suffrage and other discriminatory laws, the gradual infiltration of feminist texts from abroad, and the gradual rise of feminism and associationism in Spain combined to present a serious challenge to the official social dogma of the day.

These tensions characterise the first two films of the trilogy under discussion here, both of course made at the height of Francoism. They were mainstream popular films that, on the surface at least, displayed no interest in challenging dominant ideology, continuing the traditions of a genre that in Francoist times offered, as Barry Jordan and Rikki Morgan-Tamosunas put it, 'convenient diversions from more disruptive pursuits such as politics and ... provided an effective vehicle for conveying the conservative values of the regime' (Jordan and Morgan-Tomasunas 1998: 63–4). *La gran familia* was designated 'de interés nacional' ('of special national interest'), a category that enabled projects not only to escape mutilation at the hands of the censor but also to be awarded special extra funding (Gubern 1981). In this respect, officially endorsed on the basis of its embrace of dominant ideology, *La gran familia* seems radically different from other family-centred films (sometimes even comedies) that dared question the regime's crude mixture of Catholic ethics and authoritarian politics. Darker family-oriented films of the late 1950s and early 1960s, such as Carlos Saura's *Los golfos* (*The Layabouts*, 1959), *Stress es tres tres* (*Excess Stress*, 1968) and *La madriguera* (*The Warren*, 1969) or Nieves Conde's *Surcos* (*Furrows*, 1951), and lighter ones like Berlanga's *Plácido* (1961) or *El verdugo* (*The Executioner*, 1963), seem worlds apart from the saccharine utopianism of *La gran familia* and *La familia y uno más*. The former, despite the strict censorship of the times, were daring attempts at dissidence; the latter at appeasement. They complement the couple-centred romantic comedies of the day, such as *Las chicas de la Cruz Roja* (*The Red Cross Girls*, Rafael Salvia, 1958) or *El día de los enamorados* (*St Valentine's Day*, Fernando Palacios, 1959), and family comedies like those starring Paco Martínez Soria or Marisol.

Focusing not on the couple but on the group and the procreative function of love and sexuality, the first two of the *Gran familia* comic trilogy seemed ideal for the promotion of the regime's conservative ideology of the family. And yet, even here, the celebratory tone – somewhat reduced in the last of the series, *La familia bien, gracias* – and the naturalisation of key concepts related to family life do not entirely banish the tensions and unease caused by values identified with Catholic dogma and state decree. Reconciliatory mechanisms are even here, in these characteristic examples of the Spanish commercial cinema under Franco, surprisingly counterbalanced by disruptive elements that place in question issues related to patriarchy or the assumption by the younger generation of their social and gender roles. Even in comedy, strategies for reconciliation and resolution are complicated by questions about the contradictions and problems in Francoism's attempts to regiment the nation into social conformity. By the time of the appearance of *La familia bien, gracias* those contradictions could be exposed without any subterfuge. In this film, though, the pattern is in some ways reversed, since the new attitudes of the post-Franco era to some extent breed nostalgia for some of the old certainties, especially those attached to the family, the cornerstone of Francoism, as Franco himself made clear:

> El Estado reconoce y ampara la familia como institución natural y fundamento de la sociedad, con derechos y deberes anteriores superiores a toda ley humana positiva. El matrimonio será uno e indisoluble. El Estado protegerá especialmente a las familias numerosas. [The State recognises and protects the family as a natural institution and cornerstone of society, with rights and duties superior to all positive human law. Marriage will be one and indissoluble. The State will especially protect large families.] (Francisco Franco, *Fueros de los Españoles*, Art. 22, 1945, cited in Aguado et al. 1994: 386)

The family is a microcosm of the state, reflecting in miniature the power relations and beliefs of its leadership. In its celebration of the reproductive function of love, family comedy concentrates not on the individual, on sexuality for its own sake, but on social and institutional structures and patterns of behaviour. These films recognise the importance of the family in Francoist ideology and, as comedies, project a comic, never a satirical, image of its ideological significance, containing rather than revelling in or proclaiming resistance and protest. Even more procreative than their precursor in its hugely successful Hollywood prototype, *Cheaper by the Dozen* (Walter Lang 1950), where the married couple have only twelve children, Carlos and Mercedes in *La gran familia* have fifteen children, with a sixteenth on the way. To some extent the film addresses the country's need to continue to repopulate a nation decimated by war; but the fifteen children are also evidence of the *reductio ad absurdum* of Catholic attitudes to birth control.[1] The stress on the family, in line with religious antagonism to any form of sex unrelated to procreation, reduces the importance of passionate love, for although some of the subsidiary narratives include scenes of courtship, these are treated, in the case of the daughter infatuated by a local boy during the family's holiday on the Mediterranean Coast, rather lightly and, in the case of the children's godfather, when he too becomes involved in a holiday romance, somewhat farcically. The group-based focus of family comedy determines the narrative patterns of all three films.

The first film, *La gran familia*, concentrates on the multiple narratives of the parents' self-sacrifices on behalf of their children, the children's mini-dramas as each strives or fails to live up to his or her potential and parental expectation, and the involvement in the family of fringe figures like the godfather, crucially seen to be without a family of his own and, therefore, in ideological terms, emotionally unfulfilled. The second film, *La familia y uno más*, traces the attempts of the father to cope single-handedly, following his wife's death in childbirth, with the problems of his offspring, approaching but in the end being steered clear of a second marriage. The third film, *La familia bien, gracias*, concentrates on the children, now as adults leading independent lives, and the odyssey of the father and his friend, the godfather, as they vainly attempt to reconstruct the family in the radically changed ideological climate of Spain in the 1970s.

While the last film acknowledges the growing disintegration of traditional family life, exemplifying perhaps a common sentiment of the times, 'contra Franco vivíamos mejor' (we were better off opposing Franco), the first two only hint at tensions and difficulties, made as they are at the height of the regime's power. But as Francoism had abandoned autarky by 1962, so these films both project as well as ultimately defuse the threat of dissidence and heterogeneity. They exemplify Barthes's notion of 'inoculation', where 'one immunizes the contents of the collective imagination by means of a small inoculation of acknowledged evil; one thus protects it against the risk of a generalized subversion' (Barthes 1973: 150). In the main the first two films draw on the idea of the family as an institution that educates its members for their social roles. So, the parents keep imagining their children in the first film as eventually becoming, say, architects, doctors or diplomats. The tensions and prohibitions of various kinds that do occasionally surface here are to a large extent projected in ways that reinforce the prevailing ideology of the family, explaining away, as it were, repression and conflict as necessary by-products of the complex processes leading to the socialisation of the individual. The radical potential of tensions and disturbance is ultimately recuperated by the conservative tendency of the film, but even so, as in the Hollywood tradition, the strategy is not always entirely successful.

The parent–child relationship raises questions that are not finally answered convincingly. As commercial films the *La gran familia* series partly relies on the popularity of its major stars, in this case, in the first film, Alberto Closas (Carlos), Amparo Soler Leal (Mercedes), José Isbert (grandfather) and José Luis López Vázquez (godfather). Alberto Closas and José Luis López Vázquez appear in all three films; Amparo Soler Leal and José Isbert are killed off at the end of the first. Even though the roles of Soler Leal and Isbert are important, Closas and López Vázquez are the key players as regards all three films' preoccupation with representations of alternative forms of masculinity. While the mother and godfather figures are marginalised, they remain important components of the project to legitimise the authority of the father. The role of the mother here is as ancient as Spanish culture itself. Like Casilda in Lope de Vega's great seventeenth-century lyrical pastoral drama *Peribáñez*, she personifies the home. She is the 'angel in the house' who provides its comforts, making it a safe haven for the family. In an early scene recalling the domestic harmony of Lope's married couple, who celebrate their love at one point through speeches on Casilda's culinary skills, Mercedes ensures the return of her husband after kissing him goodbye in the morning by describing the succulent dinner menu awaiting the returning day-at-the-office hero: 'lentejas y arroz, albóndigas con salsa' (lentils and rice, meat balls in sauce). This scene, and a follow-up where she is caught haggling with stall-holders at the market, while not without domestic charm, projecting an image of marital, family harmony and togetherness, never the less reinforces the gendered role differences of the day. The wife's request for the housekeeping expenses from her husband reaffirms ideological stereotype in a gesture that belies the reality of many women's lives under Franco (Brooksbank Jones 1997: 40–94). The 'kuche, kirche und kinder' ('kitchen, church and children') ideal triumphs in this film over the lived experience of vast numbers of women who earned their living outside the home (even though many would still have had to ask for housekeeping from a husband or father).

More important to the film is the projection of the idealised woman's power over her husband through her intuitive understanding of natural justice. If the father represents discipline, the mother must be on hand – in the tradition of the Virgin Mary herself – to soften the impact of its exercise and to uphold his authority even where it oversteps the mark. From this point of view the most significant scene is one in *La gran familia* where Mercedes – significantly named (Mercies) – intervenes to protect Carlos's authority when the family rebels over his exclusion of one of the children, Carlitos, who has failed his exams, from the family summer holiday near Tarragona. The mother here fulfils her traditionally intercessional role, one that informs the entire narrative of the first film, but perhaps appearing most sharply in focus in this scene. For a moment the film seems to be staging a drama in the crisis of masculinity, advocating democracy in a culture to which it is alien, before swerving away from the wider radical implications of the scene as it reverts to its projection of a benevolent form of despotism, much more in keeping with the climate of the times, as Mercedes, in the spirit not of capitulation but of *lèse-majesté*, persuades the father to avoid confrontation by agreeing to their children's demand: 'ellos piden y tu concedes, por no perder tu autoridad' (they ask and you concede, so as not to lose your authority). The wider political meanings of the remark would not have been missed by contemporary audiences: the authority of the father, ultimately legitimated by the nation's father, Franco himself, and the very structure of order and discipline, in this microcosm of the country's social structures, are rescued from danger. Like the queen who intervenes to prevent the king from carrying out an act of injustice at the end of *Peribáñez*, so here Mercedes ensures that the authoritarian structure of the system is not prejudiced by inflexibility from the symbol of that authority. The role of Mercedes in *La gran familia* is therefore significant not only in its own terms, but also as an element in the legitimation of hegemonic masculinity.

The same is true of the roles of grandfather and godfather, played respectively by José Isbert and José Luis López Vázquez, two of the most important comic stars in the Spanish cinema between 1950 and 1970. Isbert appeared in such key films as *Bienvenido Mr Marshall* (*Welcome Mr Marshall*, García Berlanga, 1952), *Los jueves milagro* (*Miracles on Thursdays*, García Berlanga, 1957) and *El verdugo* (García Berlanga, 1963), all made in the cautiously critical auteurist tradition of the day. In these films Isbert's involvement belongs to a wider pattern of gentle ridicule of contemporary social and political realities: relations with the USA, urban problems, and religion provide the satirical targets for these landmark films. José Isbert contributes to this critique, his diminutive, gnome-like stature and rasping voice the signs of Francoism's delivery of mutant forms of humanity, the pitiful and comic equivalent of the monster in the Frankenstein (*El espíritu de la colmena* (*The Spirit of the Beehive*), Victor Erice, 1973) and other horror films (made by Jesús Franco and others) so popular in the 1960s and 1970s. Like López Vázquez he represents a complex alternative form of masculinity, tolerated because of its comic reversal of hegemonic forms, but also slightly troubling because its hyperbolic deviant expression registers the repressions and pressures to which all Spanish men had been subjected.

If Isbert's presence delivers a largely socio-political message, López Vázquez's is mainly identified with sex, something developed in all the (admittedly somewhat tame) sex comedies in which he appeared during the 1960s and 1970s, and in the role of the *padrino–búfalo* (Godfather Buffalo) he plays in the *La gran familia* trilogy. The contrast between López Vázquez as the *padrino* and Closas as the father is noteworthy in terms not only of the celebration of the masculinity projected by Closas, but also, in the process of that project, of the costs related to the achievement of that universalising hegemonic norm. In that respect the film borders on territory identified by Steve Cohan (Cohan 1997: 34–78) in discussion of Hollywood films raising similar issues in the 1950s.

López Vázquez cannot possibly be awarded the role of the father in a narrative the chief ideological mission of which is its reinforcement of domesticated hegemonic masculinity. Outside this film his roles had already identified him with farce, a tendency to a large extent, as in Isbert's case, inspired by physical appearance. But López Vázquez's portrayal of benign, ridiculous forms of conventional masculinity provide the *La gran familia* films with more than purely comic relief from their more sober or sentimental agendas. López Vázquez is here identified with animality, irresponsibility and pleasure, all attributes that in Bakhtin's terms (Bakhtin 1984) make of him too 'festive' a construction of masculinity for the specifications of the ideological blueprint. His animality is stressed through the children's reference to him as their *padrino–búfalo* (a negative term of endearment when he frustrates their more unruly desires), or, when in *La familia bien, gracias*, a visit to the zoo results in a comparison with an ape whose simian features uncannily resemble those of the uncaged *padrino*. These bestial affiliations belong to an alternative construction of masculinity that, together with his more priapic, pleasure-ruled instincts, disqualify him from the hegemonic ideal. The *padrino* is too wild, and his very profession as the owner of a pastry shop – a source of treats for his godchildren, but not of the regular ideological diet required to nourish a growing family – and his failure to be seduced by the joys of parenthood make him a comic but unacceptable alternative to everything sacred to the state. His id-driven masculinity makes him both ultimately unreliable and unattractive, even though from a distance, as a co-opted member of this family, he plainly has his place as its tolerated, even desired, almost-black sheep. Once again, the ideological family is protected through 'inoculation' by the very virus that threatens its existence. The *padrino* is a good playfellow: he has a comic appearance, he cheerfully suffers humiliation in the children's games, and he brings them cakes and pastries to satisfy some of their appetites. But he is also irascible, unreliable, quick to lose his patience with the children even, sacrilegiously, when he is baby-sitting. Once his failure at the beginning of *La familia bien, gracias* to resist the nubile charms of his female assistants is exposed he is condemned by his wife, who effectively pronounces judgement on his undesirable eccentricity, to accompany his friend Carlos on a peripatetic journey as family outcasts. The third film in the trilogy sees the children in homes of their own, but when the patriarch and his *padrino* sidekick seek refuge with members of the dispersed family each attempt results in ultimate failure, and the odd couple become resigned to a life on the road in each other's nostalgic company. At one level, the significance of some of the roles he plays in family games, especially when in *La familia y uno más* he is the paleface tied to a stake by his whooping-Brave godchildren, identifies him as a victim of an ideology that without actually meaning to cannibalise him at least thinks of him as an amusing but ultimately unsuitable role-model, the comic partner or shadow to Alberto Closas's straight man, who is, of course, the ideological ideal.

The casting of Closas as Carlos, however, is not without its ironies. Onscreen the epitome of paternal devotion and marital fidelity, offscreen he was an inveterate Don Juan, the Spanish cinema's equivalent of the endlessly divorcing Hollywood prototype, married seven times, his first marriage at twenty-one in 1942 lasting only three months, his second producing five children. But the necessary muffling of his idiosyncratic personal history in these films, which deflect attention from the erotic agenda of romantic comedy to the more diffuse ethical and generational matter of family life, is not always entirely successful.

The intensity of the couple-centred narratives of romantic comedy is replaced in family comedy by focus on the resolution of questions related to patriarchal authority and the socialisation of the children. The Carlos role is perfectly crafted to fulfil its part in this project. But the role is problematised by the star's offscreen meanings. Even though Alberto Closas rises wonderfully to the challenge – aided by all the other elements of the film's rhetoric – his offscreen life inevitably undermines the innocence of that idealised construction. In its eulogy of the traditional male the film relies to some extent on Closas's image as a *galán* (leading man), and strives to place those qualities at the service of the construction of an essentialist masculinity constrained by the approved processes of domestication. Paternity and marital fidelity are all the more convincing if embraced by a sexually desirable male with a history of sexual experience. Closas's star image as a 'galán, seductor en la escena y fuera de ella, mujeriego pero educado y reservado, amable y simpático' (leading man, seducer both on- and offscreen, a womaniser, but well-mannered and reserved, likeable and pleasant) (*La Vanguardia* 1994), plays into and dignifies his role as doting paterfamilias and faithful husband. The self-sacrifice of a *seductor* makes all the more appealing and persuasive the ideological project of domesticated idealized masculinity. Closas's *macho* qualities – his sexual aura, understated male handsomeness and strength and, above all, his relaxed self-assurance – encourage the male audience to accept domesticity as the price of a deeper fulfilment than that available to the eternal rake. The pathos of Carlos's situation, of traumatic incidents associated with the upheavals of family life, becomes all the more poignant in the context of a real man's sacrifices. Here Ortega's superior man has given way to superior offspring, the lawyers, doctors and so forth nurtured by the family, whose self-discipline and achievements will be reward enough for the family superman's self-denial (Ortega 1997: 77).

And yet there is still enough of a glimmer of the old charmer's independence of spirit and, perhaps, too, sufficient vestige of his involvement in one of the key anti-regime films of the 1950s, *Muerte de un ciclista* (*Death of a Cyclist*, Bardem, 1955) to disrupt this stylised aura of acquiescent masculinity. The memory of the pre-*La gran familia* Closas forms part of a discernible pattern of dissidence which, though ultimately recuperated by the sentimental rhetoric of the film, nevertheless enjoys fitful authority as a mechanism of transgression. In this respect it complements the scenes where in *La gran familia* a team of basketball players from Catalonia passes by in a bus with the words 'Visca Catalunya' (Catalan for 'Up Catalonia') written heretically on its side. Although the scenes in Tarragona and Luis's infatuation with a Catalan girl are in line with mainstream films' celebration of homogeneity through difference, the writing on the bus of course deliberately strikes at official Francoist policy to outlaw more or less the Catalan language.

While this scene clearly gestures at socio-political regional issues, the wild behaviour of the *petardista* (firework-freak) Críspulo, the pre-adolescent son who specialises in setting off bangers at inopportune moments, violates the ethical and psychological order of the Francoist family. He plays a key role in the mild disruption of the notion of the home as refuge from the disturbances of the outside world.

When in *La gran familia* the family sets off to look for the toddler Chencho, abducted while in the care of his grandfather and some of his brothers and sisters during a Christmas outing in Madrid's Plaza Mayor, the strangers they question about him are at best indifferent, and at worst unhelpful. The world outside the home, we are asked to note, is crowded with heartless strangers and child-thieves (Chencho has significantly been abducted by a childless couple, driven it would seem to criminality by a family and child-obsessed culture). Yet the house itself – supposedly unthreatening inner sanctum of family life – is characterised, even though through the mode of comedy, by eternal chaos, noise, and the uproar of the children's riotous games and practical jokes. The spirit of misrule is represented by the Puckish *petardista*, who specialises in disruption of his godfather's romantic ambitions (in *La gran familia* launching a rocket that lands in the middle of the *padrino*'s courtship of a fellow holiday-maker), and is never short of a banger when occasion demands, as when he hurls one as part of a strategy to jump the queue in the scene of his visit to the Reyes Magos to ask for the return of his lost brother, or in obedience to the random demands of his own addiction to the pleasures of the *acte gratuit*.

The disruptions caused by the *petardista* and the other children are controlled in comedy, where children are in any case usually – in contrast to their presence in the 'children of Franco' (Kinder 1983) auteurist films like *El espíritu de la colmena* (*The Spirit of the Beehive*, Erice, 1973) or *Cría cuervos* (*Raise Ravens*, Saura 1975) – a more positive force, helping to cement the relationship of the parents, strengthening the bonds of the family. It is, after all, the *petardista* who takes on the task himself of speaking to the highest authority to help in the search for the abducted Chencho when he asks one of the Reyes Magos to cancel his Christmas presents list in exchange for the return of his little brother. When Chencho is returned the *petardista* sends a rocket to the Almighty in gratitude for granting him his Christmas wish. The symbol of disruption is, after all, defused as a radical force and deployed in the service of ideology. Ultimately, for all his unruliness, the *petardista* belongs to the family, contributes to its welfare and defends its integrity. His wildness is ultimately contained, but while it never reaches the kind of disturbed behaviour characteristic of, say, the Ana Torrent child with murder on her mind in *Cría cuervos*, the unruliness does at least gesture towards the return of the repressed in the ideological family of the Franco years.

By the time of the appearance of the third film in the trilogy, 1979, Franco had been dead for four years, and Spain was on the threshold of radical change. This last film mirrors the disintegration of the old order, but in a way that ill accords with other, more liberated films eager to redefine the culture in the post-dictatorship climate. *La familia bien, gracias* enters Spain's brave new world somewhat gingerly. By now all save one child (María, the sixteenth child, whose birth had caused her mother's death, an unavoidable fate since Amparo Soler Leal had no desire to continue in the role) have flown the family nest. Carlos discovers that none of his offspring is prepared to have him as a lodger, as both he and the cuckolded *padrino* attempt to remind them of their traditional family duties. The conservative tone of the first two films remains virtually intact here, but this one takes a predictably different direction as, now that the social fabric of the Franco years is being shredded, Carlos and the *padrino* serve as reminders to everyone of former stability in present uncertainty. As divorce, promiscuity, abortion and other forms of anathema sweep across the country and find their reflection in the film, and as other film-makers – most notably Almodóvar – begin in other comedies to attack the very foundations of the traditional Spanish family, so this film arranges it for the two friends to visit each member of the family like the ghosts of Christmas past, or like Paco Martínez Soria in *La ciudad no es para mí* (*The City's Not For Me,* Pedro Lazaga, 1965), relying on a photo of the family, as Martínez Soria had depended on a photo of his deceased wife, to remind its survivors of forgotten ideals. While the first two films had been a kind of dramatised version of the twenty-five years of peace under Franco, the third was a nostalgic lament for the demise of a meaningful past and the arrival of an uncertain, fragmented future, its daring embrace of the new modernities really only an outdated and ill-concealed yearning for vanishing traditions.

Note

1 On population figures see Jean Grugel and Tim Rees (1997: 135). To encourage procreation, family allowances ('subsidio familiar') were introduced in 1938, and family bonuses ('plus de cargas familiares') in 1945. Both were paid to male heads of household, and only for 'legitimate' children. A system of prizes ('premios de natalidad'), as well as further material support for exceptionally large numbers of children, was also created. Particularly fecund families were featured in the newspapers of both the Party and church as shining examples. Despite these efforts, however, the policy was a clear failure. Throughout the 1940s and 1950s the birth rate declined as couples continued to limit the size of their families. Overwhelmingly this was a response to the poor economic conditions of the time: more children could not be afforded. On birth control see Brooksbank Jones (1997: 15, 84–5).

References

Aguado, Ana María et al. (eds) (1994), *Textos para la historia de las mujeres en España*, Madrid, Cátedra.

Bakhtin, Mikhail (1984), *Rabelais and His World*, trans. Helen Iswolsky, Bloomington, Indiana University Press.

Barthes, Roland (1973), *Mythologies*, London, Paladin.

Brooksbank Jones, Anny (1997), *Women in Contemporary Spain*, Manchester, Manchester University Press.

Cohan, Steven (1997), *Masked Men: Masculinity and the Movies in the Fifties*, Bloomington and Indianapolis, Indiana University Press.

Grugel, Jean and Tim Rees (1997), *Franco's Spain*, London, Arnold.

Gubern, Román (1981), *La censura: función política y ordenamiento jurídico bajo el franquismo (1936–1975)*, Barcelona, Ediciones Península.

Jordan, Barry and Rikki Morgan-Tomasunas (1998), *Contemporary Spanish Cinema*, Manchester, Manchester University Press.

Kinder, Marsha (1983), 'The Children of Franco in the New Spanish Cinema', *Quarterly Review of Film Studies*, 8, 2, Spring, 57–76.

La Vanguardia (1994), 20 September, 35.

Ortega y Gasset, José (1997), *La rebelión de las masas*, Madrid, Austral.

Shubert, Adrian (1990), *A Social History of Modern Spain*, London, Unwin Hyman.

Displacing the hero: masculine ambivalence in the cinema of Luis García Berlanga

7

In many ways, Luis García Berlanga's work touches on the question of dealing with difference in situations where there is little room for it. His cinematic career began in 1951 and spans the years of Francoist rule in Spain up to the present. Censorship was a constant feature of those years and Berlanga is perhaps best known for his subversive use of comedy as a tool of exposure. His projects were often halted or postponed and most had to be altered to some degree in order to be feasible. Berlanga states that his aim in making cinema was simply to create comedy out of the social reality of his times, an objective which by its very definition runs contrary to the austere officialdom of Franco's Spain. If, for Berlanga, utopia is a place where people are 'free', then the social climate portrayed in many of his films is anything but so. Denied the possibility of self-determination, the male protagonists of many of his films rail in vain against the oppression engulfing them from a tyrannical social and personal environment. Social and sexual relationships must pass through a period of oppression in the course of a subtle and insidious process of internal appropriation, both individual and collective, into officially sanctioned behaviour.

My aim here is to examine Berlanga's depictions of male characters in the face of Francoist rule in Spain. Undercutting the myths, symbols and mottos of the Falange Española, Berlanga's cinema provides an arena for the unseen and largely unknown popular experience of it, whereby masculinity is experienced not as heroism, as projected by the state (particularly strongly in the first few years after the Civil War), but as a process of implication. The films that I shall discuss are *El verdugo (The Executioner,* 1963), *¡Vivan los novios! (Long Live the Bride and Groom!,* 1969) and *La vaquilla (The Heifer,* 1985). *El verdugo* depicts the close alliance of state and civil society, whereby even those occupying positions in the official apparatus are seen to be subaltern, thereby revealing different levels of subalternity. *¡Vivan los novios!* explores the enclosed and oppressive atmosphere of middle-class society through the figure of Leo, whose bizarre predicament challenges traditional, patriarchal conceptions of the Spanish male. *La vaquilla*, although completed a decade after the end of Francoism, is set in the Civil War. Through its focus on five Republican soldiers, it perhaps best illustrates Berlanga's views on the absurdity of war and its attempted construction of heroic manhood. The theoretical framework for my analysis will be drawn from Klaus Theweleit's analysis of the fascist male and Antonio Gramsci's development of the concept of hegemony. Theweleit's project focuses on the myths and desires of the fascist imagination, whereby a hardened 'male' self-image is constructed from a fear and abomination of what is considered 'feminine' or fluid. Furthermore, such masculinity is linked to notions of nationhood, inflexible borders and unswerving purpose. Gramsci develops the concept of hegemony in a variety of ways (from an initial usage denoting the leadership of a class) in the course of his writings; for our purposes, we can focus on his development of it as a process which extends from the discourses of ideology to its everyday practices at cultural and political levels. Hegemony is thus an active and on-going 'interlocking of political, social and cultural forces' (Williams 1977: 108).

When bringing Theweleit and Gramsci together in a task of analysis, it is important to bear in mind the different levels or angles at which they may be employed. Theweleit confronts fascist masculinity at the level of a collective unconscious and thus relies on psychoanalytic theory to unearth the self-cohesion techniques of the fascist imagination. The portrait he draws clarifies the structures whereby fascist gender and national identity are constructed. While Francoism was an alliance of right-wing forces, the Falange controlled propaganda and censorship (the latter with the church), which led, in the early years, to a specific stress on heroic virility. Thus Theweleit's analysis of the fascist mentality is useful in under-standing some of the political imprints of the post-war years in Spain. Gramsci, on the other hand, allows for an understanding of the popular experience of fascism as a lived and uneven process of slippage from heterogeneity to homogeneity. Viewed through Gramsci's notion of hege-mony, and against a background of the portrait of idealised fascist masculinity drawn by Theweleit, Berlanga's films reveal the concessions which constitute the everyday realities of life lived under Francoism, with its attendant stress on militarism and officialdom. In particular, Berlanga's focus on male characters underlines the failure of Francoism to produce heroes in the 'fascist' mould.

The disparity between the ideology of fascism and the popular experi-ence of its practice becomes evident. An appreciation of Berlanga's cinema is thus closely tied to an understanding of Francoism. In many ways, early

Francoism was little more than a tacit prolongation by other means of the Civil War. The monolithic identity of Spain projected by Francoist ideology belied the fratricidal split implicit in its very discourse between a nation of 'true' victors and the 'enemy within', or those not in sympathy with the Nationalists. In this sense, Francoism was explicitly constructed as a form of imperialism or internal colonisation where difference was all the more insidious for not being readily visible. Quelling the Other within required the constant affirmation and reaffirmation through discourse and symbols of a Self which relied on this battle in order to exist. State propaganda distorted history as a means of establishing the 'true' and timeless nature of *hispanidad*, personified most singularly by El Caudillo, Franco himself. Thus Paul Preston states 'For the Falangists, what the past proved was that the Spanish way of being has always, in the finest hour of its history, been struggle' (1990: 31). Historical contingency was buried by myths and discourse which emphasised Francoism as a means of recovering 'authentic' origins. The frequent public diffusion of images of Franco, dressed in military uniform and flanked by senior members of the Catholic church, offered visions of an upright and universalist Spanish masculinity that not only fell within the traditional confines of patriarchy, but was also apparently sanctioned by God and the nation. Such Spanish masculinity established its heroism through visible engagement in this chronologically circular quest for 'authenticity'.

Cultural products, in particular those of mass popular accessibility, provided an ideal medium for the diffusion of such values once they had been edited and even rewritten by the censors. Early Francoist cinema, emerging from privately owned production companies, often stressed traditional Catholic values, the racial homogeneity of Spaniards, and nationalistic values of honour rooted in a mythicised past. Not only were Spaniards essentially a chosen race, but implicit in the fusion of church and nation was the projection of heroic masculinity. The actor Alfredo Mayo personified for well over a decade the fascist hero in films such as *Raza* (1941), an adaptation of a novel by Franco himself. Films of this kind drew clear ideological links between 'upright' heroes and patriotism. The individual, inevitably male, thus personified the ideals of the nation through his spirit of 'sacrifice' for the larger masses and, in so doing, not only clarified the contours of selfhood and homeland but exalted them above all others.

If fascism converts individual lives into national territories through erecting a heightened conception of manhood, then Theweleit's exploration of the 'turbulent emotional world' (1989: ix) of the fascist male sheds light on the possible links or coincidences between the construction of gendered identity and the imagination of nation. Theweleit's analysis of the writings of members of the Freikorps reveals fascism to be epitomised by an explicit gendered symbolisation, where masculinity is constructed by and placed in the service of the destruction of all that is enjoyable or pleasurable. Theweleit stresses that fascism is a system of desire best symbolised bodily through the repudiation of softness or femininity and the pursuit of hardness and self-denial as a means of self-expansion: 'In "standing erect", the fascist adopts an attitude of sexual defense and mastery; his stance was seen to produce an inevitable and unquestioned ... superiority to the rest of the world, and to ground the ... claim to world domination ... For would not any ego standing less than fully erect have dissolved long ago within the "mass"?' (1989: 50). Boundaries of distinction, such as 'self'/'other', 'high'/'low', 'culture'/'mass', permit the targeted construction of a heroic fascist masculinity which in turn builds the dream of the nation conceived in terms of racial and moral supremacy. Theweleit quotes Heinz, a Freikorps member: 'The nation first emerged from the primitive mind of a hero, struggling for inner stability on the threshold between the highest possible fulfillment and the horrible void; it penetrated to the deepest core of his being and became his vocation' (1989: 82). Conquering the weaknesses or voids of one's inner spaces, subduing the 'alien within', thus becomes the endless struggle for the nation's imperialism, a battle which ultimately seeks the warrior's own death or 'self-sacrifice'.

While Theweleit's portrayal of fascism clearly falls in line with the projected ideals of Francoist heroism and nationalism, Berlanga's films uncover the 'treacherous' underbelly of the fascist armour where softness lurks. Berlanga's characters are implicated in fascist-style behaviour not for idealistic motives of patriotic grandeur, but for reasons of sheer survival within a society where individuals are denied the choice of any other way of being. The importance of visibly acceptable behaviour and attitudes turns Francoism into a tool of social negotiation belying and yet reliant upon the unexpressed and inexpressible ambivalence which marks the characters. His depictions of popular reality thus expose the myths of Francoism through parody drawn from 'real life'; his reputation as a 'neo-realist' film-maker must therefore be understood as an exposition of the absurdity of social constraints.

Impressed by the neo-realist cinema which emerged in Italy in response to fascism, Berlanga's reworking of it into the Spanish context is accentuated with the dark humour which characterises his work and which he attributes to the tradition of *esperpento* in Spain. This emphasis on the popular, as opposed to the ideological or mythicised, offers an alternative portrayal of the 'national' which contests the official versions of the same by creating an arena for those who do not directly occupy the seats of power, despite their implication in the status quo. Alignment with subaltern characters allows a different angle on Francoism, experienced from below not as heroism but as orchestration and ambivalence. Furthermore, the subaltern are seen in their diversity, marked by economic and political differences, but grouped together and seemingly homogenised by a dominant and dominating ideological discourse within a suffocatingly enclosed national territory.

Gramsci's reworking of the concept of hegemony extends the notion of ideology from an abstract system of dominance to a 'lived' and 'living' process of social, political, economic and cultural practice. As such, it includes and runs deeper than the conscious articulations of a dominant ideology or class to embrace the everyday realities of subordination as diverse and complex. Hegemony therefore engages at the level of popular experience and includes the ties between culture and cultural production and economic and political factors. This understanding of hegemony shifts the meaning of political dominance, seen not as a top-down and fixed imposition of power but as an on-going process of consent, contestation and change. In this context, Williams stresses that hegemony:

> does not just passively exist as a form of dominance. It has continually to be renewed, recreated, defended and modified. It is also continually resisted, limited, altered, challenged by pressures not all its own. We have then to add to the concept of hegemony, the concepts of counter-hegemony and alternative hegemony, which are real and persistent elements of practice. (1997: 112–13)

Hegemony emerges therefore as plural and multi-grained, encompassing a wide range of human behaviour from force at one end to consent and acquiescence at the other, and furrowed by the cross-currents of other hegemonies.

Berlanga's male characters are repeatedly played by well-known comedy actors (Pepe Isbert, José Luis López Vázquez and Alfredo Landa, for example) who have become symbolic of popular Spanish humour. Recognised and loved by the public, names such as that of Isbert are part of the cultural fabric of the Francoist years. Berlanga's motive for choosing these actors rests no doubt on the fact that they provide the best means of conveying the 'performative', and hence popular, aspects of fascism at play. A Gramscian exploration of the male characters he portrays, therefore, both illuminates and is illuminated by Theweleit's study of the male fascist imagination. What gradually emerges is a vision of Berlanga that extends beyond any attempt to establish him within a supposed trend of internal opposition to Francoism: Berlanga's films deal with the fact of Francoism as tackled and experienced by men under fascism. Most importantly, while the discourses of fascism fall in line with Theweleit's emphasis on the construction and policing of fenced distinctions, the experience of fascism as portrayed by Berlanga is marked by crumbling borders where self and other blur in a process of interaction and splitting. Unlike the inflexible steel masculinity of fascism, the men in his films are survivors and, as such, fluid, adaptable and, above all, ambivalent.

El verdugo, perhaps one of Berlanga's most controversial films, scans the uneasy jointure of state authority and civilian life epitomised in the executioner's role. The much-loved comic actor Pepe Isbert plays the ageing state executioner Amadeo, whose daughter Carmen marries José Luis, a funeral parlour worker. As Amadeo nears the age of retirement, he and his daughter manage to convince José Luis to take over the job of executioner, if only to retain the apartment that comes with the job. Reluctantly, José Luis agrees, on condition that he can resign if ever faced with an execution. When the moment comes, however, he and Carmen have a child and need the apartment more than ever. More horrified than the convict himself at the act that awaits him, the agonising José Luis has to be dragged unwillingly by prison guards and forced to do his job. In order to maintain his family, José Luis must continually sacrifice the personal life he most values: the letter ordering him to Mallorca for the execution arrives just as he and his wife make love on a new bed. He is called away for the execution itself while enjoying a visit to the Drach caves in Mallorca with her. Once in the prison, the guards force a tie around his neck in an effort to spruce him up for the job, bringing to mind his own task of forcing the garrotte around the victim's neck. When he returns to his family after the execution, José Luis, the family man, has ceded to José Luis, the executioner. Spanish officialdom is underlined by the profusion of uniforms in the film and the stress laid on clothing. Engaged in state activity, ordinary men acquire publicly valid identities through the adoption of apparel and roles which represent an authoritarian state.

Nevertheless, the gap exists between these functionaries of Francoism and the heroic image they emulate. The film's opening scenes underline the repeated presence of the 'ordinary' man beneath the uniformed and stylised exterior and the inextricability of the one from the other: a pair of hands break bread into a bowl of soup. The camera tracks back to reveal that they belong to a prison guard having lunch. Two funeral parlour workers bring in the coffin of a recently executed prisoner, lay it against the wall and light up a cigarette. The ground is laid for the film's discomfiting juxtaposition of popular, daily existence and officially imposed death. However, the prison guard sits away from the two workers, signalling to viewers the different levels of their implication in the system and thus the unacknowledged, but discernible, heterogeneity of the Francoist apparatus. The camera then aligns itself with the workers' line of vision as a group of impersonal, formally dressed officials who witnessed the execution walk through the room: seen from afar, they have no particular identity apart from that implied by their attire, save the whispered words that the defence lawyer is among them. The 'decency' of their controlled appearance must necessarily jar in viewers' minds with the horror of the act they have just witnessed and no doubt been implicated in. As the workers prepare to leave with the coffin, a guard opens the heavy iron door again to let the executioner in: José Luis and his colleague turn their heads in amazement at the undeniable 'ordinariness' of Amadeo as he shuffles in. Dressed in a frayed suit and beret, he appears like any other elderly Spaniard. The executioner is none other than the 'common man'.

Berlanga's farcical portrayal of the grimmest public office derives its comedy from Amadeo's common sense, his instinct for survival and 'popularity'. As such, he appears the 'other' of his public persona, troubling because of his endearing conniving and common sense. Amadeo approaches his job, viewed by many as Francoism at its ugliest, with a pragmatism that is organic. Attempts to interpret him as a parody of Franco, 'the executioner', inevitably fail for reasons of his humanity and popular earthiness which remain undestroyed by his profession. Neither can José Luis ever be taken for the heroic fascist male who rejects femininity: his trajectory is spurred on by his wife and father-in-law and is justified by his private role as a father. Masculinity is seen instead as a process of slippage within a repressive and enclosed environment, where available public roles have to be adopted in order to make do. At the same time, the ideals of Francoism are stripped of the mantle of 'authenticity' and revealed as only constructs, which could be shed by a simple act of undressing.

¡Vivan los novios! moves the theme of entrapment out of officialdom into ordinary society. Repression no longer appears in the guise of authoritarian uniforms, but in the stuffy suits and 'decent' dresses of the Spanish bourgeoisie. Leo, the main protagonist of this film, is a banker from Burgos who goes to the seaside resort of Sitges with his mother on the eve of his wedding to Loli, who owns a clothing shop there. He spends his last night as a bachelor out on the town, eyeing the many female tourists around. Fascinated by the otherness that is so evident around him, Leo attempts in vain to slip stealthily out of his obligations and into two women's apartments. He befriends an Irish girl who speaks no Spanish, but is forced by his future brother-in-law to return to his hotel. Once there, he discovers that his aged mother has drowned in the pool.

The wedding goes ahead, nevertheless, the dead body awaiting burial and packed meanwhile with ice in the bath-tub. The funeral is arranged for the next day, as bride and groom become mourners now that the wedding is over. Torn by the delay in publicly acknowledging his mother's death and giving her a funeral, Leo turns in desperation to the Irish girl, but she is unable to understand him. In a wonderfully metaphorical final scene, Leo sees the Irish girl flying in a sky-kite overhead as they lead the funeral procession. He rushes after her, but is dragged back into line by the family. Despite his wild and infantile desires to be free of social obligations, Leo complies at every point with the pressures that his friends and family put on him. In any case, freedom for Leo is no more than a vision, a glimpse of difference that cannot be accessed. While the blondes in bikinis scattered through the film demarcate the traditional Catholic values of Spanish patriarchy by signalling their 'permissiveness', they also serve to highlight the extent to which Leo's 'decency' is at best a guise that he must adopt. Yet Leo's implication in this rigid system of appearances is such that even at night, when invisible to prying eyes, he can only prowl around town, unlike the easy-going foreigners, and so remain within the repressiveness of his social environment.

Leo personifies the Spanish male bound by a sense of guilt and social, if not religious, obligation. The need to 'confess' is evident throughout, implying that he is 'soiled' by his actions. Berlanga thus shows sacrifice, the repudiation of pleasure, as a social obligation which splits the individual between desire and duty. A particularly poignant scene is when Leo steals into Loli's bedroom on the eve of their wedding after his night on the town. He makes sexual advances, saying that they can then confess their sin together. As he tries to implicate her in his guilt, she notices his bare feet, which strike an absurd contrast with his suit and tie. The camera frames her squarely thrusting his feet into the air, a sign of his 'naked' shame.

Like the male characters in Berlanga's other films, Leo squirms inside the starched shirt of his public persona, but remains wearing it, ambivalent and consenting to the end. The unusual juxtaposition of a wedding and a funeral show both ceremonies to be hollow: emotions are suppressed or feigned in order to produce the socially desirable image. All the same, the homogenising force of public pressures never quite subdues the otherness within Leo and, once again in this film, the comedy arises from this gap between the projections of Francoist society and its popular experience.

La vaquilla was completed in 1985, nearly ten years after the death of Franco. Nevertheless, it is based on a script written by Berlanga, together with his long-term associate and scriptwriter Rafael Azcona, in 1957, and is the culmination of a project that was frustrated for so long not just by the censors, but also by the political allegiances of the producers concerned, anxious not to cross certain ministers in power. Despite its completion in democratic Spain, *La vaquilla*'s pertinence to this discussion lies in its setting in the Civil War and its ability thus to shed light on an emerging fascism in Spain (particularly pronounced during the war).

If the fascist preoccupation can be considered to be a continuous battle for self-aggrandisement, then this struggle should most obviously be displayed by the realities of the Civil War itself. Nevertheless, *La vaquilla* displays all too clearly the absurdity of a war where people are rent asunder by ideological differences that bear little relevance to the smallness of their provincial lives. The film's wartime setting requires a predominantly male cast. The plot consists in the officers and men from the Republican side stealing into Nationalist territory in order to ruin the bullfight planned for a day of fiesta by capturing and returning to their side with the bull. Crossing enemy lines requires the Republican hit squad to pass themselves off as Nationalists, only to discover that a young cow is kept where they expected to find the bull. The farce does not end there; the bullfighter among them shies away from the heifer and the officer in their group stops off at a brothel. Although the Nationalists never discover their true identity, the Republican venture ends in disaster with both sides shooting at each other. The motivation for this expedition exceeds that of loyalty to the Republican cause: Mariano, their guide, comes from the village where the fiesta will take place and he fears, with good reason, that the girlfriend he has not seen for two years will take up with a Nationalist during the festivities planned for after the bullfight. Sexual jealousy thus becomes confused with patriotic fervour, but is reason enough for taking on the enemy's guise, if only to further self-interest. In an early scene, two privates, one a Nationalist and the other a Republican, actually suggest to their superiors that they swap uniforms in order to access their loved ones, who are in each other's enemy territories – such a swap would after all only be an extension of the already existing practice between the two sides of swapping tobacco for paper. The adoption of feigned ideological allegiance in terms that are merely visible undercuts the 'authenticity' pursued by Theweleit's fascist warrior. A far cry from the self-sacrificing hero of fascism, the men in *La vaquilla* are soldiers by circumstance, common-sensical in Gramscian terms. This is made evident in the film's opening scenes, as the camera surveys life in the trenches on the Republican side. A medley of voices, snatches of conversations, emphasise the plurality and pragmatics of popular existence, as men talk, deal with and argue about the most mundane matters: tobacco, food, girlfriends. If the fascist male abhors and repudiates the feminine within and without, then fascism itself is rendered impotent by men who subordinate ideological fidelity to the securing of sexual fidelity from a woman. Even sexual jealousy, however, must cede to the needs of the moment: Mariano's reaction at discovering that his girlfriend is now being courted by a Nationalist is muffled by the need to remain unrecognised in enemy territory. When she passes him off as her cousin, his indignation is unvoiced. Male supremacy within fascism and patriarchy explodes when he silently gestures that he is a cuckold. In a later scene, Republicans and Nationalists strip themselves of their uniforms and splash about in the river: in the nude, the two sides blur as the water flows around them. Under such circumstances, fascism, patriarchy and ideological allegiance thus display themselves, at a practical level, as mimesis as the men are seen to hover at the edges of roles that are adopted for being appropriate rather than believed in. The soldiers in *La vaquilla* are ill at ease in their uniforms but have nothing else to wear.

Small wonder that the bull they seek turns out to be a cow. The sexual symbolism of this bizarre occurrence applies equally to their unfocused participation in the different sides of the war, as the failed attempt to steal the Nationalist bull is also a failure to snatch at once the virile core of fascism and the fascist core of patriarchically constructed masculinity: the supposed male turns out to be a female, the supposed fascist hero slides into the feminine fluidity he abhors, the supposed self slips into the other. What emerges is a picture of ambivalence, not aggression, most vividly depicted in the final scene of the film. A bull dies in the patch of no-man's land between the two zones, its flesh now food for the vultures. The comical absurdities of the film come to an abrupt halt as projections of Spanish national and sexual identity, so linked at a popular level to the image of the bull, are called into question.

Nowhere in these films do Berlanga's male characters strive to achieve heroic stature. Their concerns are embedded in the social context in which they find themselves, and their actions, however clumsy, are means of negotiation with difference. Otherness, therefore, is contended with, not rejected or resisted. Nor can the prevalent Francoist authoritarianism in which they are implicated ever totally appropriate or incorporate the common man. What emerges is a consenting relation of Self and Other that contravenes the binary opposition of the fascist imagination. Otherness is difference that can be overlapped if never totally overcome. A Gramscian analysis can perhaps highlight the weakness in the male fascist imagination, as Berlanga's films so clearly show: the concept of hegemony considers the distribution of power as a social process. Thus to expect men/heroes to form and control their lives in any absolute way is unfeasible, given the multiplicity and inequalities of human lives.

Furthermore, fascism is a chronologically regressive mythical quest for authenticity, and real life must necessarily be lived forwards. The ideologically charged discourse of fascism can only be implemented through concessions to the uneven contingencies of heterogeneous popular experience. In the hands of the common man, fascism becomes resignified through the cross-grained diversity of popular existence. The hero, then, must remain an abstraction, while men such as Amadeo and José Luis get on with their lives.

Note

I thank Steve Marsh of Birkbeck College for allowing me to read the chapter on Berlanga in his dissertation in progress.

References

Besas, P. (1985), *Behind the Spanish Lens*, Denver, Arden Press.

Graham, H. and J. Labanyi (1995), *Spanish Cultural Studies*, Oxford, Oxford University Press.

Gramsci, A. (1971), *Selections from Prison Notebooks*, London, Lawrence and Wishart.

Gramsci, A. (1985), *Selections from Cultural Writings*, London, Lawrence and Wishart.

Hopewell, J. (1986), *Out of the Past: Spanish Cinema after Franco*, London, British Film Institute.

Jordan, B. and R. Morgan-Tamosunas (1998), *Contemporary Spanish Cinema*, Manchester, Manchester University Press.

Preston, P. (1990), *The Politics of Revenge*, London, Unwin Hyman.

Theweleit, K. (1987), *Male Fantasies: Vol. 1*, Minneapolis, University of Minnesota Press.

Theweleit, K. (1989), *Male Fantasies: Vol. 2*, Minneapolis, University of Minnesota Press.

Williams, R. (1977), *Marxism and Literature*, Oxford, Oxford University Press.

Zizek, S. (ed.) (1994), *Mapping Ideology*, London, Verso.

Interview with TVE (1979), *Luis García Berlanga, mediterráneo, barroco y pirotécnico*.

Interview with TVE (1984), *A fondo*, Luis García Berlanga.

8

'When you're not a worker yourself ...': Godard, the Dziga Vertov Group and the audience

After May 1968, in the context of a French film industry totally bowled over by the general strike, Godard participated in a film-making collective, the Dziga Vertov Group, which sought to explore and find solutions to some of the problems of political film making, including the relationship with the audience. This chapter sets out to ask whether the hegemonic position of Godard as political/revolutionary film-maker (established in journals such as *Cahiers du cinéma*, *Cinéthique*, *Screen* and *Afterimage* and by theorists such as Peter Wollen and Colin MacCabe) is justified in the light of the Group's work in the context of post-1968 France.

An interesting point at which to begin our consideration is Godard's section of the collective film *Loin du Vietnam* (*Far from Vietnam*), entitled *Caméra-oeil* (*Camera-eye*), made in 1967, which, along with *La Chinoise* and *Weekend* of that year, indicates the tensions Godard felt working 'within the system', a system of film production and distribution which could apparently absorb and market even his most radical attempts to undermine it. The concerns it voices clearly inform his subsequent break after May 1968 and the work that followed.

Unlike most of the other contributions to the film (by Chris Marker, Joris Ivens, William Klein and others), which employ traditional documentary techniques in order to demonstrate the justness of Vietnamese resistance and Western solidarity movements, Godard voices his concerns in a form of direct address from behind the controls of a large Mitchell camera. The tone is one of self-conscious discomfort, 'shame', about the difficulties of making a film on Vietnam from his position in France. This reflection was brought on, he reveals, by the North Vietnamese turning down his request to go and film there, a decision which, with a mixture of self-pity and self-sacrifice, he says was justified. Therefore instead of footage of Vietnam or anti-war protest, Godard films himself, his camera, his isolation.

The major focus of what he has to say is a triple reflection on how to talk about Vietnam from afar. First he describes what he would have filmed in Vietnam had he been a US or Soviet news cameraman. He then outlines what he initially thought of filming when approached to contribute to *Loin du Vietnam*. Finally he suggests what he, or any French film-maker, *should* be filming: the struggle in France, the strikes of the workers at Rhodiaceta in Besançon.

This last point is indicative of the frustrations and contradictions in Godard's contribution, for while he can arrive at an extremely valid political insight (he alone in the film draws links between the struggle against imperialism and the force in the West, the working class, which can ultimately weaken and destroy it), it is as part of a rather self-indulgent, navel-gazing reflection on his own problems as a film-maker.

More significant, in the context of his post-1968 work, is the fact that despite that insight, or perhaps instinct, about the working class as a force for change, Godard can only see the divisions between himself, as a bourgeois artist, and the Rhodiaceta workers, his isolation from that audience: 'when you're not a worker yourself, it seems too difficult to me.'[1]

To a certain extent Godard overcame this immobilising frustration and inability to communicate in the immediate period around May 1968. He was a central figure in the cinema's May, in the Etats Généraux du cinéma (the 'Estates General of the Cinema', a large-scale gathering of film-makers, technicians, critics and students in the occupied film school, which organised the spreading of the strike, abolished existing censorship and held long debates on the future of cinema), and in the closure of the Cannes film festival. He was also an enthusiastic participant in the making of *cinétracts*, literally 'leaflet-films'; hastily made, often collaborative, anonymous films with titles such as *Le Pouvoir est dans la rue, Ce n'est qu'un début* etc. (*Power is in the Streets, This is Only a Beginning* – recognisable as slogans of the time), which were shot, often using still images, in the streets, on the demonstrations, in the occupations, sanctioned by the Etats Généraux and screened and discussed in those same factories, schools and faculties.

Godard's description of them in a *Tribune Socialiste* interview (Godard 1985: 332–7) provides an interesting point of comparison with both *Loin du Vietnam* and his later work, particularly in the conception of the audience. Godard credits Marker with the idea of the *cinétracts* and points out that their first task was resistance to Gaullist news broadcasts. They were also, however, 'a cheap and easy way of making political cinema, for a group of workers or an action committee ... screenings can take place in someone's flat, in meetings' (Godard 1985: 332).

But quite apart from this practical accessibility of the means of making and distributing a film, there is clearly a further value for Godard in this kind of work which 'facilitates a re-thinking of the cinema at a very simple and concrete level' and especially allows the relationship with the audience to be rethought, recast, leading Godard to declare 'films should be made with those who watch them'.

The problem was, however, that the possibility of direct intervention with a massively politicised audience in this very immediate way was perhaps only present while the May movement was at its height. The more order and normality were restored, the more film-makers returned to their careers as if from a month's holiday, the less Godard found it easy to envisage a continuation of that kind of film making. To his credit, like a significant minority of other French film-makers, technicians and critics, he strove to continue to involve himself in a cinema which would contribute to the struggle, which would be, in the Mao-tinged language of the time, 'serving the people'.

The three films Godard released in 1968 – *Le Gai savoir* (*Joyful Wisdom*), *Un Film comme les autres* (*A Film Like All the Others*) and *One Plus One* – are in many ways transitional, edging towards some of the basic formal principles which he was to work on in subsequent years but without the political certainties. *Le Gai savoir* proposes a 'return to zero', an explicit rebuilding of a film from its bare essentials of images and sounds, within the framing device of a conversation. The tentative approach adopted in the immediate aftermath of 1968 is given some direction for Godard by returning to the anonymity the *cinétracts* offered him, by forming the 'Dziga Vertov' film-making collective with Gérard Martin, Nathalie Billard, Armand Marco – as listed in the group's 'manifesto' (Groupe Dziga Vertov 1970: 82–8), though Jean-Henri Roger and Paul Burron among others also participated – but especially with Jean-Pierre Gorin. Especially the last because he clearly convinced Godard about the political direction the Group should take and provided a political perspective within which Godard's theoretical film-making concerns could be validated.

The Group named itself 'Dziga Vertov' after the experimental Russian documentarist of the 1920s, whose notion of *Kino-Pravda* (Cine-Truth) is seen to offer a correct analytical approach to the image but also a commitment to film 'in the name of the dictatorship of the proletariat' (Groupe Dziga Vertov 1970: 82). The choice of Dziga Vertov would indicate opting for documentary over fiction. All of the Group's films were indeed documentaries of some kind, employing the 16-mm format and usually being 60-minute films. Most of them were also commissioned by television companies and, very strikingly, all were made abroad, with British, Italian and West German television finance or, in the case of the films made in the USA (*Vladimir and Rosa, One a.m.*), money from the left-wing Grove Press.

The Dziga Vertov Group was not the only collective formed after 1968 in France. Sylvia Harvey discusses at least three others: SLON, le Groupe Medvedkine and Les Cinéastes Révolutionnaires Prolétariens (Harvey 1978: 27–33). Godard was keen to insist, however, in *Politique Hebdo* in 1972, that unlike those groups, whose main aim was 'an attempt to distribute films differently ... for us the most important thing was to apply ourselves to the tasks of production before those of distribution' (Godard 1985: 367–75). We will see later that there were certain problems with this notion.

While this might sound self-evident, there was in fact a real difference in the approach of the groups. While others were attempting, roughly speaking, to continue the relationship with the audience which the *cinétracts* had established, making films about certain struggles with their participants, then screening and discussing those films with those participants, the Dziga Vertov Group refused to consider that as the natural way forward without first posing the questions, in terms identical to those in the first issue of *Cinéthique*: 'What should be produced? ... for whom? ... and how?' (Groupe Dziga Vertov 1970: 369).

This therefore returns us to the research on images and sounds proposed in *Le Gai savoir* and to the tentative approach which says that the new films for a new audience will only be possible after decomposition and reconstruction from zero. *Pravda* (1969) can serve as an example of the Group's attempts at making progress on these questions. The film is basically a Maoist critique of Czechoslovak society, filmed surreptitiously in the streets, hotel rooms and factories of Prague in March 1969, less than a year after the Russian invasion, but is also an interrogation of the documentary form, an attempt at moving forward on the question of how to make a political film. These concerns are linked in its title, referring to the Russian Communist Party's daily paper, the main organ of the 'revisionist' ideas which led Maoists to oppose the USSR, and to the notion of 'truth' (*pravda* in Russian) in the context of film.

The analysis is constructed in four stages, each, according to the soundtrack, 'successively more profound', involving the re-editing of many of the same images with a shift in the soundtrack critique. This repetition is a common feature of the Group's films: as the closing remarks of *Pravda* would have it, 'by going round in circles, we advance'. Also common to the films is this dominance of the soundtrack, carrying most of the burden of meaning and itself frequently overburdened with quotation, recitation and self-criticism.

This 'political' documentary is seen by the Group as a new genre, that of 'theoretical film', or as 'political pamphlet' or leaflet. Hence the frequent conclusion with 'correct sound' in the Group's films, representing the 'correct' ideas explicitly and uniquely sought in 'Mao's thought', despite the paradox in the light of their critique of access to 'truth' in left-wing documentary,

Partly for financial reasons, in that European television companies were keen to finance 'a Godard' (although all but one were refused transmission), the Group concentrated on making films outside France. This seems to indicate an astonishing disinterest on the part of French revolutionary film-makers in the 'concrete situation' of their own country. Godard left for London, to make *One Plus One*, within weeks of May, as if the end of the General Strike led him to turn his back on the struggle in France, to which he did not return in film until *Tout va bien* (*Everything's Fine*) four years later. This represents a rejection of any possibility of continuing the *cinétracts* experience of direct intervention in a concrete situation with a specific, politicised audience. Intervention, indeed, in the directly political sense no longer seems to have been a key activity for the Group, who voluntarily limited their contribution to combating ideology *within* film. This is matched by a metaphorical use of Marxism in discussing film techniques, as in this example from the fifth issue of *Cinéthique*, in 1969: 'sometimes the class struggle takes the form of a struggle between image and image or sound and sound ... is the Marxist notion of surplus value not a useful weapon in the struggle against the bourgeois concept of representation?' (Godard 1985: 337–8). This means fighting imperialism within film, combating the dominant ideology by isolating, deconstructing and destroying the cinematic forms which are seen as its supports: '"the bourgeoisie creates a world in its own image" (Marx). Comrades, let us begin by destroying that image. But it also creates an image for its world. It creates the image of its world which it calls the reality effect' (Godard 1985: 337).

In referring to their work as 'theoretical' or in making analogies between film and leaflet, the Group implied that they had a clearly defined notion of their audience, the targeted recipients of the leaflet. Although on one occasion Godard referred to a 'cadre' audience, again a political, Leninist term imported into cinematic practice, there is little else to suggest that this might be the case. Despite the heavy use of Leninist (or more accurately, Maoist) terminology in the films, it remains at the level of rhetoric, since in the key respect of the relationship between a revolutionary minority and a wider audience, the Group in no way operated along Leninist lines. According to Lenin's theory of revolutionary organisation, in a pre-revolutionary situation, the revolutionary minority must address its propaganda and activities to those outside its ranks, still a minority, who might be open to its ideas. This minority outside the party or group obviously varies in composition: at times of low working-class militancy it might consist largely of students and intellectuals, while in periods of intense struggle, such as France in 1968, large numbers of workers might potentially be broken from reformist ideas.

The Dziga Vertov Group, however, addressed its films *not* in any way to the working class as a whole, *not* to the large sections of it radicalised in 1968 and questioning the electoral strategy of the left and the allied back-to-work machinations of the union leaders, *not* to the mass of students and intellectuals whose worldview was similarly shifting massively to the left in the period, and *not even* to those amongst this mass who had already reached revolutionary conclusions. The films of the Group required of the audience that it be both politically revolutionary *and* impassioned by the aesthetic questions which enthused Godard; that is an audience interested not in politics or in political films, but in 'making political films politically' (Groupe Dziga Vertov 1970: 82).

One can detect in this approach a marked *reduction* in Godard's horizons, despite the political and cultural opportunities of the post-1968 period, from attempting to learn '*Two or Three Things* ...' in 1966 to carrying out research on two or three images for an audience of 'two or three friends'.[2]

Tout va bien, made in 1972, appears therefore as the product of a double defeat, and is an attempt to learn the lessons of those defeats, to draw up a balance-sheet before thinking about the next move. First of all, it is clearly a shift away from the films made since 1968 by Godard with the Dziga Vertov Group, and while those films were always produced in a tentative, self-critical mode, *Tout va bien* is posed explicitly as a corrective to what Godard and Gorin had come to see as errors, as if the introspective self-critique conducted at the end of those films had merely provided a list of what *not* to do: with this film they attempted to lay the ground for a more positive step. As if to mark this, the film is credited to 'Jean-Luc Godard and Jean-Pierre Gorin', not to the more grandiose Dziga Vertov Group, and we can see a number of important shifts away from the Group's work as they turn, or in Godard's case re-turn, to the narrative cinema, to large-budget studio production and to employing star actors, Jane Fonda and Yves Montand.

The return to these particular means is very much tied to the other defeat, that of the May movement, and the realisation that no amount of triumphalism on a film soundtrack could mask the fact that the revolutionary left in France had stagnated in size and influence. The film therefore attempts to analyse the situation of the class struggle in France in May 1972, precisely four years on from the 'failed revolution', and to offer an assessment of the balance of forces and of what was to be done. This is again a clear break with the recent past and its revolutionary 'travelogues' and leads the film-makers to a far sharper conception of their potential audience and their relationship to it. Godard said at the time: 'I passed though a time of disrespect for the public in order now to respect them better. To respect them better means to treat them no longer as the public but as men or women there where they are. It means to be able to make films in which one no longer speaks simply about the film itself' (Monaco 1976: 240).

Subsequently he suggested that that audience was conceptualised with even greater precision, following the funeral of Pierre Overney, a Maoist activist murdered by a factory security guard, a funeral which was 'one of the last big demonstrations of the Far Left ... about 100,000. Then there was a lull. We said to ourselves "this film we're making is aimed at that 100,000"' (Godard 1980: 92).

Clearly, in the light of my earlier criticisms of the Dziga Vertov Group films, this attempt to address the remnants of the May movement, a significantly wider audience than for those films, and make an inter-vention in a concrete situation at a specific historical moment is a very positive one. Godard and Gorin attempt to achieve this by means of a narrative which introduces us to a bourgeois intellectual couple, Jacques (Yves Montand) and Susan (Jane Fonda), who both work in the media, he in advertising films, she as a radio journalist.

These two characters are then placed in a factory which has been occupied by a section of its striking workforce, thus creating a situation out of which the film-makers can provoke a generalised reflection around two linked concerns; on the one hand the specific form of the class struggle in France at that time, an important element of which was this kind of militant strike action taken independently of trade union leaders, with occupation and sequestration of bosses, and on the other the role that revolutionary intellectuals could play in it, a question which is obviously crucial to the film-makers' own social position but also to that of a substantial portion of their intended or expected audience.

While the strike, which is ultimately defeated, occupies just under half of the film, the contrasting reactions of the couple to their experience in the factory become the focus for the remainder of the film. The film-makers leave this narrative deliberately unresolved, the relationship in doubt but not settled either way, and conclude with an attempt to generalise the lessons Fonda's character has begun to learn for the audience to consider, to rethink themselves in relation to the struggle, or 'rethink themselves historically', as the narrators' voices put it in the film.

Compared to the hectoring monologues of *Pravda*, the film does succeed in opening up important questions for consideration. The phase of the strike chosen, for example, is not the triumph of the initial occupation but the moment of inertia immediately afterwards, a moment for reflection and discussion which allows questions such as 'What next?', 'How will the union or the police react?', 'Why lock up the boss?' and 'How far will they go?' to be posed for both the strikers and the audience. Even the sequence about *how* to describe, how to represent the strike or the factory conditions that provoked it, effectively manages to indicate that reality is not static, that the moments of movement, of change are what is important because, unlike the repetitions of images in *Pravda*, the reinterpretation by the strikers, illustrated by repeated images of Fonda and Montand in the role of production-line workers, has been contextualised: we are aware of the conflicting forces (the boss, the union leaders, the strikers) and their conflicting ways of explaining and representing.

Tout va bien is not an entirely successful film for a number of reasons, not least because its 20,000–30,000 entries on release fell well short of the audience Godard and Gorin had intended. The deep pessimism of *Loin du Vietnam* is not solved for Godard by his four-year research programme into 'making political films politically'. I would argue that the central flaw in his approach is the specific lack of any notion of intellectuals playing a role within a revolutionary, working-class *party* that ultimately leaves him stranded in the same position he felt he occupied in 1967, despite the sophisticated self-help routine with which *Tout va bien* concludes, of 'thinking yourself historically'.

Godard, as ever, raises such questions in the form of cinematic analogy and states: 'I believe in mass distribution where there is a mass party ... we find ourselves in countries where the revolutionary party is far from existing' (Godard 1985: 346), but sees the building of such a party clearly as someone else's responsibility, not that of the revolutionary artist and intellectual, exclusively occupied with the task of discovering new forms.

While other reasons have been advanced for Godard's retreat from militant film making after 1972 – the serious road accident he suffered in 1971, from which he was slow to recuperate, or the obsolescence of the 16-mm film format (Dixon 1997) – and while, paradoxically, this period of his work is nowadays often treated as a footnote or ignored altogether, Godard's reputation as an unrivalled radical/political/revolutionary film-maker rests in large part on a positive assessment of these seldom-seen films. Examining the conceptualisation of the audience and the nature of the political intervention adopted by Godard and the Dziga Vertov Group from 1968 to 1972 therefore constitutes one of the important starting points of a necessary reassessment of those films and that reputation.

Notes

1 All translations are the author's, with the exception of some film titles, where I have used the titles usually employed by American distributors.
2 *Two or Three Things I Know About Her* was a Godard film of that year. The reference to the tiny audience is from *Cinéma 70*: 'we were aware, when thinking about the way we were making the films, that we'd probably be unable to distribute them, that only two or three friends would see them' (Groupe Dziga Vertov 1970: 84).

References

Dixon, W. W. (1997), *The Films of Jean-Luc Godard*, Albany NY, State University of New York Press.
Godard, J.-L. (1980), *Introduction à une véritable histoire du cinéma: Vol. 1*, Paris, Albatros.
Godard, J.-L. (1985), *Jean-Luc Godard par Jean-Luc Godard*, Paris, L'Etoile.
Le Groupe Dziga Vertov (1970), in *Cinéma 70*, special issue 'Cinéma/politique', 152: 82–8.
Harvey, S. (1978), *May 1968 and Film Culture*, London, British Film Institute.
Monaco, J. (1976), *The New Wave*, Oxford, Oxford University Press.

ELIANE MEYER

Quand une femme n'en est pas une: gendered spectatorship and feminist scopophilia in the early films of Jean-Luc Godard

9

Car je ne possédais dans ma mémoire que des séries d'Albertines séparées les unes des autres, incomplètes, des profils, des instantanés.

M. Proust, *La Prisonnière*[1]

The representation of women on screen has always been a central concern for Jean-Luc Godard. It has also been the focus of much feminist critical appraisal of his films. However, despite positive critical explanations of their purpose, some images of women in Godard's films are uncomfortable to watch (anal rapes, dismembered bodies, physical attacks on women). I would like to argue that although feminist critics have, on the whole, made positive assessments of Godard's portrayal of women, watching his films still produces an uncomfortable tension. This is because they remain partly characterised by a gratuitous fixity on the female body. It is this disquieting tension between critical opinion and the experience of female spectatorship that led me to reconsider the positioning a feminist spectator of Godard's films would need to assume in order to obtain scopic pleasure.

In his later production (from the 1970s onwards), Godard's images of women tend to become fairly transparently exploitative, with for example, pornographic use of female bodies[2] or scenes of abuse.[3] As one critic puts it, 'Godard gets older but his women never grow up, in fact they seem to get younger ... [to become] the embodiment of male desires and fears' (Pajaczkowska 1990: 241). This tendency has been perceived on the whole as an instance of Godard's incorporation into the films of a feminist social critique, despite a few more nuanced opinions (Pajaczkowska, Mulvey, Loshitzky). Public opinion, however, has not always been so positive on the matter (Loshitzky 1995: 152) and many female spectators felt disquiet at the sight of those images.

In this chapter, however, it is Godard's early films that I want to consider, and the reason for my choice is twofold: on the one hand, they are his most universally popular films, and on the other, in his early New

Wave films Godard's representation of women is at its most complex and ambiguous. I would like to explore these early films (*Vivre sa vie* (*It's My Life*) and *Une Femme mariée* (*A Married Woman*) in particular), in terms of this ambiguity and ask whether the disquiet that can still be felt whilst watching them can be accounted for despite feminist critical praise. In these early New Wave films, women are often portrayed as liberated and there is no obvious use of pornographic images. However, even here, some of Godard's images of women remain disturbing, mostly in terms of their portrayal as the dangerous other, romantic heroines objectified by male fears. Indeed, as Loshitzky puts it: 'despite the celebratory reception of Godard's representation of women by many critics, one cannot ignore the misogynist tendency of his films, and in particular of the early ones' (Loshitzky 1995: 136).

The generally positive interpretations of these films (explored below), seem to make it more difficult for feminist spectators to express any disquiet that remains while watching them. It is the space of this discomfort that I would like to explore by charting the possible current of misogyny running through *Vivre sa vie* and *Une Femme mariée*. To that end, I will explore Godard's positioning of the female in these two films, in spatial and narrative and psychoanalytical terms.

But first it is important to chart some of the better known works exploring these issues and to discuss the reasoning behind their generally positive assessment of the films' representation of women. Even if there are a few dissenting voices (Mulvey, Loshitzky), most feminist critics tend to agree on this positive assessment. The reason behind it can be seen clearly. For Godard, the position of women in society or in the hierarchy of oppression, and the question of their representation, is a quasi-obsessional strand in his filmic activities. This insistent questioning, together with the evident attraction of Godard's provision of strong female roles in his films (for example, Jean Seberg in *A Bout de souffle* (*Breathless*), Anna Karina in *Vivre sa vie*), help to explain this widespread agreement amongst critics that Godard's work occupies similar terrain to feminism. One such critic claims that 'Godard remains near the front of filmmakers presenting an anti-sexist perspective ... from his early films on, Godard's sympathetic use of female protagonists has been remarkable' (Kleinhans 1972: 68). Another key reason for the generalised belief that Godard makes women-friendly films is his use of subversive filmic practices, linked by some critics to similar feminist practices aiming to subvert dominant ideology (for example, the disruption of narrative coherence) (Johnston 1976: 208).

Perhaps the most positive assessment of Godard's portrayal of women came in *Women and Film*, a left-wing, pioneering, feminist film journal whose first number in 1972 contained an article by Siew Hwa Beh on *Vivre sa vie*, which she describes as: '[a] great work in [its] exploration of sexist problems within unique structures' (Beh 1976: 180). This was followed by a third issue mainly devoted to Godard, where Kleinhans's article followed much the same line of argument. The focus of their work, however, is very much on the use of woman as metaphor for the study of oppression in capitalist society. Taken in isolation, such a reading tends to obscure Godard's representation of women *per se*. For example, the view of prostitution as a metaphor for the condition of workers in a capitalist society, or indeed for that of the artist/film-maker at the hands of producers (a recurrent Godardian theme), may obscure certain problems regarding Godard's perception of women. The issue here is that using women as a metaphor is ultimately different to giving them a voice.

This is not to say that Godard had a duty to feminism, but that the general consensus amongst feminist critics may claim too much. Indeed, it is because of those claims that exploring Godard's possibly exploitative gaze on women is important. The body of feminist criticism devoted to Godard's films made during the 1980s is mostly enthusiastic, at a time when the use of pornographic images and scenes of violence against women abound (Loshitzky 1995: 149). Kristeva, for example, on *Sauve qui peut (la vie)*, asks: 'Could Godard be the filmmaker most sympathetic to the plight of modern women?' (Kristeva 1985: 28). In the special numbers that *Camera Obscura* devoted to Godard in 1982, some of the contributors try to reclaim pornographic images and dialogue for feminist purposes. One striking example is the critical reaction to *Sauve qui peut (la vie)*, where scenes like that of a father asking another man if, like him, he has ever wanted to 'fuck his daughter up the ass', a pimp hitting a prostitute, and two men beating a woman in order to make her choose between them are claimed to be feminist. Penley argues that '[the film] affords the spectator a wide ranging iconography of the pornographic' but goes on to ask 'is the film pornographic?' (Penley and Bergstrom 1982: 52). The answer is negative, since in her view 'for all its pornographic images, the film is, rather, about the refusal or failure of a controlling male gaze, that gaze designated here as a pornographic one' (Penley and Bergstrom 1982: 52). This, however true, does not allow for any sense of revulsion a female spectator may feel at the sight of those images, and many female spectators did.[4] This is presumably what Claire Pajaczkowska, in a more nuanced appraisal, attempts to account for by arguing that there are times in Godard's counter-cinema when the attack on narrative coherence does not result in the facilitation of the spectator's capacity to think, but when the distraction of perverse sexual imagery provokes a withdrawal or a counter-attack.

Amongst these fairly generally positive assessments, it is perhaps Laura Mulvey and Colin McCabe, in *Godard: Images, Sounds, Politics*, who are the most critical of Godard's 'feminism' when they say that 'Godard has always been in the forefront of debates on politics, and representation and women have always been central to his films. Yet on this point, Godard's practice seems to be out of sync with feminist arguments' (Mulvey and McCabe 1980: 50). They argue that although Godard's films have reflected the growth of feminism, 'his use of images of women have in his early through to his late films continued to raise problems for those who follow the logic of feminist arguments'. But the main point here is that branding Godard a feminist or a misogynist does not answer any fundamental question. What needs to be accepted is that complexity and ambiguity are the concepts defining the kind of position a female spectator has to start from if she is to make sense of the images Godard provides her with. For being aware of 'the exploitation of woman as an image in consumer society and breaking down the equation to reveal its construction' (Mulvey and McCabe 1980: 52) does not prevent Godard from being complicit with those images. In other words, questioning those images does not necessarily mean that Godard does not reproduce them, as he continually moves between an investigation of the images of women and a potentially exploitative use of those images. In their analysis, Mulvey and McCabe proffer the idea that for Godard 'women represent the problem of sexuality in a capitalist society and that this position can be traced back to his romantic heritage in which woman is divided into an appearance that can be enjoyed and an essence that is only knowable at risk, deceptive and dangerous' (Mulvey and McCabe 1980: 53).

It is in the light of these comments that I would like to explore *Vivre sa vie* and *Une Femme mariée*, as they are perhaps the two Godard films which appear the most positive in their exposure of social and media stereotyping as exploitative of women. This is why I would like to go beyond this accepted reading and explore their potential misogyny. This apparent contradiction will map out the complex positioning required of a feminist spectator faced simultaneously with the cinematic evidence of Godard's understanding of women's issues and with the potentially exploitative gaze directed at women in these two films.

Mulvey's idea that Godard is guilty of essentialism, that he portrays women as the idealised and dangerous other, is perhaps best illustrated in terms of the various figurations given to female space in these two films. I will map out the positioning of the female at various levels in *Vivre sa vie* and *Une Femme mariée*, and then explore the implications of this positioning in terms of scopic gratification. By exploring this space, I do not mean to deny any positive feminist readings of these films, but rather to expand on the idea that a misogynist one may also be present. Accepting this contradiction may be the condition for a feminist spectator to ensure the obtention of scopic pleasure.

If we look first of all at the screen space attributed to women in *Vivre sa vie* and *Une Femme mariée*, it seems that gendered space is defined in terms of inside versus outside. Although both Charlotte and Nana occupy the whole spatial spectrum on screen (*Vivre sa vie* in particular uses the whole range of the cinematic apparatus to film Nana in her environment: long shot, extreme close-up, static and mobile camera, long takes and montage), the resulting images can be read in a variety of ways and with varying degrees of signification. On one level, these images of women certainly appear liberating in many ways, and it is important to note here that, at that point in the history of French cinema, Godard was in a sense providing the newly 'liberated' female viewers with the visual pleasure of self-recognition. As Ginette Vincendeau (1992) argued, female space in 1950s' French cinema was mostly claustrophobic. In the early 1960s, Godard's women, by contrast, have 'come out (side)': they inhabit the outside realm, sit in cafés and walk the streets (the potentially oppressive image of the 'streetwalker' will be examined later). 'Thus, for the *Cahiers* group, the new cinema is inseparable from its portrait of the "new woman". The portrayal of the modern woman by Karina, Moreau ... goes beyond the idealisation of Hollywood ... the modern female persona challenges these conventions dramatically' (Orr 1993: 139). Women who were in their twenties in the 1960s relate the exhilaration they felt at seeing 'themselves' on screen portrayed in Godard's films as modern, liberated women.

On another level, however, a closer examination of this spatial 'liberation' enables us to question the positive value of those images. Despite being given the run of the outside realm, Charlotte (in *Une Femme mariée*) does not claim it as female space. When filmed outside, she quickly appears distraught, runs, falls, obsessively touches her face as if to reassure herself of her existence, and even becomes 'invisible' in a scene where her lover's car is shot at an angle, making her drop out of sight. As Charlotte often appears positioned next to billboards displaying exploitative images of women used in advertising, her spatial 'unhappiness' has often been read as portraying alienation in a capitalist society. This is also true of the connection made between Nana working as a shop assistant and as a prostitute: 'This parallel is made even more explicit in the construction of the shots of her at work, suggesting that Nana is performing the same function for "Philips-Kodak-Decca" (the owners of the merchandise in the shop indicated on a sign above the door) as for Raoul, her pimp' (Cannon 1996: 288). These readings, however true, if taken in isolation could obscure the fact that the outside space is alienating not only in terms of politics, but also in terms of gender. If both Charlotte and Nana can be seen as distraught when occupying the outside world, it is also because this remains a male-dominated space.

To understand the implications of the negative power of these images, it is important to see what happens back inside the enclosed, traditionally female, space. Charlotte's uncertainty regarding her own identity does not automatically stop: her obsessive touching of her face, for example, continues throughout the scene at the doctor's, and even sometimes in her flat. But if we concentrate on the very particular space of the bedroom, there Charlotte becomes calmer, more self-assured, as if she had re-entered her proper domain, that of being conflated (in Mulvey's terms) with sexuality. This would seem to be confirmed by the shots of her fragmented body during love scenes against a backdrop of white sheeting, which has been described as the canvas against which the artist paints the female body, and also as connoting some of Godard's artistic practices: 'fragmentation ... considered definitive of Modernism marks virtually all of Godard's films ... in *Une Femme mariée*, Pierre with his head out of frame stands in front of Picasso's Arlequin with its head out of frame' (Stam 1985: 179). This reading, however, does not preclude another more chilling one, a connection possibly made by feminist spectators, that of the image of a dismembered woman's body helpless on a mortuary slab.

In his analysis of the sex scenes in *Une Femme mariée* and *Le Mépris* (*Contempt*), Stam praises Godard for his awareness of the exploitation of women through exposure to the male voyeuristic gaze, claiming that: 'Godard's work generally demonstrates a *pudeur* which derives not from a puritanical distrust of sexuality but rather from a sensitivity to the generally exploitative nature of such images within dominant cinema. The bare-breasted women [in that film] are treated with such directorial nonchalance that their nakedness hardly seems worthy of our attention' (Stam 1985: 180). Without going into a detailed analysis of Godard's filming of sex scenes, it is important here to point out that this directorial nonchalance does not automatically mean de-eroticised images or the removal of an exploitative gaze. The fact that both *Une Femme mariée* and *Le Mépris* display prominent scenes where glossy female bodies are heavily fragmented also seems to contradict Stam's comment on Godard's almost feminist cinematic sensitivity (see, for example, the very different treatment of close-up body parts in Varda's *Jane B. par Agnès V.* (*Jane B. by Agnès V.*, 1986/7), or more recently Bruno Dumont's *La Vie de Jésus*, 1997). Stam's appraisal seems to equate Godard's genuine interrogation of the dominant images of women on screen with the automatic removal of their ambiguity. However, to suggest that the potentially exploitative power of these images is defused by Godard's self-awareness would be to ignore their voyeuristic aspects. Loshitzky refers to the sex scenes in *Une Femme mariée* as pornographic (a fact apparently confirmed by Godard himself twenty years after its release) and claims, in support of her argument, that 'the first love scene showing the two lovers sitting facing each other is later quoted by Bertolucci in *Last Tango in Paris*' (Loshitzky 1995: 141).

Let us now examine more closely the relationship of Nana in *Vivre sa vie* with a possible gendered space. In this beautiful and complex film, the issue at stake is more ambiguous as, on the one hand, Nana appears happier in the outside realm (in streets and cafés) and even seems to be given relative freedom as the camera appears not to be aware of her (for example, in the shots of her walking on the boulevards). On the other hand, however, the realm of the outside for Nana is, symbolically, the locus of oppression. This is true of the streets and of bars, as Nana is a 'streetwalker' and the cafés in *Vivre sa vie* are often dominated by pimps. Indeed, prostitution is connoted by the cafés as the pimps seem to inhabit them, physically or by verbal association (Yvette recounts her entry into prostitution in a conversation she has with Nana in one of them, Nana writes to 'apply' to a brothel in another). The inside, female realm for Nana is represented by the enclosed space of the brothel, an equivalent of the bedroom in *Une Femme mariée*. Of course, in a brothel women are automatically conflated with sexuality. It is the objectification of the female characters, conflated with sexuality and locked in the space of the other, that seems to confirm a possible misogynist reading of both films.

I would like to continue by exploring the possibility of a gendered narrative space in both *Vivre sa vie* and *Une Femme mariée,* in order to show further that by fixing his female characters in a specific, gendered, narrative framework, Godard portrays cinematic versions of the romantic idea of woman as treacherous enigma. Mulvey and McCabe discuss this idea of a gendered narrative space (what they call 'sexing the point of view'), and argue that Godard's use of space varies depending on whether it is organised around a male or female central point of view: 'for example in *Pierrot le fou*, the narrative referent is fiction and fantasy, the action ... develops in great sweeps, in terms of generic violence and utopian escape' (Mulvey and McCabe 1980: 53), whereas in films like *Une Femme mariée,* where the narrative organisation centres on the female point of view, the story develops on a much smaller scale: 'Godard's use of interior space functions both figuratively and fictionally to limit the world of woman's day-dreams' (Mulvey and McCabe 1980: 53). Mulvey and McCabe claim that Godard uses this reduced space to depict woman inside, which of course 'implies an "outside", an alternative masculine sphere ... where woman's threatening qualities predominate. This image does not refer to women, but is a phantasm of the male unconscious [where] she is mysterious, elusive and destructive'(Mulvey and McCabe 1980: 54).

In *Une Femme mariée*, for example, Pierre (Charlotte's husband) describes how obsessed he is by what is hidden behind her gaze. In *Vivre sa vie*, there is a scene towards the end of the film where Nana's love interest (*'le jeune homme'*) attempts a metaphorical stripping of her self by reading Poe's *The Oval Portrait*. As Cannon states:

> Godard *is* implicated in the sexist exploitation of women in the cinema ... because Karina like Nana is objectified in the film, becomes merely another image to be juxtaposed with others, posed and explored from all angles and submitted to Godard's inquiring gaze. The fact that he self-consciously points to that personal aspect of the film in dubbing his own voice over [this] reading about an artist who creates such a life-like portrait of his wife that she dies when he completes it, by no means excuses or avoids it. (Cannon 1996: 291)

Annihilation as the price to pay for being the dangerous other is clearly present in *Vivre sa vie*, where Nana's enclosure in a narrative of death is signalled throughout the film on various levels; for example, by the association established with Joan of Arc via a screen *mise en abyme* (although of course, it is not the only connotation possible here) and the repeated offscreen sounds of a machine gun. As the ultimate obliteration, death (here as a recurring motif) only reinforces the process of the naturalisation of invisibility within which Nana is imprisoned. The invisibility that is Nana's fate can perhaps stand here more generally for the fate of Godard's women. The whole film seems to chart Nana's loss of identity, and this is perhaps best illustrated by the shot of her serving customers in the shop where their heads obliterate hers behind the counter. As Steve Cannon puts it, 'the film explores the gradual effacement of Nana's identity, her transformation into a commodity which begins with her name, the slang word for any young woman' (Cannon 1996: 288).

This, despite being rightly seen as Godard's attempt to understand the plight of women in a capitalist society, does not obliterate the fact that Nana Klein also stands here for woman, any woman, any 'little girl' even, that Godard, in his own words, attempts to know 'from the inside, while remaining outside' (Godard 1968: 229). This stripping down of Nana, this metaphorical striptease, together with the insistence on Nana being seen, looked at, from every possible angle, does put a certain emphasis on woman as spectacle, as a static image that must be unveiled in order to be understood. Although I am not denying the positive feminist readings of *Vivre sa vie*, it seems to me that the objectifying of the enigmatic Nana further reinforces Mulvey's idea of an 'outside' masculine sphere where woman's threatening qualities predominate.

As further evidence of this, I would like to cite the profusion of beautiful, near-still frames of women in *Vivre sa vie* but also in many other Godard films: Anna Karina in *Alphaville* holding Eluard's *Capitale de la douleur* and gazing out of a window is a well-known, frequently reproduced example. Whatever other meaning they may have, these images can certainly be seen to operate as an opposition between the male and female space, as Janet Bergstrom argues: 'the space/time of contemplation is never in Godard that of men ... they are ... noisily active ... in contrast, our eyes can linger on these inward looking women the way we are asked to give our attention to a painting ... we look with Godard at (not into) an interior state that cannot possibly be reached' (Bergstrom 1992: 53). The photographic techniques used in *Vivre sa vie* to frame Karina's face seem to reinforce this effect, as the lighting darkens and flattens Nana's facial features, making her face into a mask. Furthermore, Godard frames Karina in a window, clear metaphor for the screen, but also the fragile, almost intangible frontier between interior and exterior. This image of the window, so often present in Godard's films, can be viewed here to signify the opposite of its usual meaning of openness, and to represent the invisible yet forbidding barrier surrounding the woman.

Finally, I would like to explore the configuration of female space in Godard's films at another level. In the realm of fears and desires, Godard's images of women can arguably be seen to lose fullness of representation. As we have seen, the positing of an outside, sexually differentiated space, which women experience as alien and uncomfortable, and where women are objectified and perceived as dangerous, often results in Godard's films in images of fear and incomprehension. It is arguable that those images mostly find their expression in the double figure of the mother and the whore. Claire Pajaczkowska in her analysis of *Sauve qui peut (la vie)* sees Godard's women as fitting into two categories: the beautiful girls as fetishised objects of desire and violence, and the mother who, she argues, is all but absent (Pajaczkowska 1990: 242). These two figures are already present in *Vivre sa vie* and *Une Femme mariée* in the following forms. Yvette in *Vivre sa vie* conflates the two roles, as she clearly equates her entry into prostitution with the need to feed her children, and Nana herself abandons her child before becoming a prostitute. Charlotte in *Une Femme mariée* seems best to embody the mixture of fear and incomprehension in the face of motherhood, as both her lover and husband desire her to have their child in a desperate attempt to imprison her. It is, however, in her dealings with her doctor (apparently Godard's real-life GP) that her condition takes on its most chilling connotation. Her worried phone calls to the surgery for test results are reminiscent of Agnès Varda's *Cléo de 5 à 7* (*Cléo from 5 to 7*), and the analogy with fear of cancer is carried further when the doctor explains pregnancy in terms of a disease.

Certain critics have argued that this anxiety is often resolved in Godard's films by a desire for identification with the feminine (perhaps even in having female protagonists who are themselves fascinated and fearful). Pajaczkowska describes a scene in *Sauve qui peut (la vie)* where Paul Godard acts as a stand-in for the writer Marguerite Duras, and the critic states: 'this mysterious scene, where [Godard] pays homage to Duras ... by putting himself in her place, is crucial for understanding [his] central fantasy as film maker ... he can only learn from women by taking their place' (Pajaczkowska 1990: 242). In cinematic terms, this desire for identification is signified in *Une Femme mariée* and *Vivre sa vie* either by an exchange of male/female voices/gaze, or by an appropriation of one by the other. In *Une Femme mariée*, for example, female voices are denied outright when Charlotte listens to some young women at the swimming pool talking about sex. Subtitles appear on screen attempting to summarise their experience and thereby indicating a reappropriation of their discourse by the film-maker. This desire for identification only made possible by stepping into an absence further highlights the fear of women present in these films.

By questioning certain issues relating to the representation of women in *Vivre sa vie* and *Une Femme mariée*, this chapter has sought to understand the apparent tension between a fairly consensual feminist approval of Godard and the disquiet that may still be felt by a feminist spectator of his films. As these mainstream readings do not always leave much space for these uncomfortable feelings, it has also been my aim to understand the position from which the feminist spectator of Godard's early films can best make sense of the conflicting images confronting her. This position, it seems to me, can only be one of compromise.

It is obvious that nothing can take away the fascination of films like *Vivre sa vie*, or the sense of identification felt in *Une Femme mariée* with the images of oppression of women at the hands of the media in a capitalist society. However, despite Godard's genuine interrogation of these images, and despite the enthusiasm of feminist film critics, it is difficult to forget moments of unease at the sight of some of the more misogynist images in his films. The feminist spectator will have to face uncomfortable viewing, as Godard's use of claustrophobic and displaced images of women unfolds alongside what seems to be a real concern for understanding the reason why women's images accumulate their particular meanings. Ambiguity and the coexistence of pleasure and revulsion are the defining site from which feminist spectators will have to gaze if they want to derive scopic pleasure from Godard's films.

Notes

1 'All I could remember was a series of Albertines, distinct from each other, incomplete; a series of silhouettes, of snapshots.'
2 *Numéro 2* (*Number 2*, 1975)
3 *Sauve qui peut (la vie)* (*Everyman for Himself,* 1979).
4 In a public discussion with Godard in America, a woman said: 'I'm disturbed by all the scenes of abuse of women in this film and I want to know why you included them.' The angry audience agreed (quoted in Loshitzky 1995: 152–3).

References

Beh, Siew Hwa (1976), 'Vivre sa vie', in B. Nichols (ed.), *Movies and Methods: Vol. 1*, London, University of California Press, 180–5.

Bergstrom, Janet (1992), 'Violence and enunciation', in R. Bellour and M. L. Bandy (eds), *Jean-Luc Godard Son + Image 1974–1991*, New York, Museum of Modern Art pp. 51–4.

Cannon, Steve (1996), '"Not a mere question of form": the hybrid realism of Godard's *Vivre sa vie*', *French Cultural Studies*, vii: 283–94.

Godard, Jean-Luc (1968), *J.L.G par J.L.G*, Paris, Belfond.

Johnston, Claire (1976), 'Women's cinema as counter cinema', in B. Nichols (ed.), *Movies and Methods: Vol. 1*, London, University of California Press, 208–17.

Kleinhans, Chuck (1972), '2 or 3 things I know about her', *Women and Film*, 3–4: 65–72.

Kristeva, Julia (1985), 'Ces femmes au-delà du plaisir', *ArtPress*, special issue 4: 28–31.

Loshitzky, Yosefa (1995), *The Radical Faces of Godard and Bertolucci*, Detroit, Wayne State University Press.

Mulvey, Laura (1992), 'Janus, the hole and the zero', in R. Bellour and M. L. Bandy (eds), *Jean-Luc Godard Son + Image 1974–1991*, New York, Museum of Modern Art, 85–7.

Mulvey, Laura and Colin McCabe (1980), *Godard: Images, Sounds, Politics*, London, Macmillan.

Nini, Britt (1985), 'Les femmes de Godard', *ArtPress*, special issue 4: 32–3.

Orr, John (1993), *Cinema and Modernity*, Cambridge, Polity Press.

Pajaczkowska, Claire (1990), '"Liberté, égalité, paternité!": J.-L Godard's and Miéville's S*auve qui peut la vie*', in S. Hayward and G. Vincendeau (eds), *French Film: Texts and Contexts*, London, Routledge, 241–55.

Penley, C. and J. Bergstrom (1982), 'Introduction to special number on Godard', *Camera Obscura* 8, 9, 10: 2–4.

Stam, Robert (1985), *Reflexivity in Film and Literature*, Michigan, UMI Research Press.

Vincendeau, Ginette (1992), 'Topographies of the feminine: the place of women in 50s' French cinema', paper given at 'Sound Bites and Silent Dames: Women and French Cinema' conference, Birmingham University.

The fictionalisation of terrorism in West German cinema

10

Introduction

In 1968 Andreas Baader, Gudrun Ensslin and some others carried out an arson attack on a Frankfurt department store in 1968 to protest against the Vietnam War. Stirred by extensive media coverage, the public discourse about terrorism, which emerged in Germany in the years after 1968, has been characterised not only by the public fear of terrorists and terrorism, but also by a remarkable degree of paranoia about alleged sympathisers. In contrast, a critical alternative discourse evolved around the treatment of (suspected) terrorists and (suspected) sympathisers in the context of opposition to the manipulation of public opinion by the mass media.

In this chapter I will examine how West German film-makers have treated the phenomenon of terrorism in the 1970s, 1980s, and 1990s. Four films – *Die verlorene Ehre der Katharina Blum* (The Lost Honour of Katharina Blum), *Die bleierne Zeit* (lit. 'The Leaden Time', English release title: *The German Sisters*), *Stammheim*, and *Die Terroristen* (*The Terrorists*) – will be analysed as examples of a cinematic attempt to come to terms with this difficult period in German history. All these films occupy an ambiguous, hard-to-grasp area between official and critical discourses on terrorism and its impact on West German society. Made in Germany and thus exposed to the official discourse, none of the films discussed can be regarded as the alternative discourse *per se*. Since any interpretation depends on the viewer as much as on the film-maker, they should rather be seen as a twofold quest for what might constitute a politically and ethically valid role for the individual in a society almost torn apart by the debate about terrorism. In this sense, they also represent a search for identity – the attempt to position oneself through aesthetic means in society. This may be seen as a limitation by some and as the specific merit of these films by others. However, either way it does not diminish the aesthetic experience and pleasure of watching these films – even almost three decades after the first of them was made.

Die verlorene Ehre der Katharina Blum (1975)

Directed by Volker Schlöndorff and Margarete von Trotta, this film was released in 1975. It is based on Heinrich Böll's novella of the same title, but has been simplified for adaptation on the screen. A wanted terrorist, Ludwig Götten, is on the run from the police when he meets a young woman, Katharina Blum, at a party. She takes him home and provides him with further help and a hideout before he is eventually captured. Haunted by aggressive media and the police, she eventually turns against one of the reporters, kills him, and goes to jail.

The focus on terrorism is from the angle of the so-called sympathiser, but it is not really the focus on the phenomenon of terrorism that is in the centre of attention, but rather the response of state and society to it. Thus, terrorism, although obviously implied as background, does not figure prominently in the film. Rather it is the effects it has on society and individuals that the film critically examines.

The opening sequence of the film symbolises this take on the events: the viewer witnesses a policeman observing the alleged terrorist Ludwig Götten with a hand camera in the course of which symbolically the whole society (a 360-degree turn is carried out with the camera) becomes an object of observation, and Götten himself seems to be rather marginal as one among many other objects. And so he is throughout the film: physically present only in the first few scenes and in another one towards the end, the police take his appearance in Katharina's life as a welcome opportunity to examine her private life and that of other people connected with her.

This, however, is only one part of the state's response: collaboration with the mass media (here a major tabloid newspaper) ensures that public opinion is manipulated in favour of police action and turned against Katharina. Despite the use of undercover agents, which is kept secret even from one of the two public prosecutors involved, the police are not very successful in their attempts to get hold of the 'terrorist'. They are much more successful in their spying on bystanders and in the production and dissemination of unfounded accusations.

As the film tells the story from the viewpoint of Katharina, there is an obvious tendency to polarise strictly between good and evil, with very few grey areas in between, as other protagonists can only perform the roles Katharina assigns to them, and those who hurt her most are those who are described as the worst.

Thus, the most negative character in the film is the reporter Tötges, who is in a position of extreme power and influence as he covers the story for the newspaper *Die Zeitung*, which, according to Katharina, all the people she knows read. The most terrifying of all experiences in this respect is the alleged statement of her mother that she had seen Katharina's involvement with terrorism coming. In reality, the mother had been unable to talk to Tötges and died shortly after his 'visit' in the hospital. Her mother's death is then claimed by the same reporter as the direct consequence of Katharina's criminal activities.

However, the impact of the media on her life goes much further than that: heated public opinion results in threatening and indecent phone calls and letters and open public hostility by friends and strangers. Even her long-time lover, a wealthy industrialist, drops her, being afraid of his involvement in the case as he rightly suspects that the terrorist Götten is hiding in his mansion, to which he once gave Katharina a key. Only her aunt and the couple who employ her as maid remain loyal to her even if this means personal sacrifice (Blorna, her employer, loses a client as lawyer because he refuses to act on the latter's behalf against Katharina's interests). The doctor at the hospital where Katharina's mother died is perhaps the most significant example of the influence of the press on public opinion. He tells Katharina that he was going to file a suit against the reporter Tötges because of his possible causing of Katharina's mother's death. After Katharina replies that it was the business of the police and media people to destroy other people, he asks her suspiciously whether she is a Marxist.

After Katharina tries to visit Götten in the hideout she has directed him to, she arrives there only to discover that he has already been arrested. With nothing else to lose, she chooses to take revenge on the reporter Tötges and kills him at an interview that was supposed to initiate the marketing and selling of her story.

Revenge, however, is not the only way out. Although Katharina and Ludwig eventually get together again, significantly inside the prison and thus outside society, another, non-violent way out is also possible: withdrawal into privacy. This is what the only people loyal to Katharina choose: her aunt gets married and her employers stay away from the crowd of 'honourable citizens' at the funeral of Tötges, at which his death is claimed to be an attack on the freedom of the press and democracy in general. The film does not leave this claim undisputed. In a final insert it says that similarities between practices of the print media in the film and in reality were neither intended nor incidental, but unavoidable.

Thus, the film has shown the powerlessness of individuals involved or uninvolved against the state apparatus and mass media. Within the course of five days (this is underlined by the strictly chronological sequence of events with the dates inserted, the only exception being two flashbacks), an individual can be driven to extremes by a hysterical society, which thereby creates the internal enemy it needs in order to unify the majority of citizens and thus survive. Individuals becoming the direct or indirect victims of public hysteria are forced to question their own identity. They have to reposition themselves against a society that does not accept them any more as a part of it. This becomes most obvious with Katharina herself, who, however, hits back at society. Her employers and her aunt, similarly but less extremely challenged in their identity, draw a line between themselves and the 'honourable' society, they do not opt out of society, but define their identity against the public by withdrawing into privacy.

The film is clearly sympathetic to Katharina, who chooses to hit back, and tries to encourage an understanding for her choice of identity. However, this choice is not justified, its limits are shown, and another potential identity is offered in withdrawal from public life. Here lies, from the viewpoint of alternatives, an option available for individuals that are critical of society and its discourse, an option, however, that has features of resignation that are very similar to Katharina's escape into violence.

Die bleierne Zeit (1981)

Based on the true story of two sisters, the film depicts the two different paths chosen by the generation involved in the late 1960s' students' movement – the terrorism of Gudrun Ensslin (portrayed in the film as Marianne) and the 'long march through the institutions' (exemplified by the feminist movement and the struggle against the anti-abortion law) that her sister Christiane (portrayed in the film as Juliane) chose.

As in *Katharina Blum*, terrorism as such is only a marginal aspect. Central to the film is the argument about terrorism and about the state's response to it, both viewed from the very personal standpoint of the sister of one of the terrorists. And as in *Katharina Blum* both the state and the media are accused of maltreatment of both terrorists and, in this case, people who are involved merely because they happen to be relatives. There, more clearly than in any other of the films I am looking at, the state is accused of extreme injustice in its response to terrorism: the alleged suicide of the sister apparently turns out to be murder. The state, however, is reduced to prison guards and to officers of the Federal Office for the Protection of the Constitution, who appear on only one occasion outside the prison. The conditions of imprisonment, therefore, are the major point of critique: isolation from other prison inmates, mail allowed only from two close relatives, few visitation rights, visits that impose humiliating conditions on visitors, take place under strict surveillance, and are minuted by an increasing number of officers who get closer and closer to the table, leading eventually to the complete separation of the two sisters by glass and contact only via microphone.

Again, the story is told from a very personal point of view, but only this subjectivity makes it possible to introduce a more human perspective on the issue of terrorism. It is – and this is important – not the terrorist's subjectivity, but that of the citizen who rejects terrorism as politics, but is emotionally linked to the terrorist and thus able to see beyond public hysteria.

As in *Katharina Blum*, the manipulation of public opinion through the press/mass media is criticised as well. Initially only referred to in two passing remarks, the consequences of such manipulation and encouragement of public outrage are made clear in a very drastic manner by the attempted burning of the terrorist-sister's son. But this is only part of the critique of the mass media: after Juliane, the surviving sister has spent years to prove that her sister's death was not a suicide, publication of her findings is refused and thus withdrawal into the private and maintaining the memories remains the only way out and the only possibility of living, and coming to terms, with one's own past. This, eventually, is symbolised in Juliane's attempt to take care of her sister's son and to tell him her side of the story of his mother. The film's aim of presenting the personal view of the relative who is both affected and sympathetic, but not actually involved in terrorist activities, becomes finally actualised in the film's message: terrorism is an individual choice, but not the only one under particular circumstances of socialisation.

The personal perspective of one sister, however, is at the same time a perspective on the social and political conditions under which it is possible for terrorism to emerge. The relationship between the sisters is personal, yet simultaneously it reveals the difference of their choice and the implications of each choice. Marianne's son links them personally, and his fate symbolises the dangers that lie in a polarised society. The frequent childhood flashbacks explain the close personal relationship between the two sisters even under the most unbearable conditions, while they also stand as a social explanation: born during World War II, grown up in the 'leadenness' of the 1950s in Germany, engaged for social reforms in the late 1960s, their path seems only a natural course until they choose different routes after the failure of the students' movement. And their different choices make it harder for both of them to achieve their aims: they are competing to realise the same goal with different means. And it is the difference in means – violent revolution or peaceful reforms – that even makes them opponents in some sense. Juliane accepts that she is sympathetic to a number of aims her sister is fighting for, but Marianne's choice of means has made it increasingly difficult for her to realise these similar aims her way. Not sympathising with, and actually rejecting, her sister's choice, Juliane concedes that the state is right to defeat terrorism as a public threat; but her sympathy with her sister's fate means that she cannot concede the right to destroy individual terrorists when they no longer pose a real threat.

More clearly than in *Katharina Blum*, the 'terrorist identity' is explored here, but it is also rejected more clearly, and an alternative is offered beyond mere withdrawal into privacy. There are other ways to position oneself against certain features of a society without having to cross the threshold of violence. Marianne's choice of identity is explored in its values and ideals, to many of which Juliane is sympathetic, but also in the limits of their violent actualisation. The dangers that are pointed to are the inability of society fully to integrate Juliane, despite her distinct identity, leaving her outside the official discourse, which has moved well beyond the issue of terrorism. Rejecting this exclusion, the film criticises the inability of society to incorporate a variety of identities instead of aiming at uniformity. At the same time it shows the limited space left for individuals who do not comply with this requirement of uniformity.

Stammheim (1986)

Produced in 1986, this film is a documentary-like report on the trial of Baader, Ensslin, Meinhof and Raspe at the Stammheim high-security prison in 1975–76 – the last but one chapter in the story of the first generation of the RAF. The film documents the process of the trial in its main landmarks – the appearance of all major witnesses such as the federal prosecutor-general, Siegfried Buback, and the major events such as the suicide of Ulrike Meinhof and the suspension and exchange of the presiding judge. The film employs actual phrases that were used during the trial by all the people involved: lawyers, judges, defendants, witnesses, representatives of the federal prosecution office and so on. To these are sparsely added quotations from letters by Meinhof and scenes that portray the terrorists' everyday life in prison, but apart from two scenes (the removal of Meinhof's dead body from the prison and the telephone conversation between the presiding judge and one of the defendants' lawyers), not a single meter of film is spent on filming outside the setting of the Stammheim high-security prison.

Of all the films selected here, it is probably the most objective, least personalised account of one particular aspect of German terrorism. No verbal judgements, no evaluations are made; the only sense in which the film is subjective is in its selection of material from the 192 days the trial lasted altogether. All speculation is avoided, most obviously towards the end of the film when it is stated that the three remaining defendants died in 1977 – three deaths that according to the official version were suicides, but that have persistently been alleged to have been murders.

The film's aim is obviously the comprehensive documentation of the events of the trial against the first generation of the RAF. But at the same time it is more than that. Documentary material and extensive witness reports shed light on the other side of terrorism – it is not only the revolutionary romanticism in terms of which the defendants themselves describe it frequently in their court statements, it is also the killing and maiming of innocent people in bomb attacks, the robbing of banks, the killing of policemen and terrorists. This focus on terrorism itself is one of the strengths of the film, but it is a focus from both perspectives – the witnesses as the victims are heard as well as the defendants, or their lawyers, who relate the attacks on US military bases to the context of the Vietnam War. And here the semi-documentary way in which the film has been made proves particularly valuable: photographs of the actual events (the scenes of bombings in Germany and in Vietnam) are shown but no evaluation is made; it remains for the viewer to decide which side he or she wants to take, which cause he or she finds more convincing.

The main thesis of the film, namely that after Stammheim nothing will be the same again (a quotation from Ulrike Meinhof), has certainly been proven to be true. Part of this truth is that the trial revealed the RAF's terrorism, motivations and consequences. But another truth was to be discovered as well: the truth that the state in its response to terrorism on several occasions traversed the line between legality and illegality. And this is depicted in the film too – without emotions or judgement, just the facts. The focus is on three issues: the conditions of imprisonment and their use to demoralise the defendants; the constant surveillance of the defendants, including the illegal intrusion into the protected sphere of conversation between defendant and defence lawyer; and the alleged attempt to manipulate the sentence so that any appeal against it would be pointless.

So, gradually, it is not so much terrorism itself any more that is the centre of attention, but the state's response to it, and in particular the state's treatment of the terrorists. The trial, and with it the film, sheds light on state practices without forgetting about the victims of terrorism: the obvious question that is being asked and, once again, left unanswered is how far the state can or must go to defeat terrorism and to defeat terrorists.

In raising that issue, *Stammheim* goes beyond *Katharina Blum* and *Die bleierne Zeit*, where similar issues are raised. It shows the essential dilemma of the RAF's activities, namely that their desire to contribute to the emancipation of humankind eventually became reduced to its mere ability to bring about death and increased repression and control. The film thus not only reveals the failure of terrorism, but also makes the spectator aware of the fact that there was impatience and intolerance on both sides. Those of the state are shown primarily through its inability to reflect on social and political conditions that encourage the eruption of violence, as all attempts of the defendants and their lawyers to introduce a political dimension to the trial fail. Those of the RAF itself are caused by a similar inability to apply political analysis, namely the inability to understand the social and political conditions under which they tried to achieve change and the consequences of attempts to bring about such change in a violent manner. The exploration of these dilemmas in a particular area of recent German history, dilemmas that are symptomatic for society as a whole, is one of the great achievements of this film, and the fact that this is done without judgement brings this film probably closest to being an alternative discourse on terrorism.

In its objectivity, the film also manages to give a much more detailed survey of the range of distinct identities that are possible within a society that is, after all, the most democratic that had ever been established on German soil. In the context of the Stammheim trial, the film makes clear that it is possible to retain human decency and fairness without rejecting this German society or being rejected by it. The flipside of the 'heroic' terrorist identity of fighting for the oppressed everywhere is exposed in terms of the innocent victims this struggle has cost, while at the same time the darker shades of an identity that seeks the defence of the strong state at any cost are questioned as well. To have shown the difficulty of defining one's identity in a complex setting such as this with all the errors possible in such a process is probably this film's greatest value, as it challenges the official discourse in its heart, namely in its claim to universal validity.

Die Terroristen (1993)

As the title suggests, terrorism is indeed what this film is about: terrorism as the symbolic act, as the one big blow that solves all the problems, as the one action that provides its protagonists with eternal fame. The symbolic act is to be the killing of the 'fat one', the federal chancellor. The problems to be solved are, among others, the emerging nationalist feelings in the course of German unification and the boredom of life in general. The eternal fame that *The Terrorists* – two men and a woman in their late twenties/early thirties, whose backgrounds remain largely unexplained – want to achieve is being part of Germany's chart of most wanted terrorists.

Their failure is almost absolute. Although they manage to rob a bank, the enthusiasm about German unification at the turn of 1989/90 makes this bank robbery so insignificant an event that not a single paper, TV or radio station mentions it, let alone investigates it. While the female among the three terrorists is busy writing pamphlets, the two male terrorists plan the attack on the chancellor with great care and expertise: a radio-controlled toy car carrying the bomb is to accompany the chancellor's car, get under it, explode and kill him. Everything seems perfect and certain to succeed, except for the fact that no one checks the batteries in the radio control. Their failure to explode the bomb is only matched by the incompetence of the security staff that accompany the chancellor: they return the whole device to its terrorist owners with an apology from the 'boss' and 200 Deutschmarks compensation. Devastated by this disaster, the three would-be-terrorists decide to abandon their operation and get away with the remainder of the money. This, however, is dependent on one condition, namely to return the flat they had rented in a condition that ensures the return of their deposit. The estate agent is, of course, dissatisfied and refuses to return the deposit – so all the hate and self-hate are projected at him, and one of the two male terrorists kills him. Escape seems the only way out of this ultimate failure. Despite being ordinary criminals on the run now, an accident turns them into terrorists after all. A neighbour comes by after they have left, discovers the bomb car, plays with it, and blows up the whole house. The next morning the three now feared terrorists read their story and pamphlets in the papers – to perfect this realisation of their dreams they have their photographs taken and add their pictures to the chart of Germany's most wanted terrorists displayed at a railway station.

All this is packed in a black comedy which has its particular value in the fact that it is able to show how ordinary people can become terrorists – partly because of their own frustration about society, but really because someone else makes them what they want to be, someone determines they are terrorists. Their own attempts to become terrorists had failed; only the accidental setting off of the bomb device by a neighbour and the interest in that event, in combination with the killing of the estate agent, taken by the newspapers makes them terrorists for a deed they did not commit, and suggests motives that they did not have in connection with this crime. Thus, the main thesis of this film can probably be best described as this: it is forces outside the influence of the individual, such as the state or the media, that create and determine who a terrorist is and what terrorism is, and they do this in accordance with their own agenda, so that the individual would-be terrorist plays only a marginal role in the scenario.

Therefore, the film, although it does use the first generation of the RAF as a starting point, is more than just a replay of their failure in the chronologically similar sequence of bank robbery, extensive but often pointless planning, failure to achieve their actual aims, substitute killings, and accidental involvement of bystanders. This makes the reality of terrorism a conditional one – no act of violence in itself carries the quality of terrorism, only its interpretation does, and this power of interpretation does not lie with the individual terrorist. This is an interesting twist in the usual story where the terrorist sees himself or herself as a revolutionary rather than a terrorist: here all initial attempts to become recognised as terrorists fail. And the critique that is implicit in this goes beyond a critique of terrorism or the state's response to it or the role of the media. It is a critique of society in general, a critique of its preoccupation with itself, and its inability to listen to voices from outside the dominant discourse.

The film is also, and perhaps most of all, about the desperate quest of three individuals for their identity and for a way to express this identity in action and have it recognised, accepted and confirmed by society. With a society preoccupied with itself and its drive to redefine its identity in larger and more national terms than ever before since the end of World War II, the opportunities to do so are rather limited. Once again, there is no room for individuals questioning their own identity and challenging the society in its claim to define the individual's identity for him or her. In this challenge the three terrorists succeed only partly, and thus a bitter taste of an almighty, society-determined public discourse with no room for individual voices remains.

Conclusion

With the exception of *Die Terroristen*, and to some extent *Stammheim*, terrorism itself is not the main focus of the four films discussed here – rather it is the response to it and the effects on society, and the individuals within it, of this recent phenomenon of violent protest in German history.

This is most obviously the case with *Katharina Blum* and *Die bleierne Zeit*. The two films criticise what they perceive to be the official approach to terrorism: not the terrorist but its supporter is the real danger to society. Yet, by focusing not on terrorism but on the state's response to it, and on the individual affected by it, the two films cannot make a convincing counter-argument about terrorism, but only about its effects. Assuming that this was their creators' original intention, the films succeed in delivering a powerful and emotional critique of West German society – supported by and supporting the state's response to terrorism, the media manage to manipulate public opinion abusing the power of the discourse which is so obviously a political one.

Stammheim which focuses on the clash between two different political motivations and the implications they bring with them, namely a political and a legal approach to terrorism, in part manages to balance the argument, but being conceptualised more or less as a documentary account of the trial, all it can achieve is to contrast the official discourse with the terrorists' view and that of their lawyers. In such a documentary conception, however, it is not possible to establish an alternative discourse: the viewer is merely presented with the material and the views of both parties, any conclusions are then left to him or her, and that holds true for choices of identity as well. More clearly than in *Katharina Blum* and *Die bleierne Zeit*, potential identities are offered that allow the preservation of fairness and dignity without rejecting society as a whole or being rejected by society.

Only in *Die Terroristen* is terrorism an issue in its own right, a kind of terrorism that is matched in its failure only by the incompetence of the state and the media to recognise it, and by their resulting tendency to declare more or less unrelated issues to be acts of terrorism. This symbolises the power of definition that is inherent in any discourse that has established itself as the dominant one and is in a secure enough position to be able to control which voices are to be heard and which not. This power of definition extends to individual identity as well, making it very hard for the individual to determine his or her identity. It thus also stands for the difficulty, if not impossibility, of establishing alternative discourses and identities, of participating in the dominant discourse as an outsider, or of being accepted into society with a different identity – terrorism becomes a fetish, for those who want to be terrorists and for those who profit from it, that is, the media and the state, and it is the latter who determine the nature, agenda and actuality of terrorism and the identity of terrorists, not the individuals involved.

What this points to is an interesting question: is alternative discourse on an issue of such enormous social and political importance as terrorism at all possible? As regards the analysis of these four films, the answer is a qualified no, as all of them at least manage to add, even if selectively only, to the established discourse.

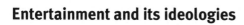

Entertainment and its ideologies

DAVID GILLESPIE

Of human bondage and male bonding: male relationships in recent Russian cinema

This chapter intends to look at a particular feature of Russian culture over the centuries, as it has developed in Russian cinematic art over the past two decades: the practice of structuring the narrative around a 'pair' of protagonists, whose friendship or confrontation leads to the elaboration and resolution of drama and conflict.

The Hollywood tradition of expressive masculinity essentially demonstrates two scenarios: either the final and decisive shoot-out between the male protagonists is the ultimate confrontation of good and evil (cf. *Dirty Harry*, the vast majority of Westerns, any film featuring James Bond); or the male-centred buddy-buddy relationship, perhaps fraught at first, helps defeat the enemy through concerted effort and ultimately friendship (cf. the male bonding of the *Lethal Weapon* series, and its various imitations). Historically, Russian cinema has generally eschewed such melodramatic tensions in favour of pursuing ideological debate, and has largely ignored both of these dynamics. It remains curiously dialogic, as various (mainly male) characters representing different worldviews argue and debate, perhaps fall out, but eventually come to a resolution. The dynamics of dialogue serve to highlight the salient issues facing contemporary Russian (or Soviet) society, and the various solutions at hand to resolve them. Whereas in the Soviet past these issues focused on the defeat of the class enemy in the name of the victory of Communism, in recent years they have been bound up with questions of freedom and subjugation, national and personal identity, and the search for truth and justice in the post-Stalin world.

Russian intellectuals have always taken pride in the continuity of their culture through wars, revolutions or economic collapse. Dialogism is not confined to the relatively new art of cinema; rather, it is a feature of literary discourse first examined in the works of Fedor Dostoevskii. In their varying ways, the two most eminent Russian literary scholars of the twentieth century, Mikhail Bakhtin and Iurii Lotman, have drawn attention to the structural binary oppositions of Russian culture. Mikhail Bakhtin first examined the tension between 'high' and 'low' cultural forms in his celebration of the 'carnival' in Rabelais. Bakhtin's thesis is that in *Gargantua and Pantagruel* official – that is, closed, authoritarian – discourse is subverted by popular, sometimes coarse and vulgar, forms (clowning, joking, laughter and parody) to make way for the dynamic and the new (Bakhtin 1981, 1984). Iurii Lotman, together with his colleague Boris Uspenskii, has noted the 'persistent opposition' throughout early Russian culture (up to the eighteenth century) of 'old' versus 'new', which equates with 'paganism' versus 'Christianity', 'Russia' versus 'the West', 'true faith' versus 'false faith', the 'social bottom' versus 'the social top' (Lotman and Uspenskij 1984). In short, 'old' Russian culture is engaged in a polemic with 'new' Russian culture, with the ultimate aim of establishing true meaning and identity.

Lotman also affirms the persistence of cultural memory over the centuries. The main dramas of the nineteenth- and twentieth-century classics are played out as a duel, both real and metaphorical, between opposing male protagonists, and these binary oppositions recur in Russian film. In Pushkin's *Evgenii Onegin* the eponymous hero shoots Lenskii in a duel, but does not get the girl (neither Olga nor, eventually, Tatiana). Lermontov's Pechorin also wins out in a duel, and though Grushnitskii dies, Pechorin loses both Vera, his true love, and Princess Mary, the cause of the original confrontation. Moreover, the death of both Lenskii and Grushnitskii signifies the death of romantic idealism, and the victory of pragmatic opportunism, even cynicism, in contemporary Russia. The metaphorical duel between Andrei Bolkonskii and Pierre Bezukhov in *War and Peace* over the eternal questions, such as how to live and what is happiness, ends with the death of Bolkonskii on the battlefield, and his realisation that pure intellect cannot be the source of true happiness. Pierre, on the other hand, finds some sort of contentment through his exposure to simple folk wisdom and an elemental understanding of life. Goncharov's Oblomov represents a Russia of happy indolence and unfulfilled potential which is opposed to the perceived Teutonic efficacy of Shtolts, in an irony-laden allegory of Russia's relationship with the West. In Dostoevskii's *Crime and Punishment* the student Raskolnikov loses his battle of wits with the prosecutor Porfirii Petrovich, and with it his belief in the perfectibility of man and the power of his reason. In Pasternak's *Doctor Zhivago* the bloodthirsty revolutionary Strelnikov shoots himself after one of several meetings with the poet and mystic Zhivago as they both vie for the love of Lara, the beautiful, wilful embodiment of Russia. In Solzhenitsyn's *Cancer Ward* the ex-prisoner Kostoglotov wins the moral argument with the Stalinist bureaucrat

Rusanov, but the price of his life and freedom is sexual impotence. The question in this novel is one that is echoed across the massed ranks of post-Stalin literary works: is the price of freedom too high?[1]

It is significant, therefore, that the oppositions, debate and dialogue of classical Russian literature recur in Russian cinema. By looking at male–male relationships through the prism of pre-existing cultural models, I do not intend to discuss the image of man (described recently as the 'crisis of masculinity', the 'collapse of male self-confidence' and 'gender angst') in Russian film.[2] The films to be discussed below are as follows: *Voskhozhdenie* (*The Ascent*), directed by Larisa Shepitko in 1976; *Kholodnoe leto 53-ego* (*The Cold Summer of 1953*), directed in 1987 by Aleksandr Proshkin; *The Servant* (*Sluga*), directed in 1988 by Vadim Abdrashitov; *Utomlennye solntsem* (*Burnt By the Sun*), directed in 1994 by Nikita Mikhalkov; *Musul'manin* (*The Muslim*), directed in 1995 by Vladimir Khotinenko; and *Kavkazskii plennik* (*A Prisoner of the Mountains*), directed in 1996 by Sergei Bodrov. I will conclude with a discussion of *Nostalgiia* (*Nostalgia*), directed in 1983 by Andrei Tarkovskii. These are, of course, very disparate films. Some of them (especially those made between 1987 and 1994) feature the juxtaposition of male protagonists as a confrontation of good and evil, representing the attempts of Russian culture to exorcise the demon of Stalin. Others use the pairing of male protagonists as the frame for a time-honoured larger debate on Russia's identity in terms of its relationship to something alien, 'the other', and thus ask questions about the future. What unites them all is their exclusion of women within a predominantly male discourse. The female, if present, serves the purpose merely of the prize to be won or lost. The literary and cultural paradigms within which all of these films work are evident.[3]

Shepitko's *The Ascent* is based on the 1972 novella *Sotnikov* by the Belorussian writer Vasili Bykov, and remains faithful to the original text in all but one key area. Both film and novella are set in a snow-bound Belorussian landscape during the last war. Sotnikov is a partisan who, along with his comrade Rybak, is sent by his commanding officer to find food in a local village. They encounter a German patrol, and, after a brief gunfight, Sotnikov kills one of the Germans. He, though, is wounded, and beginning to feel the effects of advanced pneumonia. In a scene of excruciating intensity, Rybak drags his wounded and sick comrade across the snow to shelter as the German patrol comes looking for them. They eventually take refuge in a peasant house, and hide in the attic when the Germans come. Just as the Germans are about to give up their search and leave, Sotnikov's pneumonia gets the better of him and he has a fit of coughing. They are captured, along with the innocent housewife who sheltered them (against her will and better judgement), and the village elder (ironically, since Rybak had wanted to shoot him as a traitor). They are taken to the German base and subjected to interrogation.

Rybak has so far been physically and morally the stronger, helping and protecting his sick comrade, and implacably opposed to any accommodation with the enemy. Like the true positive hero of countless works of Soviet war fiction, he is devoted to the cause of defeating the enemy. In contrast, Sotnikov is frail, and obviously dying. Nevertheless, under interrogation and torture with a hot iron, Sotnikov remains unbowed and unbroken. He will not reveal the whereabouts of the rest of the unit. When Rybak is summoned to the interrogation room, the mere threat of torture turns him into a collaborator. Rybak then tells Sotnikov that he pretends to collaborate, in order to stay alive and save them both. Rybak becomes a traitor, but Sotnikov, the housewife and the village elder are all hanged. Death here is religious martyrdom, as Sotnikov's head is filmed surrounded by ethereal light.

The decisive influence on the relationship between Sotnikov and Rybak is that of Portnov, the Russian Nazi collaborator who is Sotnikov's interrogator. Dressed all in black, he is obviously an incarnation of pure evil, significantly a former Communist who has switched allegiance. Sotnikov, despite his physical weakness, has the spiritual strength to reject him; Rybak, apparently the stronger, surrenders his soul to him, and directly participates in the death of Sotnikov by kicking away the stool on which his former comrade stands with his head in the noose. Sotnikov ascends to heaven; Rybak is plunged into a living hell of cowardice and betrayal.

The twin themes developed here through the interaction and juxtaposition of male protagonists are strength and cowardice, loyalty and betrayal, spirituality and depravity. It is no accident that the film has a religious dimension (then very much frowned upon in Soviet culture), as Portnov is the Mephistophelean figure who sees hidden weakness and exploits it through temptation. Moreover, Bykov's original story has a sharp ideological focus (not submitting to the enemy at all costs), but Shepitko cleverly debunks the myths of Soviet war fiction. Portnov as a Communist would be the 'positive hero' through whose efforts the enemy would be defeated; however, here he is working for the enemy. The film therefore suggests that the service of Nazism is fundamentally little different from the service of Communism. The religious allegory that is absent in the novella furthermore gives the film another, neo-Slavophile meaning: the enormous sufferings visited upon the country in the last war forge a spiritual strength that is above ideology, and that will survive and grow in future generations (as shown in the figure of the small boy inspired by Sotnikov's dignity in death).

Almost twenty years later, the relationship of hangman with his intended (and unknowing) victim is the driving force behind Nikita Mikhalkov's Oscar-winning *Burnt by the Sun*. The film is set in the Stalinist terror of 1936, at the country dacha of Sergei Kotov, a famous Red Army commander loved and respected by his men and formerly hero of the Civil War. Played by Mikhalkov himself, he is a real man of the people, a Russian patriot who prefers the peasant bath-house to a sauna, and Russian folk-dancing to Western-style tap-dancing. His nemesis is the young and dashing Mitia, recently returned from the West, who works for the secret police. Mitia had bought his return to Russia by betraying his former friends in the White emigration in the West, and now prepares to betray Kotov, his former friend and mentor.

Their opposition is played out on several levels. Mitia used to be the lover of Marusia, now Kotov's wife. Mitia's betrayal, we learn in the after-titles as the film closes, will go further, for after Kotov's execution Marusia will be arrested and will die in a prison camp. Essentially, though, the decent, simple and honest Russian values personified by Kotov are betrayed and destroyed by the totalitarian evil embodied by the cosmopolitan and Westernised Mitia. The interplay of the two protagonists here develops as a nationalistic and worryingly xenophobic reading of twentieth-century Russian history.

As in *The Ascent*, there is a third male character in *Burnt by the Sun* whose influence on the central duo is decisive. Stalin appears in iconic mode as a portrait on a huge banner that floats over the landscape, dominating it and everyone in it, at the end of the film. Mitia salutes the image he serves so ruthlessly, and which Kotov had hitherto served with faith and devotion. Stalin is also the dominating influence in the relationship of the two protagonists in another explicitly anti-Stalinist film, *The Cold Summer of 1953*.

As the title indicates, the film is set in the aftermath of Stalin's death in March 1953, and shortly after secret police chief Lavrentii Beria's now infamous amnesty for criminals. Two political prisoners, Sergei Bosorgin (nicknamed Luzga) and Nikolai Starobogatov (nicknamed Potapych), have been released from camp and are spending their five years of exile in a remote riverside village. Sergei used to be a captain in the Red Army and, during the war, was the only one in his unit to escape German encirclement. Naturally enough for those times, he was suspected of being a traitor and imprisoned. Starobogatov, a much older man, was imprisoned back in 1939, as a result of a trip abroad (he was accused of being an English spy). Starobogatov is an engineer by training, and his appearance and behaviour mark him out, alongside his surname (literally: 'the wealth of old'), as an intellectual of the old school.

Their peaceful, almost idyllic life is destroyed when their village is over-run by seven heavily armed and ruthless recently amnestied criminals. They kill the only policeman and terrorise the local population as they wait for a boat to take them away. The village becomes a microcosm of Soviet society, where violence and injustice reign, people are cowed and distraught, and there is that most ubiquitous feature of Stalinist society, the traitor-informer. The criminals have nothing but contempt for the 'politicals', and subject them to abuse and beatings. However, in the ensuing battle Sergei and Starobogatov pick the criminals off one by one in a shoot-out that owes much to the Hollywood Western, but Starobo-gatov and a peasant girl are killed.

On a superficial level this is a straightforward shoot-'em-up, with clearly defined good guys who triumph over adversity, injustice and overwhelming odds (albeit at a high price). On another level the film shows the ultimate victory of legality and morality over criminality, and thus also represents a key concept in the glasnost years of Mikhail Gorba-chev, when the film was made. Both in the late 1980s and in the mid-1950s Russia emerged into the light after the darkness of repression, and the ghosts of the past are slowly, painfully, laid to rest.

These themes come into sharp focus through the interrelationship of Sergei and Starobogatov. Both are representative of the social types ensnared by the Stalinist terror: the soldier and the old-fashioned *intel-ligent*, one the warrior-saviour, the other the thinker and repository of old-world values. Both are reduced to the same level by their arrest, and both fight against a common enemy. In this fight they recover their self-worth, courage and identity. The film is therefore an allegory of the re-emergence of humanity, morality and dignity in the post-Stalin years.

The fight of Sergei and Starobogatov is above all with tyranny and its legacy. Another key film of the glasnost period, and with a similar theme, is *The Servant*, another political allegory but one that disturbs with its psychological insights. The director Abdrashitov concentrates on the highly ambivalent master–slave relationship of former driver Pavel Kliuev, now a celebrated choirmaster, and the former political bigwig Andrei Andreevich Gudenov. The story is told in both the narrative present and flashback. In Pavel's flashbacks Gudenov is clearly a Stalinist-type bureau-crat who literally gets the red-carpet treatment when he visits enterprises. In the present he bemoans the loss of faith by the younger generation. Gudenov's enemy is Bryzgin, a liberal who represents the values of justice and democracy, and who describes him in demonic terms as an enemy of virtue, of the past and tradition, and 'the genius of chaos'. Gudenov is a Soviet Mephistopheles, who can literally make a whole football team dance to his tune, is able to read Pavel's mind, anticipate his actions, fuel his desires and even find him a wife. He can also then split them up.

Pavel, though, revels in his own subordination to Gudenov, and there is more than a hint of sado-masochism, not to say homoeroticism, in the alternating themes of power and subservience. 'Your habits will become mine,' says Pavel to his master. 'That was said by the slave,' is Gudenov's smirking reply. Pavel does indeed want to be subservient and manipulated, he wants his will to be controlled by another, he wants Gudenov to dominate everything in his life, including his marriage.

The film's ending is downbeat, as Pavel kills Bryzgin and is then arrested. His need to act the slave leads to self-destruction. Significantly, the police come for him as he conducts his choir at a concert: he may be going through the motions, but ultimately he is not in control. Abdrashitov's film has a bleak message for Soviet society struggling towards some idea of freedom and democracy in 1988, and suggests that the much-deplored passivity and indolence of Russians have their roots in a deeper, altogether more intractable psychological malaise.[4]

A *Prisoner of the Mountains* is an adaptation of Lev Tolstoi's story of the same name, but updated to take place during the course of a contemporary war in the Caucasus, probably Chechnia. Two Russian soldiers, Zhilin and Kostylin, are taken prisoner by rebels and held in a mountain village. The village elder Abdul-Murat wishes to exchange them for his own son, who is held by the Russians. Kostylin is later killed after an unsuccessful escape attempt, but Zhilin is allowed to go free.

The developing relationship of the two Russians during their captivity provides the thematic focus of the film. Kostylin is a professional soldier, much older than Zhilin, who sees his captors simply as aliens and enemies who deserve to be killed. Zhilin is a young conscript who does not understand why he is fighting an unnecessary and wasteful war, and covers his ears during combat. He is at least respectful towards his captors, and tries to communicate with the mountain tribesmen. Through the differing attitudes of Zhilin and Kostylin towards an alien culture, the film explores Russia's own search for itself; through imperialist confrontation with 'the other', Russia struggles towards its own identity in a changing world. The director Bodrov has made a film which is more than an anti-war film, and more than an adaptation of a nineteenth-century classic. Moreover, A *Prisoner of the Mountains* explores questions of Russia's borders, both geographical and psychological, as if confronting its Russian audience with the age-old question: where does Russia go now?

Bodrov's film can be seen as a companion piece to Khotinenko's starkly anti-Russian (some would say unpatriotic) *The Muslim*, which is similarly based on a clash of cultures, here Russian and Muslim. A Russian soldier, Kolia Ivanov, returns to his native village after eight years in captivity while fighting in Afghanistan, and encounters drunkenness, crime and corruption throughout the community. He has since converted to Islam, does not drink, does not condone the thieving all around, and is regarded as an alien by villagers who simply do not understand an alien culture. Indeed, the modern Russian villagers we see in *The Muslim* thrive on thieving and greed, and are easily seduced by Western culture in the form of pornographic films showing at the local cinema.

The contrast between Russia and 'the other' is at its sharpest in the relationship between Kolia and his drunken, aggressive brother Fedka: one embodies the values of tolerance, honesty and moderation, the other living only for the next drink, determined to defile and destroy anything that is not familiar or native. Fedka at one point tries to force Kolia to kiss the icon of St Nikolai, but even in the face of violence Kolia refuses. Kolia is eventually killed by another Afghan veteran who believes that Kolia had betrayed his unit when captured. It should be borne in mind that 'Kolia Ivanov' is just about the most common male Russian name there is. His death is the metaphorical death of Russia itself.

Khotinenko's film makes a statement on the spiritual and moral wasteground that is post-Soviet Russia. The Russian village, for centuries regarded as the home and repository of true Russian spirituality, is consumed by its own venality and degradation. Kolia, as a paragon of goodness and purity, can find no place there. The Russian identification with Western values goes no further than the search for dollars and the titillation of sex films, and the clear inference is that Russia has lost its true way and identity. Khotinenko's film has a brutal message for crisis-ridden Russia in the 1990s, and one which is explored through the conflict within a single family.

In all of these films the central male–male relationship has been viewed as a duel of ideologies, with the future of Russia itself at stake. These clashes are played out against the backdrop of the topical issues of the day, and thus are part of their time. Tarkovskii's *Nostalgia* is also concerned with border consciousness (where does Russia begin and the West end?), but also transcends the immediate socio-political context. Gorchakov is a Russian writer in Italy researching the life of an eighteenth-century Russian musician, Sosnovskii, who spent time in Italy. Gorchakov feels ill-at-ease and alone, sometimes speaking Italian, sometimes Russian and sometimes a mixture of the two, all the while looking for a point of identity in the unfamiliar Italian landscape. He meets a recluse, Domenico, who prophesies the end of the world, unless a personal sacrifice is made. Domenico thus reminds Gorchakov of the 'holy fool' of Russian culture, regarded by the masses as the bearer of spiritual truths, although outwardly appearing an imbecile. Domenico kills himself in

Rome before a crowd of curiously uninvolved onlookers, and Gorchakov also then sacrifices himself by fulfilling Domenico's last wish, carrying a lighted candle across a body of water. However, the world is not saved: faith no longer unites people.

Through his encounter with Domenico, Gorchakov finds an accom-modation between Russia and Italy; moreover, in mirrors he sees not his own image but that of Domenico. It is not hard to see Tarkovskii, too, seeing his own situation – that of self-imposed exile and alienation – in that of Gorchakov. Through the Russia–Italy axis Tarkovskii explores issues of confrontation–accommodation that have dogged Russian culture for centuries in a timeless, extra-political, almost metaphysical context. More than any other Russian director of the post-war period, Andrei Tarkovskii has crossed the psychological Russia–West border in search of meaning and identity.[5]

All of the films discussed have a narrative structure of dialogue and/or opposition of male protagonists as part of an exploration of socio-political or historical questions. All of these directors are thus working within a clear Russian cultural tradition, one noted and attested by the leading Russian scholars of the twentieth century. Russian cultural forms in the late 1990s were still struggling to escape the dead hand of the recent past and point to a future, and continued to use familiar and time-tested forms and structures. It is fair to say, though, that whereas in Russia in the 1990s literary culture had declined and seemed unable to cope with the advent of the market and a host of other, generally unsavoury issues, cinema reacted quickly and effectively. The opposition of, and tension between, the dual themes of tyranny and morality, slavery and freedom, 'self' and 'other', and, ultimately, Russia and the West dominated Russian cinematic discourse, and look set to do so for the foreseeable future.

Notes

1 Barbara Heldt, in her definitive analysis of the treatment of women in Russian literature, highlights the predominance of the male over the female in literary discourse: 'There is no lack of general pronouncements about how women act or feel or think in Russian literature: these, however, have been overwhelmingly made by men. The unflattering have been more than amply "balanced" by the flattering. In fact, in Russian fiction the elevation of the Russian woman is matched only by the self-abasement of the Russian man. His is a long and tortuous road to enlightenment, while *she* grasps the essentials of life, if not immediately then certainly firmly and intuitively when the time comes [to fall in love] ... There is no novel of gradual female development, of rebirth or transformation as we find in Austen or Eliot; while some male characters learn and grow through intellect or experience, the changes in women are mysterious givens of nature, of Womanhood. The heroines of male fiction serve a purpose that ultimately has little to do with women: these heroines are used lavishly in a discourse of male self-definition' (Heldt 1987: 2).

2   Lynne Attwood has written succinctly on this: 'This supposed male oppression at the hands of women was exacerbated by the oppression exerted by the state. On the one hand, the Soviet Union's extensive welfare system, which met all of its citizens' basic needs, stifled their drive and initiative. At the same time, it exerted such tight control over their behaviour that it destroyed their independence and autonomy. Damage to Soviet manhood is said to have been particularly acute in the Stalin era. Even though the image of the muscle-bound Stakhanovite seems to glorify masculinity, the state was at its most intrusive, and men at their most impotent' (Attwood 1998: 367).

3   I do not, for reasons of space and scope, intend here to discuss in detail the binary oppositions of the cinema of Socialist Realism in Russia. Suffice it to mention Ivan Pyriev's 1939 classic, *Tractor-Drivers* (*Traktoristy*), where the forward-looking and dynamic Klim wins the hand of the fair Mariana from the boorish Nazar. He also wins the friendship of Nazar by showing him how to work his tractor to maximum effect; Nazar then leads the singing at the wedding of Klim and Mariana. In other words, socialist men resolve their differences through increased efficiency and production yields. Otherwise, the homogeneity and sheer predictability of male–male conflicts in films of 1933-53 has been well summed up by Peter Kenez: 'Socialist realist films included three stock figures with depressing regularity: the Party leader, the simple person, and the enemy. The Party leader was almost always male, ascetic, dressed in a semimilitary style, unencumbered by a family or love affairs. The simple person could be male or female and was allowed to have interest in the opposite sex. Sexual relations were always chaste, the viewer could never see more than a kiss, and these relations often needed to be straightened out by a Party leader. The enemy, whose function was to wreck and destroy what the Communists were building, was always a male. On occasion, but rarely, he attempted to win over the simple person to his side by lying and subterfuge, but mostly he limited his activities to blowing up things' (Kenez 1992: 158).

4   *The Servant* bears more than a passing resemblance to Pavel Lungin's 1990 film *Taksi-bliuz* (*Taxi Blues*), which explores the increasing domination of one man by another against the background of a Moscow changing under the pressures of perestroika, with the consequent blurring of sexual and psychological identities.

5   In his diary Tarkovskii notes the following: 'Working all the time in Italy I made a film that was profoundly Russian in every way: morally, politically, emotionally. It is about a Russian who has been posted to Italy on an extended visit, and his impressions of the country. But I wasn't aiming at yet another screen account of the beauties of Italy which amaze the tourists and are sent all over the world in the form of mass-produced postcards. My subject is a Russian who is thoroughly disorientated by the impressions crowding in upon him, and at the same time about his tragic inability to share these impressions with the people closest to him, and the impossibility of grafting his new experience onto the past which has bound him from his very birth' (Tarkovskii 1987: 202).

References

Attwood, L. (1998), 'Gender angst in Russian society and cinema in the post-Stalin era', in David Shepherd and Catriona Kelly (eds), *Russian Cultural Studies: An Introduction*, Oxford, Oxford University Press, 352–68.

Bakhtin, M. (1981), 'Forms of time and of the chronotope in the novel', in *The Dialogic Imagination: Four Essays*, Austin, TX, University of Texas Press, 84–258.

Bakhtin, M. (1984), *Rabelais and his World*, trans. Helene Iswolsky, Bloomington, Indiana University Press.

Gillespie, D. and N. Zhuravkina (1996a), 'Nikita Mikhalkov's *Utomlennye solntsem*', *Rusistika*, 13: 58–61.

Gillespie, D. and N. Zhuravkina (1996b), 'Sergei Bodrov's *A Prisoner of the Caucasus*', *Rusistika*, 14: 56–9.

Heldt, Barbara (1987), *Terrible Perfection: Women and Russian Literature*, Bloomington and Indianapolis, Indiana University Press.

Johnson, Vida T. (1997), 'The search for a new Russia in an "Era of Few Films"', *Russian Review*, 56, 2: 281–5.

Johnson, Vida T. and G. Petrie (1994), *The Films of Andrei Tarkovsky: A Visual Fugue*, Bloomington and Indianapolis, Indiana University Press.

Kenez, Peter (1992), *Cinema and Soviet Society, 1917–1953*, Cambridge, Cambridge University Press.

Lawton, A. (1992), *Kinoglasnost: Soviet Cinema in our Time*, Cambridge, Cambridge University Press.

Lotman, Ju. M. and B. A. Uspenskij (1984), 'The role of dual models in the dynamics of Russian culture (up to the end of the eighteenth century)', in *The Semiotics of Russian Culture*, Ann Arbor, Michigan Slavic Contributions 11, 3–35.

Tarkovskii, A. (1987), *Sculpting in Time: Reflections on the Cinema*, trans. Kitty Hunter-Blair, Austin, TX, University of Texas Press.

Entertainment – but where's the ideology? Truffaut's last films

12

> If French cinema were compared to a house with a sloping roof, Truffaut would be the ridge-pole of tiles that joins the 'auteur' side to the 'commercial cinema' side. He was balanced between these two slopes, and made use of each. Since his death, the two sides have lost their point of connection. (Jean Douchet, 1989)[1]

This tribute to Truffaut's capacity to combine cinema as art with cinema as entertainment was written five years after his death, but the bridging quality it identifies had been present from the beginning of his directing career. Despite their critical scorn for the French film industry of the 1950s (the 'tradition of quality') and the limitations imposed by shoestring budgets, Truffaut and the other young directors of the *Nouvelle Vague* sought, in their earliest films, to emulate their cinematic heroes (Hitchcock, Renoir, the best Hollywood studio directors) by combining artistic integrity with story-telling that engaged a wide audience. Truffaut – more than the other New Wave-ists, with the exception of Chabrol – continued to judge the success of his films in terms of their accessibility and the pleasure they brought to a public of casual, non-specialised filmgoers: 'I make films that resemble those I liked [as a child] ... films that are made to be accessible to everyone ... I tell stories with a beginning, a middle and an end, even if I know very well that in the end the interest lies elsewhere than in the plot' (Truffaut 1988: 530).

This commitment to popular story-telling produced an uneven but reasonably consistent degree of commercial success, so that Truffaut's production company, the *Films du Carrosse*, was increasingly able to attract co-investment for his projects. By the time he came to make what were to be the last three films of his career, *Le Dernier métro* (*The Last Metro*, 1980), *La Femme d'à côté* (*The Woman Next Door*, 1981) and *Vivement dimanche!* (*Finally Sunday!*, 1982), Truffaut was financially equipped to enhance his film narratives with some of the expensive pleasures of high-investment commercial cinema: star actors, meticulous recreation of period and place, high-quality film image and colour. With budgets of four (*La Femme d'à côté*), seven (*Vivement dimanche!*) and eleven million francs (*Le Dernier métro*), at a time when the average cost of making a film in France was 3.51 million (Prédal 1991: 396), Truffaut's three final films were glossily produced, generically varied and if not star-studded at least star-sprinkled works, which both confirmed his status as an *auteur* and proved that the appeal of his cinema went well beyond a small elite audience of intellectuals and *cinéphiles*. *Le Dernier métro* – commercially the greatest hit – won ten *césars*, the French equivalent of Oscars, and was the fifth most successful French film at the box office in 1980/1, with 3.3 million tickets sold

It makes sense, then, to discuss the last three films as successful ventures in terms of the entertainment industry. They clearly do not belong in the category of the blockbuster (although *Vivement dimanche!* rivalled *Superman 2* at Parisian box offices when they opened in the same week), but these are films that could, and did, attract large audiences, and apparently satisfy them. The films' capacity to entertain can also be observed in the response of UK students, even those resistant to 'difficult' foreign films, who seem to find viewing late Truffaut films unproblematic and largely pleasurable, although most of their experience as spectators has been of mainstream commercial cinema. However, to refer to a 'serious' director as a purveyor of entertainment is generally to question his or her artistic and ethical integrity. Entertainment suggests easy pleasures, a refusal to engage with 'serious' issues for fear of losing the audience, and thus a tendency to endorse rather than contest hegemonic values. The accessibility and popular appeal of Truffaut's films laid him open to the charge of 'selling out to the system', as the film critic Jean-Louis Bory put it in 1974.[2] One not untypical review of *Le Dernier métro* accused the film of employing the classic devices of popular fiction (a happy ending, a clear delineation of characters as 'good' or 'bad') to provide an inappropriately 'comforting and comfortable vision' of the war years in France, and indeed of life itself (Affron and Rubinstein 1985: 188). The narrative strategies of entertainment films tend to be equated with ideological conservatism, and though for Jean Douchet the capacity to combine auteurism with popularity was a rare and valuable achievement, for many critics Truffaut's commercial successes undermined his credibility as an *auteur* with anything critical or interesting to say.

In *Only Entertainment* (1992), Richard Dyer both disputes the automatic identification of entertainment with conservatism, and suggests that the preoccupation of film studies with the ideological subtext of films has meant a lack of engagement with 'entertainment *qua* entertainment' (Dyer 1992: 3–4). Even in work that deals specifically with mainstream commercial film, he argues, the qualities that constitute entertainment have been seen chiefly as the 'sugar' on the 'pill' of ideology, with the main focus remaining on the latter. In this chapter I propose first to take the 'sugar' of Truffaut's last films seriously, by asking what produces their entertainment value, and second to pose the related question of their ideological implications. Are these films that, precisely because they are pleasurable and relatively easy to watch, leave spectators completely unmoved and unchallenged in their attitudes and beliefs? To what extent does the *auteur*/commercial dichotomy identified by Douchet map on to a struggle within the text between progressive and conservative meanings?

Why are these films entertaining?

Genre

Truffaut's last three films constitute a virtuoso performance by a director whose work had always been characterised by variety. Each of the films employs the framework of a different genre, which functions – as genre functions in most commercial cinema – to provide the spectator with a point of access to the fiction. One important aspect of entertainment (to which I return below) is escapism, the capacity of fiction to transport the spectator temporarily into an imaginary world and thus suspend the real anxieties of the everyday. Entry into that imaginary world requires, none the less, a degree of recognition, for total unfamiliarity makes the suspension of disbelief impossible. However, recognition is not solely dependent on perceived similarity between the fictional world on the screen and our own, lived experience, for our mental 'maps' of reality are constructed as much by the fictions we consume as by empirical knowledge. Genre provides a familiar framework based on other stories we have watched, heard and read, a set of visual and aural signifiers that produce expectations of the narrative to come, but within which variation and surprise remain possible. None of the films under discussion here – indeed none of Truffaut's films – could be described as pure 'genre films', but *Le Dernier métro* and *Vivement dimanche!* in particular make productive use of generic codes familiar to most spectators.[3]

In the case of *Le Dernier métro*, the genre evoked is the Occupation film, a subgenre of the period movie set in occupied France and dealing with the hardships of everyday life and the difficult moral and political choices between resistance and collaboration. Though some 60 feature films about the Occupation years were made in France under de Gaulle's presidency (Hayward 1993: 250), it was after his death, in the 1970s and 1980s, that preoccupation with this traumatic period produced a flood of books and films, known collectively as the *mode rétro*. Since enjoyment is not ahistorical but 'works with the desires that circulate in a given society at a given time' (Dyer 1992: 7), *Dernier métro*'s success is not unrelated to its deployment of the iconography and themes of the *mode rétro*, and its topical concern with historical memory. The film signals its generic affiliation through its extensive use of period details that have become, through their repeated use in cinema, immediate signifiers of a whole era: extracts from what purport to be cinema news bulletins of the period, low-slung black Citroen cars that mean 'Gestapo', German uniforms set against quintessentially Parisian streets, women painting stockings (including the seams) onto their legs in response to rationing and shortages, the last metro itself with its overtones of curfews, the underground and final journeys. Truffaut's film uses the accrued associations these scenes and objects carry as an economical means to evoke an era, carrying the spectator into an immediately recognisable fictional world that promises (and delivers) a story of resistance and collaboration, suspense and escape or capture, ending with the redemptive conclusion of a victory won not only by the Allies but also by the Free French. *Le Dernier métro* also plays on the pleasures of spectacle offered by the 'heritage' genre. The elegant recreations of 1940s fashions, the use of authentic period music (particularly the yearning Piaf-like songs of Lucienne Delyle), offer the agreeable illusion of access to a lost past, which the predominating sepia and ochre tones of the visual image touch with nostalgia.

Vivement dimanche! also provides a sense of affectionate nostalgia, but this time for a cinematic rather than a historical past. The film carefully deploys, at both the diegetic and the formal level, features of *film noir* and the 'whodunnit' murder mystery of the 1940s and 1950s. From the opening sequence of the first murder, where the camera pans slowly across a dark, watery landscape to the accompaniment of tense, thriller-style music, and the low-angle shots reveal only the legs of the murderer, the type of fictional world we are entering is clear. Signs of the *film noir* are everywhere: the whole film is shot in black and white, the lighting (achieved in part through the use of authentic 1950s lighting equipment (Baecque and Toubiana 1996: 551)) is appropriately high contrast, stylised rather than realistic; although the setting is contemporary many of the clothes (for example, Fanny Ardant's tailored jackets and long raincoats) evoke the 1940s; three-quarters of the film takes place at night so that there are numerous shots of dark, rainy streets. The plot revolves around murders, mistaken identity, the search for evidence to clear the name of the innocent hero, a search that in its turn leads to more deaths and revelations of infidelity and crime. The pleasure of the search, leading to the final discovery of the murderer, is sustained throughout, and interwoven with the developing relationship between Barbara (Fanny Ardant), the capable secretary, and Vercel (Jean-Louis Trintignant), her falsely accused employer. The power struggle between these two, conducted both in witty, hostile dialogue and through physical fights, recalls the mixture of hostility and attraction in the Bogart/Bacall films of the 1940s. If Barbara brings the gender script into the 1980s by making the agent of inquiry and detection a woman, the classic *femme fatale* role allotted to women in the 1940s *film noir* still makes her appearance in the person of Vercel's seductive, unfaithful first wife. Even the failure of the narrative to provide answers to all the questions it poses (why, for example, was the car of the first victim left with its doors open and lights on?) recalls the labyrinthine and partially unresolved complexity of, for example, *The Maltese Falcon* (1941).

Both *Le Dernier métro* and *Vivement dimanche!* then set up, and to some extent fulfil, spectator expectations that are intertextual, generated by viewings of other films and playing on the pleasure of re-entering familiar fictional worlds. *La Femme d'à côté*, the middle film, is less clearly situated in terms of genre, though the social world it inhabits is familiar both because (unlike in the other two films) it refers in a realist way to contemporary France, and because the mileu it evokes is commonly the site of narrative action in French films. With its affluent, middle-class setting, centring primarily on the commuter village near Grenoble in which the main protagonists live, and on a tennis club where they also meet, it provides a suitable visual framework either for light social comedy or for the kind of psychological *drame intime* that is a staple genre of French cinema. In fact *La Femme d'à côté* is a love story of extraordinary intensity: Bernard (Depardieu) and Mathilde (Ardant), having put an end to their passionate but painful relationship some years before, find themselves living as neighbours in a small village, each with a new partner. The film charts their reluctant but uncontrollable return to each other and ends with their deaths, as Mathilde shoots first Bernard, then herself. More than in either of the other films, the spectator is invited to identify with the emotions of the protagonists, and it is in the intense involvement in a helplessly passionate love ('ni avec toi, ni sans toi', 'neither with you nor without you' is the film's epigraph), set within a banal domestic world whose familiarity has its source both in lived reality and in the cinema, that – as I shall argue below – the primary pleasure of viewing lies.

Stars

Use of genre, then, relates Truffaut's films to a ready-established set of signifiers, and situates the spectator in a partly familiar fictional world. Many of the earlier films had also employed genre as a structuring device (for example, *Tirez sur le pianiste* (*Shoot the Pianist*) in 1960, *La Sirène du Mississippi* (*Mississippi Mermaid*) in 1969), the only difference being that the comfortable budgets of the 1980s allowed Truffaut to recreate genre periods and settings more lavishly. Similarly, though he had occasionally employed big star names in the past (and indeed many of the unknown actors cast in his first films had since achieved celebrity), Truffaut's last films offer the public a number of star attractions. A star name in the cast is a standard way of increasing a film's chances of box-office success, for the star exerts a fascination regardless of the film's other qualities, and brings to the role a set of ready-acquired connotations that may be exploited to develop the fictional character. Catherine Deneuve brought to the role of Marion Steiner (*Métro*) the persona of the cool, enigmatic yet secretly passionate woman, built up both by earlier film roles and by media constructions of her private life. By the time *Le Dernier métro* was made, Deneuve had also long been a 'semi-official ambassador for French fashion' (Vincendeau 1994: 44), so that to see her dressed in Lisèle Roos's elegant 1940s costumes was another of the film's pleasures. In fact Deneuve is perhaps the French actress most identified in the 1970s and 1980s with France itself (a status acknowledged by her modelling for the bust of Marianne, symbol of the Republic, in 1985), so that her role as a woman who saves both a Jewish husband and a French cultural institution from the brutalities of Nazism could be read as an enjoyably heroic representation of France. Similarly the Resistance in the film is primarily represented by the actor most closely identified with masculine French identity, Gérard Depardieu.

If Deneuve incarnates what the majority of the French are happy to see as French femininity – elegant, articulate, her air of control concealing a passionate (hetero)sexuality – then Depardieu is probably her masculine counterpart. His films of the 1970s had established him as a rough, proletarian anti-hero – again a persona supported by media treatment of his own biography – who combined masculine sexual potency with an appealing vulnerability. Bringing these two icons of Frenchness together, Truffaut plays on the mixture of hostility and attraction between, on the one hand, Deneuve/Marion's aloof glamour and secret desires and, on the other, Bernard/Depardieu's coarse-grained sexual confidence and underlying sensitivity. In *La Femme d'à côté* Truffaut also builds on the ambivalence of the Depardieu persona to create another Bernard, this one a contented, socially established husband and father, whose emotional fragility surfaces in his uncontrollable passion for Mathilde, and is expressed, in part, through a violent attack on the woman he loves that recalls the 'tearaway' character of his earlier films. The phenomenon of stardom, and its place in entertainment, is inherently intertextual.

Truffaut's choice of Fanny Ardant for *La Femme* and *Vivement* meant a move away from the use of stars, although Ardant was a well-known face because of her role in a popular television saga, *Les Dames de la côte* (*The Ladies of the Coast*), shown on the French second channel (Antenne 2) in the winter of 1979. Jean-Louis Trintignant, who plays opposite Ardant in *Vivement*, was not a star in the iconic sense of a Deneuve or a Depardieu, but had none the less appeared regularly both in the cinema and in the gossip pages throughout the late 1950s (thanks mainly to his role in *Et Dieu créa la femme* (*And God Created Woman*), 1957, and offscreen affair with Brigitte Bardot), and on into the 1960s (starring in Lelouch's successful *Un Homme et une femme* (*A Man and a Woman*), 1966, Rohmer's *Ma Nuit chez Maud* (*My Night at Maud's*), 1969). Trintignant's role in Truffaut's film in fact combines certain features of two of his most famous roles: he has the timidity and dependence on a strong woman of the young man he played in *Et Dieu créa la femme* whilst (in terms of narrative structure) playing the romantic hero role of *Un Homme et une femme*. The casting of stars not only plays to the spectators' fascination with a famous personality, but also provides the fictional character with a satisfyingly 'full' individuality that may be hard to establish within the time constraints of a feature film.

Utopianism

The experience of a world more 'full' and complete than the everyday is part of the pleasure of mainstream cinema. Richard Dyer describes this as 'utopianism': 'the image of "something better" to escape into, or something we want deeply that our day-to-day lives don't provide' (Dyer 1992: 18). Dyer defines entertainment's 'utopian sensibility' in terms of a number of categories or qualities, each of which offers pleasure through the temporary provision of what 'real' life – for reasons that may be existential or historical and political – denies. Although Dyer's book is concerned with a type of cinema far more explicitly commercial than that of Truffaut, some of these categories – energy, abundance, intensity, transparency and community – can help to explain the spectator pleasures provided by the three final Truffaut films.

Le Dernier métro deals with a period of conflict and terror, and in this sense is far from utopian, but it also represents a world in which the enemy is clearly defined, consensus can be assumed, and identification with an inclusive, purposeful community is made easy. The film's narrative focuses spatially, temporally and diegetically on a project of communal resistance: the theatre troupe, an eclectic bunch in terms of age, status, sexual orientation and degree of political commitment, work towards the production of a play that represents the defence of a liberal, humanist culture against Vichy censorship and Nazi/Vichy anti-semitism. Spectator sympathy is further developed through scenes of humorous offstage banter, through the relationships that form and dissolve between members of the cast, through the plot line that shows the theatre's Jewish director concealed in the cellar, dependent on the theatre's survival both for his life and to maintain a reason for living. In the concluding scene, the film's love story, the historical plot and the narrative of the theatre's survival converge in a triumphal ending whose 'feel-good' quality is accentuated by the rich musical score and the shots of Deneuve and Depardieu in radiant close-up. *Le Dernier métro*, as I shall argue below, makes quite complex demands on the spectator, but one part of spectator response is simply pleasure in this sense of inclusive and productive community.

Of the three films it is *Vivement dimanche!* that seems the most obviously 'utopian', for it is a witty, fast-moving and light-hearted film that has no pretensions to realism. The central narrative is that of a quest for the truth, as Barbara seeks to uncover the true identity of the murderer: not only does she succeed, thus proving the innocence of the falsely accused Vercel, but her discovery also rewards her with Vercel's love. As in *Le Dernier métro*, the central narrative and the love plot converge in a triumphantly happy ending: the reward for the protagonist's determination and courage is not only to achieve her goal, but also to win the man (men, in *Le Dernier métro*) she wanted. Such narrative closures carry an enjoyable dose of escapism. The film also entertains through a quality of vibrant energy, present in Fanny Ardant's acting style (Barbara is played as a self-possessed, sharp-witted woman with immense *joie de vivre*), in the script's playful humour, in Georges Delerue's varied musical score, and in the invitation to share the director's enjoyment of a shared cinematic past.

Conversely, *La Femme d'à côté* is a film that creates a plausible, everyday world the better to absorb the spectator in an inexorable descent towards near-madness and death. If Dyer's concept of utopianism seems relevant here, it is because fiction entertains not only by imagining greater happiness than we normally have access to, but also by representing painful emotions in a way that is more intense, less adulterated by banality, than life normally allows. Dyer's category of 'intensity', defined as 'the experience of emotion directly, fully, unambiguously, "authentically"'

(Dyer 1992: 21), refers precisely to this type of cinematic pleasure. *La Femme d'à côté* follows its two main protagonists Bernard (Depardieu) and Mathilde (Ardant) from their chance re-meeting eight years after the break-up of their affair, through their renewed passion for each other and attempts to escape back to the safer happiness each had found, to their shared death. The narrative drive away from domestic security and towards each other is relentless, intensified by the main actors' plausible acting of desire and pain, by the poignant musical score, and by the use of increasing amounts of deep blue in the screen image as the dénouement approaches. As Mike Figgis put it in a warm appreciation of the film in *Sight and Sound*, 'This is a very good film. I've seen it twice now ... Both times it made me sad (which is good). Let's face it, most films are very boring and vanish quickly from memory' (Figgis 1995: 67). *La Femme d'à côté* offers an intensity of emotion that makes the spectator sad, but also produces a memorable and cathartic pleasure.

Auteurism and commercial cinema: double viewings

I have concentrated above on some of the features of Truffaut's last films that make them accessible and pleasurable to a wide audience, hence commercially successful. Each of these films, though, is also clearly marked as an *auteur* film, a term often synonymous with 'difficult' and 'avant-garde'. One of Truffaut's auteurist characteristics, for example, is self-reflexivity, a tendency within his classically linear narratives to puncture the fictional illusion and draw attention to the processes of film-making. This occurs to some extent in each of the final films. What I want to argue is that this disturbance of the spectator's 'suspension of disbelief', rather than working against the process of entertainment, becomes part of the entertainment, or in other words that for most spectators a degree of self-awareness is central to the pleasure of these films. As Jean Douchet points out, Truffaut's films produce a remarkable convergence between two apparently antithetical types of cinema.[4]

We have seen that in *Le Dernier métro* the skilful deployment of generic signs – and those of a genre that tapped into a national mood – is one aspect of the film's popular appeal. The film uses the resources of genre to absorb the spectator into its fictional world, and to invite identification with a group of likeable characters. At the same time, though, the film deploys genre in a less transparent way, making certain conventions of genre visible and thus inviting audiences to recognise how we (that is, the producers and consumers of fiction) structure the world through stories and – in this case – (re)construct the past. For one thing, the genre codes are sometimes so explicit as to invite recognition *as* codes. The film's opening sequence is shot in what is patently and unmistakably a studio set, and one that recalls numerous other film reconstructions of wartime Paris. From the outset, the spectator simultaneously engages with the fiction and (subliminally rather than self-consciously, at a single viewing) observes its construction.

This 'double viewing' is facilitated by the fact that this is a film about the making of fictions. The use of a theatre company as a metonymic image for the French under the Occupation works, at one level, to align *Dernier métro* with Resistance genre films: through identification with the central characters, the spectators find themselves on the side of a 'Resistance' project, for to keep the theatre open and get the play on stage means both to defend the independence of French culture and to save the life of the Jew in the cellar. Collective identification with the 'good' forces and with their victory is undoubtedly one of the pleasures that Occupation films offer, especially in a period of anxious national retrospection. However, the *mise en abyme* structure of the play within a film produces another effect: that of constantly drawing attention to the fictional nature of the film itself, and hence to the way that the past is remembered. A degree of self-awareness about the fictional construction of the Occupation years also fitted well with a mood of national self-doubt about the period.

If the puncturing of the fictional illusion is pleasurable, this is also because it is achieved with humour and playfulness. When Bernard, during rehearsal, replies to the line of dialogue 'Why did you say that?' with the answer 'Because it's in the script!', the sudden shift from one level of fiction (the play-script) to another (the film-script) provokes a smile, as well as a momentary recognition that Gérard Depardieu (who plays Bernard) is also speaking from a script. In the famous final sequence, we observe a bitter farewell scene between the widowed Marion and the wounded Bernard, only to have the camera reframe to reveal that this is the concluding scene of a new play, directed and attended by a liberated Lucas Steiner. The recognition that we have been tricked is all the more enjoyable because it grants us the hoped-for happy ending, but it also displays the artificiality of this happy ending, the fact that it could equally well have been told otherwise. Similarly, whilst broadly speaking the film provides the neat moral divide that typifies the genre – the 'good' theatre troupe are on the side of Resistance, the evil Daxiat (plus a few briefly glimpsed French policemen and a sadistic German officer) represent collaboration and Nazism – the narrative and thematic centrality of the theatre also undermines any simple view of moral identity. The central characters act out roles not only on but also off stage: Marion saves

Lucas by performing the cool, uncommitted theatre owner, to the extent of refusing to employ Jewish actors; Bernard plays the clown to avoid shaking Daxiat's hand, and conceals his Resistance activities beneath the mask of the frivolous young actor. The implication is that the retrospective judgement of behaviour under the Occupation is necessarily complex, for intention can only be read through the evidence of shifting, conflicting performances. In *Le Dernier métro*, then, Truffaut provides entertainment that draws on the resources of genre, and of a specific genre that answered a national mood of uneasy retrospection. The film's self-reflexivity, its playful emphasis on the fictional nature of its own enterprise, works with rather than against its capacity to provide enjoyment.

Similarly, whilst *Vivement dimanche!* works for the audience as affectionate pastiche of a familiar, durably popular genre, it also invites them to recognise and enjoy the detachment implied by pastiche. The film is punctuated with humorous moments that run counter to the narrative dynamic of the murder and detection script. The police chief's interrogation of his suspects is constantly interrupted by episodes made comic by their incongruity, such as the inexplicable appearance of an Albanian political refugee, or the officer's own eccentric obsessions (such as his preoccupation with the relative ages of himself and Vercel). Barbara is engaged in rehearsing an amateur production of a Victor Hugo play when she learns of Vercel's problems, so that again (though less centrally) a second level of fiction draws attention to the constructed nature of the primary narrative – a point accentuated by the fact that she spends a considerable part of the film dressed in her costume from the play, which resembles that of the principal boy in a pantomime. The film's in some senses very conventional dénouement, when, with the mystery successfully solved and his innocence proved, Vercel marries the pregnant Barbara, is disturbed by a concluding sequence that abandons the happy couple to concentrate filming on the choir of children, as they kick a lens dropped by the photographer amongst themselves. None of these elements blocks absorption in the main storyline, but each appeals to a shared awareness of the generic framework, and of the fun of departing from it.

La Femme d'à côté works, far more than the other two films, by absorbing the spectator in the emotions of the protagonists, a process apparently at odds with the detachment provoked by self-reflexivity. None the less, here too Truffaut makes the recognition of the fictional process an element of entertainment. Like a classical tragedy, the film opens with the narration of the ending. As an ambulance speeds towards the village where the lovers' bodies lie, Odile Jouve, manager of the tennis club and confidante of both lovers, narrates to camera an outline of their story, and introduces the narrative proper with 'It all started six months ago.' But narration to camera breaks the illusion of watching an unmediated reality, a fact accentuated by the instructions Madame Jouve gives to the camera-man. This, and the return to Madame Jouve as narrator at the end, are the only points in the film at which the fictional illusion is explicitly disturbed, but they frame the whole narrative *as* a story, and a number of other elements in the film reactivate this awareness that the extremes of love are both lived emotions and stories we tell ourselves. Twice in the film reference is made to cinematic representations of fatal love: once when Bernard recounts to Odile the plot of a film he has seen (in which a woman fears being held by men, and her lover cuts off his arms for her) and once when Bernard and his wife Arlette have a night out at the cinema, and watch a film of adultery and murder. When Mathilde collapses into depression and is hospitalised, she wants to listen only to love songs that tell stories close to hers: '*Ne me quitte pas*' ('Don't leave me'), '*Je ne suis rien sans toi*' ('I'm nothing without you') ... In this film, however, the recognition of the ubiquity of stories of tragic love, and the sense of inevitability produced by the framing narrator, have the effect not of detachment but of intensifying the film's emotional charge. Madame Jouve recalls the narrators of classical tragedies, and confers upon the particular story of Mathilde and Bernard some of the status of myth, an effect heightened by the numerous echoes of their story found elsewhere in the narrative.

Entertainment and ideology

Truffaut's last films, then, are entertaining in two ways: conventionally, through their employment of well-established genre codes, star actors and utopian qualities, all of which facilitate the spectator's pleasurable absorption in and identification with a fictional world; less conventionally, through a self-reflexivity more often seen as incompatible with popular fiction, but here used with a light touch to engage audiences in the recognition of how and why stories are told. Truffaut appears to assume (his success suggests rightly) that his mass audience possesses a 'postmodern' capacity simultaneously to indulge and reflect on its own desire for fictions. This respect for the average spectator's intelligence, as well as for the popular liking for stories with a 'beginning, middle and an end', seems to me to be one of the more engaging aspects of Truffaut's films, and to represent a mild form of ideological positioning in its refusal to patronise a 'mass' audience.

Apart from this cleverly incorporated element of self-awareness, does the films' commitment to pleasing the audience simply mean ideological passivity, a conservative reassurance that Western (French) society in its capitalist, patriarchal form is sound and unchangeable? Certainly they avoid any explicit engagement with social or political issues: Truffaut once explained why he could never make a 'war film' in the Hollywood sense by the fact that to do so 'one would have to let man in the plural count for more than man in the singular, and I can't imagine doing that'.[5] Yet the pleasures these films provide for the casual spectator are not simply reassuring and reactionary. In terms of sexual politics – always, as I have argued elsewhere, ambivalent in Truffaut's work[6] – it is the case that each film departs from the patriarchal script of active male subject/passive female 'other' by making female agency absolutely central to the plot: the primary narratives are those of Marion (who saves both the theatre and her husband), Mathilde (who determines the film's fatal conclusion) and Barbara (who uncovers the truth and saves her man). Male heroism is almost wholly absent, with the emphasis placed rather on the conflicts within masculine identity in the late twentieth century. As Mike Figgis remarks of Bernard's odd career as a model-tanker driver in *La Femme d'à côté*, 'It's not the sort of job Tom Cruise would do' (Figgis 1995: 67), and it is equally hard to imagine the Hollywood hero in the role of Lucas or Julien Vercel, who spend their respective films hiding in secluded places while their womenfolk sort out their problems.[7] Nor do the films make the formation of a heterosexual couple the *sine qua non* of a happy ending. *Le Dernier métro* concludes rather with a happy triangle, *La Femme d'à côte* portrays passionate love as wholly incompatible with the social institution of marriage, and the wedding-and-babies ending of *Vivement dimanche!* is humorous and ironic. Whilst the central narrative in each case revolves around heterosexual love, there is a degree of challenge to the primacy of heterosexuality as the privileged form of love relationship. In *Le Dernier métro*, two key members of the theatre team are gay and a third (Nadine) either gay or bisexual, and the revelation of Arlette's romantic and sexual preference for women makes Bernard's relentless efforts to seduce her look presumptuous and silly. In *La Femme d'à côté*, the film's only happy and durable couple are homosexual. There is no sense in either film of a political point being made: if the films seem to claim anything it is the right of gays to indifference, rather than to difference.

Beyond the question of sexual politics, the films display an attitude to people that is attentive, inclusive rather than exclusive, concerned more to explain than to blame, so that evil characters are a rare phenomenon in a Truffaut film. This generous humanism is rarely contestatory, but nor could it be described as reactionary. Viewing Truffaut's last films provides some of the pleasures typical of commercial mainstream cinema – absorption in a compelling illusory world, a utopian degree of energy, sense of community, intensity of emotion – and in doing so identifies the spectator with a worldview that is far from radical, but is compassionate, curious and open. The films also refuse the hierarchical distinction between 'entertainment' and 'art' cinema, by rendering pleasurable the recognition of fiction as interpretative framework, through which we frame our lives and histories.

Notes

1 'Si on comparait le cinéma français à une maison avec un toit avec deux pentes inclinées, Truffaut en serait le faîte, la ligne de tuiles reliant la pente "auteurs" à la pente "cinéma commercial". Lui-même, tenté par l'un et par l'autre, jouait de ces deux tendances. Depuis sa mort les deux pentes s'écartent l'une de l'autre.' Jean Douchet, 'La rue et le studio', *Cahiers du cinéma*, 419/20, May 1989, quoted in Prédal 1991: 394. All translations are by the author unless otherwise stated.

2 Bory made this accusation in an article in 1974, extending the same reproach to the directors Claude Chabrol, Jacques Demy and Eric Rohmer. Truffaut replied with a long, detailed letter defending his integrity as an *auteur* and disputing the idea that this is incompatible with commercial success (Truffaut 1988: 528–36).

3 For a fuller discussion of Truffaut's use of genre see Holmes and Ingram 1998: ch. 4, and pp. 138–9.

4 Some recent Hollywood films – those of Quentin Tarantino, for example – have also (in a very different way) made self-reflexivity a central element of entertainment.

5 From an interview translated from *France Observateur* in *Sight and Sound*, 31, 1 (Winter 1961–2): 37. Quoted in Williams 1997: 402.

6 See Holmes and Ingram 1998: ch. 5.

7 That said, Hollywood cinema is not all active heroes and passive heroines: Truffaut may well have had in mind some of the heroes of *his* hero Hitchcock. In *Spellbound* (1945), for example, Ingrid Bergman's psychoanalyst heroine investigates and finally solves both the plot's central mystery, and the problems of her patient/lover, played by Gregory Peck. Though physically and in personal style a much more 'masculine' figure than Truffaut's heroes, Peck's role in the narrative is *functionally* a passive one.

References

Affron, M. J. and E. Rubinstein (eds) (1985), *The Last Metro*, New Brunswick, Rutgers University Press.

Baecque, A. de and S. Toubiana (1996), *François Truffaut*, Paris, Gallimard.

Dyer, R. (1992), *Only Entertainment*, London and New York, Routledge.

Figgis, M. (1995), 'A French Affair', *Sight and Sound*, 15, 10: 67.

Hayward, S. (1993), *French National Cinema*, London and New York, Routledge.

Holmes, D. and R. A. Ingram (1998), *François Truffaut*, Manchester, Manchester University Press.

Prédal, R. (1991), *Le Cinéma français depuis 1945*, Paris, Nathan.

Truffaut, F. (1988), *Correspondance*, Paris, Hatier and Livre de Poche.

Vincendeau, G. (1994), 'Catherine Deneuve and French womanhood', in *Women and Film: A Sight and Sound Reader*, London, Scarlet Press, 41–9.

Williams, T. (1997), 'World War I in Truffaut's *Jules et Jim*', in W. Gortschacher and H. Klein (eds), *Modern War on Stage and Screen*, Lewiston/Queenstown/Lampeter, Edwin Mellen Press, 401–14.

Performance in the films of Agnès Varda

13

The work of Agnès Varda is, like most important work in cinema, hard to categorise. The reaction which her films demand from their audience is complex, and cannot be pinned down to one side of an easy dichotomy of 'entertainment' or 'ideology'. Both play their part in the way her films function, although openly ideological intention, defined as the hope of putting across a particular attitude to society, is really confined to one or two 1970s' films which are directly concerned with the women's movement. Apart from these, however, Varda's observation and reflection on the society that surrounds her is always vital to the interest of her films, and they certainly depend on an ability to analyse and question, even if any conclusions to be drawn are uncertain, ambiguous and avowedly subjective. As regards entertainment, all her films – fiction and documentaries, feature-films and shorts – rely on an ability to engage the audience at a level other than the purely intellectual, through emotions, laughter, narrative interest and, perhaps most vitally, through a sense of wonder.

Varda's films are immensely varied, not only in style but in the subjects which preoccupy her. A number of themes can, however, be traced throughout her work, and one of these bears very directly on the subject of this book, and also on the way in which Varda conceives her own role as a film-maker. This is the question of performance.

Performance is a central feature of several of her major films, from *Cléo de 5 à 7* (*Cleo from 5 to 7*, 1961) to *Jacquot de Nantes* (1990) and even to *Les 100 et 1 nuits* (*The 100 and 1 Nights*, 1994). Its evocation raises immediately questions of the reasons for it, which Varda's films explore both from the point of view of the performer and of the performed-to, in other words the audience. As soon as the audience becomes an issue the subject of entertainment becomes central. The vast majority of the performances we shall be looking at in Varda's films are of a kind which have entertainment as a primary goal – popular song, conjuring show, puppet show or the musicals of Jacques Demy. The questions raised around this subject can be roughly summarised as: whom does the performer seek to entertain?; what makes the performance successful and rewarding for both performer and audience?; and what rewards may – and should – be expected?

I hope to trace a development in the answers to these questions by looking at the ways in which performances are used in four of Varda's major films: *Cléo de 5 à 7*, *Daguerréotypes* (1974–5), *L'Une chante, l'autre pas* (*One Sings, the Other Doesn't*, 1976) and *Jacquot de Nantes*. The development which I shall follow is not a simple chronological one, and I shall look at *L'Une chante*, which essentially develops questions raised in *Cléo*, before dealing with *Daguerréotypes*, made two years earlier but containing a more complex exploration of the function of performance and representation.

In *Cléo de 5 à 7*, the central character, Cléo Victoire, is a glamorous young singer of light variety pieces; the film follows her through the two anxious hours as she awaits the results of a medical analysis which may show that she has cancer. We see Cléo perform twice in the film, in two key scenes: a rehearsal which takes place in her flat, and later, a solo 'performance' in a Paris park.

Cléo is a performer and an entertainer, but it would be difficult to frame that description more actively, to say that she, herself, *entertains*. She has no control over what she performs – her songs are written for her by two pleasant but distracted young men who do not care to find out what she would wish to express – and even less does she have a relation- ship with her audience. Her songs are destined for recording (even the rehearsal is for a recording session); the act of performance always takes place alone. The audience is then left to fate. There are two examples in the film of the typical meeting of songs and audience; in both cases, as Cléo's voice comes from a taxi radio or a café jukebox, the listeners hardly listen at all. Even though Cléo happens to be present, she is not in fact performing and so any relationship between performer and audience *through* the performance is quite impossible to her, and although she attempts to interest those present in the music, she has no success.

Cléo's work thus seems negative and alienating. 'Performance' has been reduced to a set of almost automatic actions repeated for the benefit of a notional 'audience', hazily conceived and never seen, reduced to a lowest common denominator of taste. To appeal to a group so vast, and so little known, Cléo's only strategy is to conform to a supposedly general fantasy: an alluring, sexy young woman, whom every man wants to go out with and every woman wants to be. In a sense it is irrelevant whether this is accurate or not; the image has been chosen because it is *assumed* to be attractive. Neither Cléo nor her songwriters and managers would be able to locate anyone specific whom it is intended to attract.

I have said that Cléo's work seems 'negative and alienating', but this is not inevitable. Within the film Cléo's attitude to it changes, and in the two key scenes which mark this change we get a first glimpse of what performance can, and should, imply in Varda's terms.

The first of these scenes is the performance of the second song which Cléo is asked to rehearse, 'Sans toi'. Cléo is supplied with words and music, but 'Sans toi', with its macabre clichés describing the singer's impending death, chimes directly with Cléo's current terror.

As the connection becomes more obvious, so the angle from which Cléo is filmed changes. At the beginning of the song she is framed with her accompanist, manager and companion, grouped around the piano; however, the changing angle substitutes the dark background of a partition, against which, finally, she stands out, in close-up and brightly lit. Although the change is clearly accounted for by the layout of the set, the effect of the dark background and highlighting is that of an actual performance, with Cléo spotlit as if on a stage. Thus Varda illustrates for us the change in consciousness which the song provokes in Cléo. The shock of recognising that the song is describing her own situation obliges Cléo to listen to the words, and to interpret them (the French word for an individual performance of music or drama is *interprétation*, which clearly implies the active mental engagement which Cléo has not previously shown). She becomes an active performer, and at the same time she becomes her own audience, listening to what she is singing and applying it to her own experience.

Here, already, we reach the essence of what real performance implies for Varda, the first vital element in her exploration of the concept. In order to have genuine power, performance must touch the real experience of either performer, or audience, or both, and re-present it. The vital concept of representation is of course a very problematic one; I am here using it to imply *the existence of preliminary experience*. Without a preliminary, true, experience, performance in Varda's films is always a failure. The negative counterpart to such true experience is the received image, the cliché. In the context of performance, cliché implies that instead of referring to actual experience, the performer relies on an interpretation of experience which is already familiar and accepted. Cléo's sexpot image is such a cliché, already tried and tested by the music industry and used as a model to which the real Cléo is adapted. Cliché, in brief, is the representation of a representation.

'Sans toi' of course contains clichés, but for Cléo (and through Cléo, for the film audience) they become once more directly linked to real experience. The song proves the desperately-needed trigger for self-awareness in Cléo, forcing her to express her actual fears. The genuinely despairing images regain their original power. This process of repossession is filmed almost triumphally – admittedly against a dark background – reflecting the fullness of experience which full engagement with her performance brings to Cléo.

In the second performance scene in the film, Cléo descends the steps of the Parc Montsouris in the manner of the star of a Broadway spectacular. The song she sings speaks of her pride in her physical beauty and the power that it brings her, and she sings it with enjoyment. Again, there is no audience within the filmic space (although there is of course the film audience to whom both performances are explicitly directed by lighting and camera angle); again, therefore, Cléo seems to be her own audience. However, she is here much more autonomous than in the 'Sans toi' episode: she has chosen the song, she has chosen the moment and the manner of performance, and her pleasure in it is evident. We understand that the words do relate to real experience. Cléo's journey through Paris has enabled her to become aware of other people, but also of herself in relation to them, and here she sings with self-awareness, both of the pleasure which she derives from her beauty and of how precious that (now fragile) pleasure in it is. Her manner is certainly based on a cliché – of the Broadway/Hollywood star entrance – but Cléo in choosing this cliché takes control of it, putting 'herself as showgirl' on display in joyful self-parody, accepting this role which in rushing out into the streets after the rehearsal she had been desperate to escape from. Now aware that she can look beyond her image, she is able to come to terms with it and take pleasure in it.

Performance then is central to *Cléo*, but it is a one-sided vision of performance, since we see only what the act of performance can offer to the performer. Cléo learns that the skill which she already possesses can be a valuable way of expressing her own feelings and formulating them for herself, but her transformations of experience are only shown as positive when they are for her alone. Her fortuitous audience for 'Sans toi' is in fact quite uncomprehending. A hint of the vital relationship with the audience perhaps comes in scenes where Cléo herself is the fascinated (and horrified) audience of various street entertainers; their various manipulations of their bodies make an impact on her because she relates them, viscerally, to her own fear. However, she does not relate this to her own reasons for performing, at least not visibly.

L'Une chante, l'autre pas also presents as one of its protagonists a young singer and entertainer, Pomme. Pomme is in some ways an anti-Cléo: after one or two sessions as a backing singer she has rejected the world of variety and taken complete control of her performance and of her image. She writes all her songs herself. She is politically engaged (in the women's movement), and operates somewhere between the fields of the 1960s' folksinger and performance art. Most importantly, she performs before an audience, and throughout her career, which the long temporal sweep of *L'Une chante* allows Varda to follow as it develops, a constant preoccupation is the relationship between performer and audience.

The starting point of Pomme's career, in fact, is the need to perform before an audience whom she knows, using her technical skill to express her experience and theirs in a way which will transform and clarify it. This initiating scene takes place on the canals of Amsterdam where Pomme has gone with a group of other women to have an abortion. Pomme's song is at once the response to a *need* to make sense of the common experience and a gift to her companions in misfortune. Performer and audience are here very close – literally in the same boat – but not identical, so that Pomme's transforming moment is a big advance on Cléo's: she is able to share her self-awareness as she gains it.

She also gains a sense of vocation which springs from her relationship to her audience, but that relationship, as the film goes on, becomes more complex. When we see Pomme performing at a demonstration, her intended audience is already more diverse than that of Amsterdam. However, the militant/festival atmosphere allows the assumption of common concerns to be effective. The structure of the film means that we come to this performance through a long flash-forward, and the Pomme of the demonstration appears a first, satisfactory, resolution of the character's adolescent uncertainties, which is then explained by the subsequent flashback to her experience in Amsterdam. However, *L'Une chante* is a film where the characters' progress conforms quite strictly to a fashionable dialectical concept: resolution leads to new internal contradictions, which have to be resolved in their turn, and so on. One of the main contradictions inherent in Pomme's new identity as a performer lies in her relationship to her audience: this is growing larger, and she needs to continue to perform outside particular, often highly emotional circumstances which unite those present round common emotions and aspirations. Appealing to a shared genuine experience, while necessary for success, becomes problematic. Pomme solves the problem in part by deliberate universality – for example, listing all the clichés of womanhood which she and her audience reject, without, however, committing herself to affirming what she might be – and in part by increasingly elaborate abstraction. Neither strategy is entirely successful.

The former is illustrated by a 'gala in a northern suburb'. The glimpse we are given of the audience shows a scattered group, almost entirely male, dreary both in expression and in clothing in contrast to the highly coloured, even frilly, image projected by the group. Between performance and spectators there seems to be an abyss. The show is a moderate success – that is, it is moderately applauded – but the connection which drew the women at the demonstration to drift towards Pomme, and to call her by name, is visibly absent.

Pomme's most elaborate spectacle ends in a major failure, although this is attributed not to lack of communication with the audience, but rather to practical problems of money, group relations and performance space. However, there is a suggestion that the failure is in part due to a misunderstanding of the nature of successful performance. The images we see of the project in rehearsal show an elaborate piece of performance art, involving an apparently pregnant Pomme, perched on stilts covered by voluminous skirts, and a large cast in eye-catching costumes; clearly the work is expensive, and it is equally clear that there are tensions among the cast, and yet the subject of the spectacle is ill-defined and at best not much different from the songs which Pomme had once sung to simple accompaniment. The problems in connecting with reality are dramatically epitomised when the falsely pregnant Pomme protests at one of the dancers' real pregnancy: 'we can't have two pregnant women in this show'. The concerns of the show are steadily drifting away from the concerns of the performers, both personal and economic. Elaborate alternative performance art, in other words, risks getting 'stuck in a rut', succumbing to visual splendour for its own sake, and finally foundering through detachment from – once again – 'true' experience.

In the latter part of *L'Une chante*, Pomme returns to performance after an interlude as a wife and mother in Iran. In these last performances Varda shows us another possible solution to the problem of performer–audience relationship within a specifically socio-political context. The elaboration of Pomme's pre-Iran work has been considerably reduced, and reduces further in the course of the three or four performances shown. Shots of the small all-female group on tour show that their needs are not great – they are content with two battered mini-vans – and that they seek out audiences in unlikely places, such as small, run–down country towns, where novelty value and low population combine to allow a direct relationship between group and watchers. The songs are chosen to relate to the singers' own experience – for example, the satisfactions of pregnancy and motherhood. This subject is vital to the understanding of Pomme and to the film in general, but it has always been controversial within the women's movement. Not only does it not reflect the experience of all the audience, but some vehemently oppose it; on the other hand, it is undeniably the truth of *a certain* experience. On this basis, the group combines their performance with debate with the audience. This is entertainment in the Brechtian sense, with the aim of making its audience think: the value which the film puts on it coincides with the 1970s' fashion, but it also corresponds to a conviction, which we shall see elsewhere in Varda's work, that satisfactory entertainment must consist of an exchange between audience and performers. In *L'Une chante* this, the second vital element in true performance, is everywhere emphasised.

L'Une chante is the film where Varda is most clearly concerned with the relationship between performance and ideology. In this the film reflects the debates of the period, relating them specifically to the women's movement, which was Varda's own interest, but raising issues which were discussed in many different contexts in the years between 1968 and the late 1970s. Perhaps there are signs even in this work, however, that Varda was more attracted to the idea of enchanting an audience (provided it is in the right way, without sterile cliché) than of provoking it to intellectualised argument. Certainly Pomme's performances remain steeped in utopian imagery, even when not overly spectacular – the flower-child aspect of the affair may itself seem a cliché now, but was fairly clearly not intended as such at the time.

Two years before *L'Une chante*, Varda made *Daguerréotypes*, a portrait of the street in which she lives and its inhabitants. *Daguerréotypes* is a reflective documentary on its subjects' lives, but it is also an essay on the function of film making, and indeed of representation more generally. Central to *Daguerréotypes* is an extended performance by a café conjuror called Mystag, a performance which – much more clearly and deeply than in previous examples – is used as a metaphor for Varda's own procedure. The metaphorical importance of Mystag is announced from the first shots of the film, where he serves as introduction, so that the whole film is framed by him, as if it *is* his act. Thus, he is equated with the film-maker, and the film is equated with a conjuring trick, and although he does not reappear until perhaps a third of the way into the film, the conjuror as controlling spirit of the film is never quite forgotten.

In *Daguerréotypes*, Varda's interest in the process of performance/ entertainment is centred on the audience. We neither know nor particularly care what Mystag gets out of his performance – what counts is *how* he holds his audience. Mystag is a highly effective operator before fairly unsophisticated spectators, but the effect which he achieves parallels what the film-maker hopes to achieve before her more sophisticated ones.

So, what are the vital elements in Mystag's success? First is his use of elements of the audience's day-to-day experience in ways that both reflect and extend this experience. His audience consists of small shopkeepers who handle a wide variety of goods, and it is from these goods that Mystag selects his props – a rich and evocative selection, which underlines to the cinema audience what creative potential is contained in the rather drab world of the rue Daguerre. His handling of the objects also reflects their daily use. For example, bank-notes are ruffled as they are in every shop when the till receipts are counted – the cinema audience is reminded of the parallel by an intercalated sequence – but, in Mystag's hands, they multiply. One could argue that this is a visual translation of economic reality, but the effect does not depend on such an intellectual response. It is more the concrete expression of a fantasy which all struggling shop-keepers and most other people can relate to. Likewise, Mystag handles his butcher's knives as the butcher does in his shop, but he operates on his own arm. Again, this evokes fantasy, but the visceral fear is no sooner evoked than evacuated: the unmentionable has happened but no harm is done. The effect is to remind the audience of the power of these objects which they handle every day and believe they know well, and then to present a world in which they act differently and can be treated in ways normally unthinkable.

The success of this for the audience depends on their intimate experience of the objects concerned, and their secret wishes or fears that they might act in the way Mystag shows them to. It thus depends absolutely on the audience's experience. However, it also depends on a framing device which allows these transformations to take place in a world at once familiar and unfamiliar. Mystag himself is both similar to and different from his audience. His chattiness as well as his props connect him to them on one level, and yet he is not quite of their world. He comes from Elsewhere – the other side of Paris, remarks the film-maker in voiceover, but it is not clear if his audience are aware of this; in any case, he also carries information about exotic places, Africa and India, which suggest a much more distant Elsewhere. He dresses in strange robes. But these distancing devices are themselves retrieved before their unfamiliarity becomes too radical for the audience to cope with. Mystag's conjuror's garb is comfortingly returned to ordinary experience by the very force of cliché, here presented as a largely positive influence in that it allows for controlled strangeness.

Clearly, Mystag's performance works here for two audiences, one of which – that of the film – is in addition watching the other reacting, as an audience, to the show. Varda's filming adds to the performance a layer of 'commentary'. It is very important, however, that the commentary for the supposedly more sophisticated cinema audience does not tend to deconstruct Mystag's spectacle or to expose the illusion. On the contrary, the camera is enlisted in order to assimilate the cinema-spectator's experience with that of the primary audience. In filming the conjuring tricks, tell-tale gestures are edited out in order to make the illusion more perfect, thereby making suspension of disbelief easier even to the cynical.

More importantly, it is the editing which makes the connections described above, intercutting Mystag's tricks with shots or short sequences of ordinary street activities which provide a parallel through objects or through gestures. Although Varda has to draw attention to these parallels, we understand that to the café audience they will be obvious for the most part. There is the odd exception – when Mystag prefaces his fire-eating act with a mysterious description of 'the mystic East' with its fire-eating fakirs, we hear him speak in voiceover above a shot of the baker withdrawing loaves from his furnace. This rather more abstract parallel is less easy to attribute directly to the people of the rue Daguerre, given the film's insistence on their unimaginativeness; it could credibly be an unconscious connection – perhaps made by the baker alone – but it could equally well be a reminder to the cinema audience alone that the difference between everyday reality and magical fantasy need only be a question of interpretation.

For this seems to me to be the ultimate success of Mystag's act, and the implied aim of the film. In *Daguerréotypes* Varda chose a deliberately unspectacular subject with which she sets out to seize the spectator's attention, something which she can only do by transforming the ordinary street into something either intellectually or emotionally worthy of interest. While not denying the intellectual possibilities – this tightly knit urban/rural community is clearly of sociological interest – the film from the start emphasises the emotional appeal to a sense of wonder and mystery. The Chardon Bleu, with its strange herbal concoctions in dusty jars and its gentle, drifting, absent owner, could serve as the setting for a fairy tale (told by Mystag?) but it is also, and remains, a run-down little shop in a real Parisian street run by an old couple who, when wrapped up in winter coats to buy the evening's pork chop, look like anyone we might meet – and overlook – on the way home from the cinema.

Rather than persuading the audience to question what it sees, Varda asks us to surrender to mystery while remaining aware that what she is actually describing could not be more mundane. Within the film she provides a rather more blatant example of the same technique, and an illustration of how enjoyable the experience can be to an audience. However, while Mystag never asks more than a temporary suspension of disbelief, Varda's film leaves an enriched sense of the possibilities to be found in the world, which almost inevitably remains with the spectator once out in the street.

In terms of the elements we have previously identified as vital to Varda's concept of performance, Mystag's show is clearly 'true' and successful. He draws on the real experiences of his audience, and twists them into new and unexpected forms. His act is absolutely dependent on the participation of the watchers, not only by willing co-operation in the illusion but often by actual presence on stage. Mystag demands that his audience take risks, first with their possessions, then physically, and in persuading them to do so he creates an intense and very active bond with them. However, the performance, and its value, end when Mystag leaves the stage. The effect of the film remains in the spectator's mind outside the cinema, but there is no suggestion that Mystag leaves a lasting impression. We may therefore come away with the impression that Varda's achievement is more successful than Mystag's. Such a judgement introduces a third element to our picture of truly valuable performance/ entertainment, which will become central in *Jacquot de Nantes*. This is the call for continued creation – for the audience's consumption of creative fantasy to be itself transformed into the desire to create independently, to continue the illusion.

Jacquot de Nantes was the film which Varda made to celebrate the life of her husband, the film-maker Jacques Demy. He participated in the film, made during the last few months of his life, and its content was defined by the spoken memories which he confided to Varda. *Jacquot* can be read as the story of an apprenticeship in the production of 'true' performance/ entertainment. The film is, like *Daguerréotypes*, framed by a credit sequence which introduces the theme in a metaphorical way from the start. After a lyrical introductory sequence in the present, the film opens, in fact, with a curtain *closing* on a puppet show. Once down, the curtain serves as back- drop for the complete credits, including catering crews and electricians' assistants, a list which has been left to the end of films since the 1950s. This beginning-coded-as-ending clearly alludes to the end of Demy's life, and prepares us to read all that follows as a flashback; a flashback, however, on a performance, both theatrical and cinematic, since we are given the ending-codes for both forms. As the curtain closes (just before the credits) the camera turns to the young Jacquot, staring riveted at the stage, saying determinedly to his mother: 'It's not over. Sometimes the curtain opens again. I'm waiting.'

Jacquot the child is thus first introduced as a spectator – although an exceptional spectator both by the intensity of his experience and by his attention to the way in which the puppet show works, which already foreshadows his move from passive to active participant. In the course of the narrative sequences of *Jacquot*, his attempts to translate his experience into his own performances will develop in sophistication and in success – and, of course, the intercalated sequences from Demy's films remind us of the eventual triumph.

The rapt spectator of that early sequence is soon impelled to reproduce what he sees. Taken by his mother to an operetta, he translates the experience into his own performance in two separate sequences, each of which isolates a different aspect of the conditions in which performance can work. When he sings one of the numbers from the show in order to demonstrate to his father what the latter has missed, the scene is a cosy family one. Jacques is not even at the centre of the screen. His reproduction is necessarily approximate and there is no sign of an appropriate environment. On the other hand he is impelled by the need to 'speak' directly to an audience close to him both physically and emotionally.

A little later, another scene shows Jacques in a deserted corner of the garage, again reworking his experience of the operetta. This time the performance is more sophisticated; he has procured a blanket to represent the elaborate costumes, and a few crates to set up a makeshift stage. He is surer of the words and the tune, and accompanies his singing with appropriate histrionic gestures. However there is no audience. Here the important aspect of performance which Jacques is 'learning' is the need to set up a separate space which can delineate what needs to be a heightened, magical world. He is presumably well aware that he cannot possibly create the true effect that the operetta had on him simply by singing in the kitchen. The improved rendition also suggests that he is aware that performance requires some technical skill, or at least some work. None the less, we do not get the impression that this is a rehearsal. At this stage, Jacquot seems content with an imaginary audience, an extension of himself who can be relied upon to react appropriately.

In the course of the film Jacques will arrive at a more sophisticated version of performance/entertainment, notably in the developing understanding which he gains of the need for entertainment, even when based on fantasy, to relate to and to transform experience in order to win over his audience. His early experiments are not yet at this level, however; his first aim is simply to reproduce spectacles he has already seen. This is already true of the operetta; it is equally true in the much more important episode of his own puppet show.

This first real initiation into the creation of spectacle extends over a considerable part of the film, and the first striking element about it is the trouble which Jacques goes to in order to reproduce the illusion. His first attempt seems doomed to failure; he has the apparently excellent idea of making rounded, three-dimensional puppets out of potatoes, but they turn black overnight and he abandons them in disappointment. The film also briefly abandons the subject, but Jacques returns to the attack. This time he turns to cardboard cut-outs; a more satisfactory solution, although, for this kind of show, the loss of the third dimension is a real impoverishment. The film shows the immense care which he takes with these cut-outs, and also with the creation of the appropriate performance space. In order to give his box-stage the aura associated with theatre, he even steals two angels from the cemetery, in a scene which refers to René Clément's famous post-war film *Jeux interdits* (*Forbidden Games*, 1949); Jacques, however, will use his booty to reproduce the rituals not of death but of life. There is perhaps something more in the parallel, as like the children in *Jeux interdits* Jacques still understands only imperfectly what is involved in what he is doing, and his main search is for an accurate reproduction of a form.

The actual show is, accordingly, a disappointment. Jacques assembles an expectant audience of smaller children; but they, too, are expecting a reproduction of their experience of the professional Guignol, and despite all his efforts Jacques's version is not close enough. His audience refuses – or is unable – to suspend its disbelief, and the cry 'That's not stardust, it's sand' effectively shuts down the Demy Guignol.

It is interesting to look at this valuable failure in terms of the elements of performance. What, exactly, is it that is missing? Certainly, the attempt to re-create, with inferior means, a ready-made spectacle (re-presenting a representation, and thus entering the realm of cliché which we have already seen corresponds in Varda's world to a false concept of entertainment) is an important element. The same element can be seen, later, in the film *Solange's Adventure*, another early failure. However, in neither case is the failure directly attributable to the cliché – indeed in the case of the Guignol the cliché, had it worked, was all that the audience asked. The problem in both cases is first technical, and in both cases the failures are vital to later successes in that they supply technical experience in strictly controlled conditions. This is not a new pattern – we have seen that Pomme, too, serves an 'apprenticeship' as a choirgirl and as a backing singer, experiences which frustrate her because they are divorced from her concerns but without which she would be unable to produce the 'true' entertainment in which she finds her vocation.

In the case of *Solange* the technical failure is straightforward and the film never reaches an audience at all. However, the Guignol does meet its audience, who reject it because of a missing *illusion*. This is interesting because, in Jacques's next effort at production, the illusion is equally defective technically speaking, but the audience – admittedly more sympathetic *a priori* – finds this charming, and applauds Jacques's drawing of the Pont de Mauves more than a direct photograph of it. Why does *Le Pont de Mauves* keep its audience, while the puppet play, *Cendrillon*, loses it? I think the answer can be found in the connection between reality – experience – and illusion, but that it is slightly more complicated than simply to say that *Cendrillon* is a cliché while *Le Pont de Mauves* represents a lived experience (although this is true). There is also the issue of what in the spectacle appeals to the direct experience of the audience. The moment of success or failure hinges on the moment of *recognition*. In the case of *Le Pont de Mauves* recognition occurs confronted with an element within the story: 'Oh yes: there are the girders [of the bridge]'; and the rather amateurish drawing is taken for granted – the family have seen the bridge but they have never seen this little film before. On the other hand, the children at the puppet show recognise sand – which they know from experience – standing in for stardust, which they have never known, in the context of a play which they have seen before in other circumstances where the stardust was not recognisably something familiar. Jacques might have surmounted the failure by the Mystag technique of claiming sand as sand and somehow transforming it to stardust – thus placing the recognisable element within the world of the illusion – but that would have demanded technical skills presumably beyond him, and in any case he is not yet sophisticated enough to recognise the need for it.

The later small films that the young Jacques creates in the course of the recreation of his apprenticeship show the increasing realisation both of his technical skills and of his understanding of the role of experience. *The Ballerina*, essentially a technical exercise, none the less is not a pure cliché: apart from the spectacle of the ballet (which we have no reason to believe that Jacques has seen), the cardboard dancer reproduces the movements that he remembers his young neighbour Reine demonstrating to him in her bedroom. *Night Attack*, apart from its immensely skilled technique, takes its charm from its setting in a very recognisable Nantes. However, the ultimate confirmation of the potential success of transforming experience is of course to be found in the clips from Demy's famous and popular films interspersed throughout *Jacquot de Nantes*. Demy's films are in many ways the epitome of the entertainment cinema: musicals, and mostly fantasies. Varda's insertion of the clips in conjunction with episodes from Demy's youth show them on the contrary as re-presentations of everyday experiences, if those experiences are certainly reconstructed by Varda in such a way as to emphasise the visual parallel, they are none the less always entirely mundane. Perhaps the most spectacular example is the cooking sequence from *Peau d'Ane*, where the pantomime world of fairy tale is shown to have its beginnings in the Demy kitchen. *Peau d'Ane* is one of the stories treated by the professional Guignol, and indeed we see Jacques at a performance of it soon after his unfortunate experiment with *Cendrillon* – an indication that the lesson was well learned and that, in his sophisticated adulthood, it became possible to treat the 'cliché' world of fairy tale successfully.

Jacquot de Nantes thus provides a very full illustration of Varda's concept of 'true' entertainment, which seems to be presented coherently throughout her work. The vital elements which ensure validity are first a rigorous truth to lived experience, without which entertainment is condemned to endless repetition of itself in the empty shell of cliché, and second a continual exchange between performer and audience, which relies on a sense of *shared* experience and on a need for communication. The most important content of such communication is seen to be the potential worth of experience, the successful performer being one who not only reproduces but in some way enhances possibly mundane reality. The enhancement can come through a simple declaration of value – especially in the case of female experience; for example, in Pomme's affirmations of her pleasure in the particularities of 'being a woman' – or it can consist in connections between everyday objects and the evocations of fantasy, appealing to dreams and desires both conscious and unconscious. This chapter has concentrated on those films which show, as it were, the work in progress, but the problem of transformation of experience underlies all Varda's work. Ideally, the transformation is transmitted to the audience, who can then use it creatively in their own lives. There are instances where the transformation seems to be a purely internal process, produced and received by the same person – who is thus both 'performer' and 'audience' and who uses performance to gain self-awareness; but the fullest expression of entertainment always implies transmitting that awareness.

In brief, Varda's films illustrate that the kinds of performance which are most often branded as 'simple entertainment' – be they popular songs, conjuring shows or children's puppet plays – have an immense potential for creative action on all participants. Performance in Varda's films, although very rarely highly cultural and even more rarely openly didactic, is never 'mere entertainment'.

WENDY EVERETT

Singing our song: music, memory and myth in contemporary European cinema

14

The subjective and non-representational discourse of music, with its unique ability to access remote and inaccessible times, places and emotions, plays an important and an increasingly dynamic and self-conscious role within the quest for identity and the interrogation of memory and history that dominate contemporary European cinema, and in particular the autobiographical films which are one of its essential components. However, whilst retaining the link between music and anteriority which has consistently characterised classical narrative, these films undermine traditional scoring practice in a number of ways: music is foregrounded, in defiance of its traditional supportive and compliant role; and it is used self-consciously, drawing attention to its status as signifier, and to its function in constructing the very past which it purports to represent or recall. Nowhere is this shift in the status and function of film music more tellingly revealed than in the frequency with which recordings of popular songs feature within the non-diegetic sound-track, in a radical departure from the rules of classical narrative film making. Within the parameters of the complex and mysterious relationship between music, memory and identity, this chapter will focus in particular on the function of popular song in autobiographical film. It will show how this seemingly innocuous innovation not only resites and redefines the role of music in cinema by, for example, destroying traditional distinctions between sound and vision, sign and referent, popular and private, but also makes an important contribution to current debate on the significance of mediation and reception in the filmic articulation of memory, history and myth.

Whilst I shall be concentrating upon films (and, in some instances, television films) which are autobiographical in intent, since in them concerns of memory and identity are paramount, I am not, of course, claiming exclusivity for them; indeed, many of the features I notice, and the conclusions I reach, may apply equally to fictional works. Similarly, although the films I have chosen are European, that is to say, have been made in European countries with predominantly European funding, this is a reflection of personal interest and enthusiasms, and is not intended as a judgement of, or comparison with, those made elsewhere. Nevertheless, it is certain that the overwhelming concern with memory and history which has marked Europe, particularly through the tumultuous changes and uncertainties of the twentieth century, has strongly shaped its cinema(s); and it is fascinating to observe that these issues are increasingly being articulated within the naturally fractured, unstable and contradictory discourse of autobiography. History, memory and identity are of course tightly imbricated; and if it is the case that the concept of history has changed in the course of this century, via moments of existential crisis and denial, from one of certainty to something closer to the constant and insecure reappraisals of experience which constitute memory (Sorlin 1991: 175), it is equally clear that identity itself is a consequence of the ability to remember: 'Our memory is our coherence, our reason for feeling, even our action. Without it we are nothing' (Buñuel 1985: 4–5); 'Memory defines who we are and shapes the way we act more closely than any other single aspect of our personhood' (Rose 1992: 1). Moreover, it is memory that enables us to perceive life/time as a continuum; to decipher the present, and to shape the future. Remembering is thus understood as an essentially dynamic process of inquiry; a shifting dialogue between present and past within which memories themselves change afresh each time they are recalled (Young 1993: 730–43). Given this concept of memory as flux, it will be recognised that the aim of autobiography cannot be the (mere) nostalgic reconstruction of a static past, but is an open-ended renegotiation of past by present, and of present by past, which almost certainly involves, and quite probably exists because of, the need to reach behind conscious memories to the unworded, unrepresented memories buried deep in the subconscious mind. Such memories cannot be produced at will, but are released involuntarily by a trigger device, most frequently a physical sensation such as smell, taste, touch or, of course, hearing music.

We can therefore distinguish two basic types of memory involved in the autobiographical process: voluntary memory, characterised by the concern for authentic detail, which is, in cinematic terms, most obviously revealed in visual components such as sets and props, and is often mistakenly considered to be the aim of autobiography rather than part of its process; and, second, the fundamental desire to rediscover the forgotten landscapes and sensations which lie beyond voluntary recall, but which may flood back unexpectedly, at any moment. The elusiveness of such memories, particularly those which mark the first five or so years of childhood, reflects the incompatibility of the infant's non-linguistic, inarticulate and overwhelmingly physical experience of the world, with the (primarily linguistic) schemata used by the adult for storing and classifying memory. Language, it seems, whose gradual development marks our transition to adulthood, has no means of dealing with the complex and pre-linguistic experiences of infancy and early childhood. As a consequence, the only way such memories can be triggered is through a physical sensation that in some way recreates the original, directly touching 'the unconscious memory trace, the record left behind by a total situation out of the past' (Schachtel 1949: 22–3).

It is a truism that music is able to express nostalgia and loss, and to recall the distant past, yet it is only the relatively recent recognition of hearing as one of the earliest developmental senses that has identified the significance of music in relation to unconscious memory, to the pre-Oedipal, pre-linguistic state, and loss of plenitude. Since the infant hears before it sees, recognising the timbre of its mother's voice long before it can identify her face, the association between music, particularly song, and the maternal appears to be established before birth, and the centrality of the auditory realm to the formation of subjectivity is clear (Rosalato 1974: 80). This is a particularly interesting development in film theory, where Jacques Lacan's work on the importance of vision and the image in the formation of the subject (the mirror phase) has, not surprisingly, tended to dominate. For Guy Rosalato, however, the voice itself functions as (acoustic) mirror, in that the subject simultaneously emits and receives sounds; thus the child's first sounds constitute, at least in part, 'a reprise, a hallucinatory evocation of the sonorous features of the maternal: a sort of auditory restaging of the *fort-da* game' (Rosalato 1972: 39). The capacity of music to affect the emotions is therefore seen to emanate from its early association with the mother; with Kristeva's maternal *chora*, and from its apparent ability to restore plenitude and the lost maternal object (Kristeva 1980: 286).

Given that our early experiences of music are fundamental to our emotional development, argues Storr, it is surprising that autobiographies tend to concentrate on place and events, and to ignore music almost entirely (Storr 1997: 126–7). Whilst this statement is clearly something of an over-generalisation, it is none the less true that the majority of written autobiographies privilege the visual aspect of remembering. However, the near universality of the reproduction of just such musical milestones in autobiographical films perhaps suggests that what we can more usefully deduce from Storr's observation is simply further proof of the problems involved in expressing through language those total early experiences of which music is a part. Incidentally, I suggest that we might well see this as evidence that film, far from being inadequate to deal with the inner experiences of autobiography (Bruss 1980: 296), is actually a particularly privileged site for the articulation of its concerns (Everett 1995: 3–10), not least because of the simultaneity and immediacy of its multiple signifiers.

It is within this relationship between music and anteriority – in particular, the close link between voice and self, or voice and mother – that the phenomenon of the popular song must be situated. It would seem that for all of us, even those whose main interest is classical rather than popular music, popular songs remain firmly embedded in the mind, constituting part of its 'mental furniture' (Storr 1997: 126). In the light of this, it might seem paradoxical that film, always keen to exploit the emotional power of music, should have eschewed these songs for so long, yet outside the special case of the musical, popular songs rarely featured in the score before the late 1960s (Brown 1996: 564–6). The explanation, enshrined in the rules governing the role of music in classical narrative, itself reflects wider issues concerning the nature of musical discourse, and the imperfectly understood relationship between it and the iconic images of film. Indeed, the very impenetrability of musical structures to the non-specialist, allied with music's power to affect the emotional and even the physical responses of its listeners, characterises it as a potentially disruptive force which the narrative must tightly contain. Traditionally, therefore, film music was accorded an essentially subservient role: to support the dramatic impact of the narrative without drawing attention to itself; in other words, to be 'inaudible', or at least inconspicuous (London 1936: 37, Adorno and Eisler 1947: 132, Gorbman 1987: 73). As a consequence, music which was either particularly complex or particularly familiar was avoided because it might distract the spectators from the narrative (Thomas 1991: 72, Lindgren 1963: 139). Writing in 1992, Flinn noted that despite the increasing critical awareness of the centrality of its role, film music still tended to pass largely unnoticed, to have 'the rather curious distinction of being at the periphery of most people's concerns about the cinema' (Flinn 1992: 3). Her comment also perhaps reflects Storr's more general point, which is that in a culture such as the Western one, dominated by the visual and the verbal, music tends to be perceived as peripheral and perplexing (Storr 1997: xi).

Thus, despite the synaptic potency of popular songs, their ability to bridge temporal and spatial distance, and to recall particular epochs or persons from our past (Monaco 1987: 110), their potential inclusion in films was considered too risky, particularly in the light of their ability to 'wrap themselves around whatever emotion you happen to be carrying when you first heard them' (Potter 1993: 84–5). The danger was that the personal connotations they would carry with them for each spectator would automatically introduce into the narrative uncontrollable and disruptive elements of the 'outside' world.

However, in autobiographical films, which are essentially open-ended explorations of the process of remembering and of the shifting relationship between past and present, and self and other, not only do directors want the memory-trigger mechanism of songs to be recognised, but they also actively seek the personal and creative involvement of each spectator. Indeed, it is perhaps a requisite of the fragmentary nature of the discourse that the spectators should contribute their own memories to their reading of the film. This aspect, fundamental to the creation of both individual and group identity, also partly accounts for the widespread popularity of these films; the way in which audiences, irrespective of age, background or even nationality, respond by claiming to have seen in them a reflection of their own childhood (Davies 1992: 21). Accordingly, not only do popular songs abound in autobiographical films, but they tend to be actively foregrounded in a variety of ways which intentionally destabilise the narrative and redefine the relationship between image and music.

A few examples must serve to indicate the degree to which recordings of popular songs figure in the soundtracks of autobiographical films. In England, for instance, Terence Davies's *The Long Day Closes* (1992) contains more than twenty such songs; and Dennis Potter's (semi-)autobiographical trilogy, *Pennies from Heaven* (1978), *The Singing Detective* (1986) and *Lipstick on Your Collar* (1993), is densely packed with, and even structured by, popular songs. Indeed, the opening episode of *Lipstick on Your Collar*, which was first broadcast on Channel Four on 21 February 1993, featured six songs in less than an hour. So central is the role of songs in articulating memory that Potter, for his part, describes the evolution of the narrative as 'an attempt to express attitudes to the music' rather than vice versa (Cook 1995: 163). In France, we can, for example, cite André Téchiné's *Les Roseaux sauvages* (*The Wild Reeds*, 1994), in which he completes a score containing orchestral music by Barber, Strauss and Wagner with some half-dozen popular songs which marked his own adolescence. Interestingly, this film is one of a series of nine autobiographical works, commissioned in 1994 by the French television channel ARTE, for which nine different directors, including Chantal Akerman, Claire Denis and Patricia Mazuy, were each invited to recreate the period of their adolescence using (and this was in fact the main condition imposed upon them) popular music of the period. Leaving aside the fact that such a condition was unlikely to be necessary, given the quasi-universal inclusion of popular music in autobiographical films, we can note that the series provides a fascinating insight into the way that music functions as memory trigger simultaneously for the individual whose memories are being recounted, and for the viewers, for whom (depending upon their age) the songs will also recall powerful personal memories. Diane Kurys also uses popular songs to frame her schooldays in Paris in the 1960s in *Peppermint Soda* (1977); the Hungarian director Márta Mészáros uses pop and rock music to express her teenage rebellion in *Naplû gyermekeimnek* (*Diary for my Children*, 1982); and 'I've got a lovely bunch of coconuts' serves as a protective mantra for the unhappy child remembered in Lasse Hallström's *Mit liv som hund* (*My Life as a Dog*, Sweden, 1985). In *Toto le héros* (*Toto the Hero*, Belgium, 1991) Van Dormael includes a wide variety of popular and children's songs, as well as actively exploring music as memory trigger through his use of Charles Trenet's 'Boum', and within the film's semi-autobiographical framework songs provide the means by which we can distinguish the moments of personal memory. In *Jacquot de Nantes* (France, 1990), Agnès Varda's fascinating attempt to film the 'autobiography' of her dying husband, Jacques Demy, songs from his own films offer the route into his mind. The presence of popular songs thus emerges as a key characteristic of autobiographical films, no matter which countries or periods they recall.

However, even more significant than the proliferation of these songs is their insistent foregrounding; it seems that all the directors are fired by the need to stress the central role of music in remembering. This aspect may be made explicit by the title of the film, possibly echoing that of a song, or containing an unambiguous reference to music or singing: examples include *Lipstick on Your Collar, The Long Day Closes, The Singing Detective*. The songs almost inevitably accompany the credits and/or opening sequence of the film, setting the scene, establishing the mood and the period, and situating the remembering I in his or her remembered context; but in so doing, they are made to stand out, to draw attention to themselves and their function in a way which clearly breaks all the traditional rules. Such examples reveal clearly that song not only acts as trigger in suddenly recalling long-buried memories and sensations, but also constitutes a predominant feature of voluntary memory, hence its repeated use as a way of recapturing past events or atmospheres. Songs can therefore function as historical trace alongside other remembered objects (furniture, wallpaper, radios, toys, photographs), supplying proof of the authenticity of the past they nostalgically recall.

Despite its nostalgic, even utopian function (Flinn 1992: 9), music in autobiographical film escapes the stasis of these other trace objects, through its radical foregrounding, the reasons for which are clear in the light of the popular view of nostalgia as 'memory without pain' (Monaco 1987: 93). For, as we have already noted, autobiographical films are concerned with memories which are intensely personal, whose locus is extra-linguistic, and which are frequently painful and difficult, to such an extent indeed that they may actually have been suppressed. Thus the recreation before us on the screen of the nostalgic childhood world, with its almost obsessive attention to detail, to which the faithful reproduction of authentic recordings of songs may seem to belong, is not the aim of the film but, in a sense, merely its starting point; the context in which the total experience of childhood memory may resurface. The concern of autobiography cannot therefore be the recreation of a static past, memory as utopia, but is an exploration of the present via the processes of remembering; of the way the mind travels through the temporal landscapes of memory, and it is, of course, no coincidence that autobiographical films are so often narrated as journey. Within this journey, neither the memories nor the songs which are their vehicle should be seen as static exhibits in Caughie's 'museum of collective traces' (Caughie 1992: 11–13). Unlike photographs, songs are not evidence of 'having-been-there' (Barthes 1984: 91); they do not testify to 'time's relentless melt' (Sontag 1977: 15); instead they constitute a meeting of past and present, a threshold between the shifting selves and times of identity which may lead to a new understanding of both.

This positive view of song as meeting place of the multiple tenses and viewpoints of the self is shared by many different cultures, not least that of the Australian Aboriginal, for whom songs not only mark territorial boundaries, but also guide the individual's journey from past to future, from memory to identity. Their notion of song as 'map and direction-finder' (Chatwin 1987: 13) seems particularly suited to the demands of autobiographical film in which, even when songs exploit their nostalgic potential, they do so ironically and self-consciously. Potter considers that it is this combination of ironic self-awareness and nostalgic innocence in songs that enables him to turn fiction 'inside out', to move the narrative inwards from description to process: 'you can use the power of nostalgia to open the past up and make it stand up in front of you. That is why I use popular songs' (Potter 1993: 22, 96). Thus, when popular songs accompany the credits and/or opening sequences, in what appears to be something of a filmic cliché, various devices which draw attention to them will destabilise the narrative, and focus the spectator's attention on the process of remembering. For example, Terence Davies's *The Long Day Closes*, which is an account of his childhood in Liverpool in the 1950s, opens with a slow tracking shot along an empty and derelict street, before the camera turns into one of the houses, and pauses, motionless, in front of a broken staircase. As the sequence ends, we see Bud (Davies's alter ego) sitting halfway down these stairs in the house which is now restored to its former state. This apparently simple sequence reflects, however, the densely layered signifiers of memory. The somewhat disturbing artificiality of the street set and the heavy rain can, for instance, be recognised as tentative explorations of the artificiality of memory, whilst its dark and confusing contours indicate the problematic nature of retrospective vision. A peeling poster advertising *The Robe* (the first ever cinemascope production) both acknowledges the centrality of film within the memory construct, and is accorded a subjective status by Bud's opening words, as he asks his mother for money to 'go to the pictures'. The child's position on the stairs, neither at the top nor the bottom, but at the indeterminate halfway stage which exactly parallels that of early adolescence, contributes a third-person viewpoint which is at odds with the unmarked and unidentified perspective and time of the exterior part of the sequence, and illustrates the multiple and fragmented viewpoints of memory.

Nevertheless, the true complexity of the scene emerges only through the relationship of these visual elements with the song which accompanies them. Throughout the sequence we hear a nostalgic recording of Nat King Cole singing 'Stardust', the Hoagy Carmichael song which was extremely popular in post-war Britain. It clearly has personal significance for Davies, since it both instigates the memories which are the film, and transports him into his open-ended journey through time. The song is featured non-diegetically, which is to say that it is not contained by the narrative in any way, instead being presented as part of the process of remembering. To some extent, we could equate its function with that of a narrative voiceover, for it appears to speak with authority, but its status remains unmarked. However, by situating its melody and lyrics within a visual context, Davies exposes the processes of remembering; and since it is likely to be recognised by at least a proportion of the audience, for whom it will awaken a range of entirely personal memories and responses, the song sites memory in the interplay between screen and spectator.

The song, which is acknowledged as part of the personal memories of the director/protagonist and of the spectators, simultaneously interrogates these memories, by revealing their essential artificiality. The voice we hear is smooth and glamorous; its distinctive American quality marks it as exotic, as the product of an alien culture. Moreover, by juxtaposing song and film poster, Davies identifies the cinema as the primary source of the popular American culture to which this film, like his memories, pays tribute. In other words, just as the song recognises itself as both public construct and intimate memory, so too the self which it strives to reflect is acknowledged, at least in part, as its construct. The memories which constitute identity are largely fictional, not so much 'formed' as 'framed' or even 'faked' by the tool which mediates them (Chambers

1997: 237). It is important to recognise in this idea one of the fundamental attributes of autobiography: that to describe oneself is, essentially,
to create oneself (Lejeune 1971: 84), and that the 'self' thus created is
factitious.

Such processes are made explicit by the lyrics of 'Stardust': dealing
with separation and loss, the song self-consciously acknowledges its
nostalgic power: as reflection of the past, 'the music of the years gone by',
it is sutured into our very being, thus 'a song which will not die'. But this
apparent nostalgic innocence, to which it so helpfully draws our attention,
is modified by the visual signifiers which we have already noted, and also,
of course, by the song's position on the soundtrack. It is preceded by the
Twentieth Century-Fox logo theme, and a brief extract from the soundtrack of *The Happiest Days of Your Life* (1950); thus 'the music of the years
gone by' recalls the notion of (schooldays as) the happiest days of your life,
an ironic association, in the light of the memories which the song will
instigate, and an unambiguous warning of the dangers and dishonesty of
nostalgia. Whilst we hear (in the extract from *The Happiest Days of Your
Life*) the sound of a gong, followed by Margaret Rutherford's ironic 'Tap,
Gossage, I said "tap" – you're not introducing a film', we recognise that
introducing a film is, of course, precisely what Davies is doing, and that
his 'song which will not die', the remembered 'reality' of his childhood, is
itself largely a filmic construct. The use of a popular song as part of the
opening sequence of *The Long Day Closes* is thus far from innocent, and
its function greatly exceeds the simple establishing of a spatial and
temporal context, for it also instigates an examination of the fundamental
issues of autobiographical discourse in which the spectator is directly
implicated, not least the central and dynamic function of music.

If the relationship of song and other filmic signifiers is a central
element of this discourse, no less important, of course, is the fact that the
essential physicality of music (Blacking 1976: vi–viii, Steiner 1992: 44) is
enhanced in song by the joint articulation of words and melody, music
and language. For Barthes, in particular, it is this combination of voice
and melody, 'the materiality of the body speaking its mother tongue',
which enables song to intensify both the memory of the original
experience (*jouissance*) and the keenness of its loss (Barthes 1977: 179–
89). The particular significance of songs in autobiographical films
reflects their hybrid status as both verbal and non-verbal, both music and
discourse, which enables them to transgress the boundaries between
public and private, self and other. Here we might usefully consider a
further sequence from *The Long Day Closes*, also composed of two distinct
elements: an exterior shot of Bud walking slowly through a fairground
with his mother and sisters, and an interior shot of him sitting on his

mother's knee. As in the previous example, both elements are accompanied by a single song, 'She walked through the fair', also popular in the
1950s, and likely to be familiar to at least some of the audience. As the
song describes walking through the fair, we see Bud doing just that; in
fact, his pace closely mirrors the slow rhythms of the song, and although
this is for the child a moment of carnival, of enjoyment, the overall
atmosphere is reflective and quiet. As we hear the words 'And then she
went homeward / With one star awake / As the swan in the evening / Moves
over the lake', we cut directly to the interior scene, and into Davies's
increasingly intimate memory of his mother singing that song to him. As
we watch, the recorded voice is first joined, and gradually replaced, by that
of the mother. Clearly, this change reflects the gradual interiorisation of
the song; its move from public to private status. At the same time, we can
see that the same interiorisation is occurring for the mother, since
singing to Bud reminds her that her father used also to sing it to her when
she was small. Although Bud is interested by this information, he is
unaware of her sadness; unlike us, he does not notice that her eyes have
filled with tears. However, in using the song to recall his own childhood,
the adult Davies attains a new understanding of his mother's sadness, of
her lost past. The song is therefore performing multiple functions as its
status is increasingly internalised, and in so doing it illustrates Potter's
comments about using nostalgia to move inwards from description to
process.

It is the essentially unstable status of the songs which equips them
perfectly to express the multiple and conflicting textualities of memory,
whilst their self-conscious foregrounding within the films creates the
slippage and doubling fundamental to autobiographical discourse. Their
function far exceeds that of nostalgic device or memory trace, for as the
films reveal, they form part of the dynamic process of the creation of the
self; for ultimately, of course, that is the purpose of autobiography. Playing our song thus becomes singing our song as we are directly implicated
in the remembering process; and the fact that the song was not written by
us, and has already been used by countless other individuals, is irrelevant,
for in singing it, it becomes our own. We are all, as individuals, subject to
the process of enculturation which enables, or perhaps obliges, us to
share a past crystallised by the banalities of popular song, and yet we are
determined to forge a unique identity with the help of that common, but
still entirely subjective, musical discourse.

References

Adorno, T. and Eisler, H. (1947), *Composing for the Films*, London, Dennis Dobson.

Barthes, R. (1977), 'The Grain of the Voice', in *Image, Music, Text*, selected and trans. Stephen Heath, New York, Noonday Press.

Barthes, R. (1984), *Camera Lucida: Reflections on Photography*, trans. Richard Howard, London, Fontana.

Blacking, J. (1976), *How Musical is Man?*, London, Faber and Faber.

Brown, R. (1994), *Overtones and Undertones: Reading Film Music*, Berkeley, Los Angeles and London, University of California Press.

Brown, R. (1996), 'Modern Film Music', in G. Nowell-Smith (ed.), *The Oxford History of World Cinema*, Oxford, Oxford University Press, 558–66.

Bruss, E. (1980), 'Eye for I: Making and Unmaking Autobiography in Film', in J. Aulney (ed.). *Autobiography: Essays Theoretical and Critical*, Princeton NJ, Princeton University Press., 296–320.

Buñuel, L. (1985), *My Last Breath*, trans. Abigail Israel, London, Flamingo.

Caughie, J. (1992), 'Half Way to Paradise', *Sight and Sound*, May, 11–13.

Chambers, I. (1997), 'Maps, Movies, Musics and Memory', in D. Clarke (ed.), *The Cinematic City*, London and New York, Routledge, 230–40.

Chatwin, B. (1987), *The Songlines*, London, Jonathan Cape.

Cook, J. (1995), *Dennis Potter: A Life on Screen*, Manchester and New York, Manchester University Press.

Davies, T. (1992), Interview with Wheeler Winston Dixon, *Cineaste*, XIX, 2–3, December: 20–3.

Everett, W. (1995), 'The Autobiographical Eye in European Film', *Europa: An International Journal of Language, Art and Culture*, 2, 1, Spring: 3–10,

Everett, W. (ed.) (1996), *European Identity in Film*, Exeter, Intellect.

Flinn, C. (1992), *Strains of Utopia: Gender, Nostalgia, and Hollywood Film Music*, Princeton NJ, Princeton University Press.

Gorbman, C. (1987), *Unheard Melodies: Narrative Film Music*, London, BFI and Indiana University Press.

Gorbman, C. (1998), 'Film Music', in J. Hill and P. Church Gibson (eds), *The Oxford Guide to Film Studies*, Oxford, Oxford University Press, 43–50.

Kristeva, J. (1980), *Desire in Language*, New York, Columbia University Press.

Lejeune, P. (1971), *L'autobiographie en France*, Paris, A. Colin.

Lindgren, E. (1963), *The Art of Film*, second edition, New York, Macmillan.

London, K. (1936), *Film Music*, London, Faber and Faber.

Monaco, P. (1987), *Ribbons in Time*, Bloomington and Indianapolis, Indiana University Press.

Olney, J. (ed.) (1980), *Autobiography: Essays Theoretical and Critical*, Princeton JN, Princeton University Press.

Potter, D. (1993), *Potter on Potter*, London, Faber and Faber.

Rosalato, G. (1972), 'Répétitions', *Musique en jeu*, 5, 37–45.

Rosalato, G. (1974), 'La vie: entre corps et langage', *Revue française de psychanalyse*, 38: 1, 79–94.

Rose, S. (1992), *The Making of Memory*, London and New York, Bantam Press.

Schachtel, E. (1949), 'On Memory and Childhood Amnesia', in P. Mullahy (ed.), *A Study of Interpersonal Relations*, New York, Science House, 3–49.

Sheringham, M. (1993), *French Autobiography – Devices and Desires*, Oxford, Clarendon Press.

Sontag, S. (1977), *On Photography*, London, Penguin.

Sorlin, P. (1991), *European Cinemas, European Societies 1939–90*, London and New York, Routledge.

Steiner, G. (1992), *Heidegger*, London, Fontana.

Storr, A. (1997), *Music and the Mind*, London, HarperCollins.

Thomas, T. (1991), *Film Score: The Art and Craft of Movie Music*, Burbank, Riverwood Press.

Young, J. (1993), *The Texture of Memory: Holocaust, Memorials and Meaning*, New Haven CT, Yale University Press.

JULIA DOBSON

Transatlantic crossings: ideology and the remake

15

The remake occupies a complex position in the wholly interdependent network of relationships between entertainment and ideology. Indeed an examination of the discourses which surround the remake provides fruitful indications of popular assumptions central to our perceptions of the means and consequences of entertaining ideologies. Discussion of the remake has been included as an element of critical debates around entertainment (Dyer 1992), authenticity (Mazdon 1996) and cultural constructions of national cinemas (Vincendeau 1993), but the model of the remake itself has rarely been the central subject of critical analysis. The relationship between 'original' and remake will be explored here not in terms of an oppositional ideological difference, but rather in the context of the different narrative strategies employed in the films which may serve to disseminate a single dominant ideological discourse.

The omnipresence of ideology in all social and discursive practices is emphasised in Althusserian critiques of cultural expression, as Belsey asserts: '... ideology is not an optional extra deliberately adopted by self-conscious individuals, but the very condition of our experience of the world, unconscious precisely in that it is unquestioned, taken for granted'(Belsey 1980: 5). Ideology entails a misrecognition of the subject's relationship to the world, a process which, within the filmic medium, is conventionally fostered through the projection of the illusion of unified subjectivity (visual and narrative identification with a character or a star), through absorption in a coherent narrative and through the positing of unproblematic narrative closure. Such investment in the narrative and the subsequent misrecognition manufactured between subject and projected world can serve to naturalise the existing dominant social, political and economic structures. Indeed much film theory posits the cinematic apparatus as constituting an ideal site in which such projections and identifications can be realised and reinforced.[1] However, displaying a marked contrast to these assertions, popular and critical discourses around the phenomenon of the remake have significantly underplayed both the ideological power of the shared cinematic apparatus common to first text and remake, and the constructed nature of the 'original'. In the context of the relationship between entertainment and ideology, the validity of such oppositions between 'original' text and secondary remake demands closer inspection.

The number of Hollywood remakes of European films has increased markedly since the mid-1980s, in parallel with the growth in remakes of established film classics and film adaptations of literary works. All these models exploit the security of an already successful narrative in order to formulate a supposedly new product, whose success has an ambiguous relationship to the target audience's knowledge of its predecessor. It remains clear that most films which are remade are chosen specifically because of their already proven box-office success, an aspect which is of paramount importance to the Hollywood film industry in its budget rationales and search to identify and satisfy the common denominators used in the global marketing and distribution of its products.

It must be stressed, however, that the historical relationship between French and Hollywood film industries has been based neither on simple oppositions nor on mutual exclusivity. The *policiers* of the 1950s demonstrate considerable cross-fertilisation of French and American cinemas (Vincendeau 1992a) and the New Wave arguably regarded Hollywood as less conservative than the French *cinéma de qualité*, although Godard's later description of the relationship as '... a two-way fascination and a one-way exploitation'(Vincendeau 1996: 173) remains a pertinent reminder of the financial scale and distributive impact of the respective industries. In its acceptance of and emphasis on the binary opposition between a highly conventional, formally and thematically conservative, budget-led Hollywood remake in relation to a progressive, less mainstream,[2] *auteur*-led French original, the prevalent model also implies that ideology is somehow added to the narrative on its transferral to Hollywood, and thus is only explicitly present in what is presented as the corrupted and culturally inferior remake. The dominance of such factors points towards an over-reliance on the opposition between original and remake – the classic dialectical use of a binary divide which enables both sides to construct their identity strategically in reference to their opposite, and which consequently provides support for increasingly problematic definitions of national cinemas. In the context of the contemporary global film industry, the GATT talks, national and international funding, distribution structures and other extra-textual constructions of cultural identity are clearly implemented in the support of the binary opposition of French and Hollywood productions.

The problematic construction of the relationship between original and remake is thus multifaceted, yet in the context of this discussion, I would argue that the fundamental point which both transcends and undermines any binary opposition remains the fact that the dominant ideology present in both mainstream French and Hollywood cinemas is that of capitalist patriarchy. In the light of this it would be both naive and erroneous to posit an 'authentic' and ideology-free French original which has been corrupted through the remake to serve the cause of ideologies that can be identified as specific to the Hollywood film industry, or indeed to any one national cinema. Such a move would in itself encourage the naturalisation of the French text and the ideological discourses at play within it. My discussion of these films will thus explore both French text and remake as different articulations of a dominant ideology. What interests me here is the different mechanisms employed in the films to naturalise the ideological tenets of capitalist patriarchy. In focusing on the ideology of gender and, more specifically, on the constructions of femininity which are operational within the narratives, this discussion inevitably marginalises other elements. The construction and articulation of masculinity and sexuality, the hypocrisy of government-sanctioned murder and the ethics of surveillance are coherent themes in *Nikita* (Hayward 1998), yet their striking absence in the remake can, for reasons of space, only be noted here.

Gender constitutes a fundamental factor in the construction of subjectivity, and thus represents a vital consideration for a dominant ideology's construction and reinforcement of the models of subjectivity which best serve its political, social and economic value-systems. Indeed concepts of remaking, imitation, parody and performance are of central concern to a wide range of gender theories. Through an illuminating analysis of Beineix's *Diva*, Zavarzadeh argues that various stages of cultural transference and displacement are implemented within cultural media in such a way as to permit representations of women's encodement in gender that are no longer viewed as politically acceptable in other arenas. The cinema spectator is thus only made intelligible to herself or himself by participating in the construction of a narrative in which men and women are situated within 'the universalising codes of capitalist patriarchy' (Zavarzadeh 1991: 204). He cites two examples of these codes as the reinstatement of the virgin/whore binary and the successful inscription of a threatening feminine into the patriarchal order as acceptable narrative closure. Both these codes prove valuable in an examination of the films under discussion here.

The space available in this chapter restricts the number of illustrative examples possible, and a degree of familiarity with the films chosen –

Besson's *Nikita* (1990), remade by Badham as *The Assassin* (1993),[3] and Clouzot's *Les Diaboliques* (1954), remade by Chechik as *Diabolique* (1996) – must be assumed. These four films are particularly relevant to this context as they share an initial and superficial focus on potential subversions of gender 'norms' – not the corrupted figure of the *femme fatale* who rarely escapes punitive closure, but female killers. What proves most interesting, however, is the films' explicit limitation of possible gender subversion, as the main drive of the respective narratives serves to assimilate and contain the clearly signalled gender disruptions through the ultimate reinscription of the central female characters within conventional constructions of femininity. In many ways these films can be read as narratives of rehabilitation.

Besson is widely seen as a director who attempts to transgress perceived boundaries in his desire to 'bring the speed and action of Hollywood into line with narrative structures that are French' (Hayward 1998: 40); his next film, the Hollywood production, *Léon*, was, however, described as 'French' by American audiences and 'American' by French cinemagoers (Austin 1996: 132). *Nikita* has provoked both critical and commercial interest (the film achieved a first-run audience in France of almost 4 million). *The Assassin* was also commercially successful[4] and the narrative and central character have been subsequently adopted and exploited not only by Hollywood through the remake under discussion here, but through an American television series and a Japanese remake.

Whilst *Nikita* and its remake arguably achieve the same ideological goals, their textual differences[5] are central to an appreciation of the variant devices available within the same broad narrative of rehabilitation of a potentially subversive 'feminine' threat to patriarchal gender representation. Narrative structures of rehabilitation are clearly evident from the first sequences of the film. The eponymous heroine's drug dependency and criminal behaviour are 'cured' by her training at the government agency. This enacts her first rehabilitation, from animalistic, dehumanised social outcast to functional individual, who is forced to acknowledge the power of the state over her free will. Her reintegration into society and into a romance subplot affirms further institutional and emotional rehabilitations, and she is doubly remade through her new civil identity and secret code name. However, it is the gender aspect of these rehabilitations that requires closer attention, implying an ultimate rehabilitation which serves to eliminate the threat posed by a subversive 'feminine'.

Nikita is first introduced as an inhuman or at best androgynous character. In order to be successful as an agent in the outside world it seems she must become conventionally feminine. As Austin remarks, 'Besson seems to be presenting the autocratic state as a purveyor of both gender stereotyping and of high culture' (Austin 1996: 130). The familiar elements of the nature/nurture debate on gender are inconsistently and ambiguously present throughout the film and inform its representation of Nikita's identity. She is seen to undergo training in femininity in the same way as she learns martial arts and IT skills. In *Nikita* the process of Nikita's assisted and gradual transformation to the conventional glamorous 'feminine' is foregrounded and epitomised in a scene in which she learns to use a lipstick in front of a fully lit theatre dressing-room mirror, a sequence which evokes both the masquerade and the spectacle of conventional 'femininity'. However, in the remake the process is hidden and the spectator is required simply to witness the striking physical contrast between the 'before and after' of a necessary makeover. The question posed by the enigmatic teacher in the remake is not whether the main character, Maggie, can 'learn' femininity and the advantages of explicitly adopting such codes as part of her cover, but whether she can be transformed from an ugly duckling into an elegant and acceptable swan. The heroine is presented as empowered through the revelation of her essential femininity rather than through her perfected skills in constructing a gender identity. The emphasis upon process and artifice varies greatly between the two films, yet the attainment of a visually conformative femininity is ultimately presented in both as a re-establishment of natural attributes and as a major factor in the central character's emotional development and personal happiness.

The adoption of various disguises is central to the heroines' missions, but there is no subversive agency in these transformations, as the potential of masquerade is undermined by the limitations of dressing up for a role determined by others. Nikita is seen to exploit archetypal feminine roles; that of the *femme fatale*, portrayed through the indispensable little black dress in which she performs her first mission, and that of the maid delivering room service, the servile feminine of her second mission. The trope of masquerade may indeed appear central to *Nikita*. In a reading of the films which draws heavily upon Butlerian theories of gender performativity, Brown concludes that this aspect of the film and its remake contributes to its success, which '... indicates the emerging acceptance of feminine identities that encroach upon even the most masculine of domains' (Brown 1996: 69). These disguises may serve on one textual level to maintain the superficial theme of the ambiguity of appearance and the artificiality of gender identity, yet I would argue against Brown that they contribute ultimately to the removal of Nikita's potential disruption of patriarchal gender codes. Hayward demonstrates convincingly that, in *Nikita*, the threatening implications for patriarchal culture of successful cross-dressing are undermined by an ultimately reductive and misogynist representation of the feminine (Hayward 1998: 111-15). Taken further, this point reveals that the pattern of disguise represented also corresponds increasingly to the presentation of Nikita's roles as examples of playful 'dressing up'[6] rather than controlled and competent disguise, and consequently contributes to the central mechanism for the rehabilitation of gender subversion within the film; the presentation of Nikita as child.

The recurrent presence in Besson's films of characters who retreat into childlike behaviour has been identified elsewhere (Hayward 1998: 127), but my specific argument here is that the subversive potential of a self-reflexive and active femininity is neutralised through its narrative containment within a dominant 'infantasy'. Nikita is consistently presented as childlike throughout the film: within the institutional spaces of the government agency she cries out for her mother, throws tantrums and plays tricks on her colleagues, she is presented with an archetypal birthday cake chosen by Bob as a suitable gift, and the camera presents us with recurrent close-ups of her dangling vulnerable feet, always short of reaching the floor. On return to the outside world her apparently successful socialisation and congruity are disrupted by her raucous songs and the childlike exuberance which she demonstrates for the adult activities of both shopping and sex. This portrayal is reinforced through her relationships with the central male characters. As Vincendeau remarks, the narrative constructs a father–daughter relationship between Bob and Nikita (Vincendeau 1993: 23) and indeed Nikita's relationships with all men are characterised in this way. Despite the reversal of traditional gender roles apparent in their first meeting, her partner Marco soon adopts a protective role and repeatedly addresses her through childlike games and expressions. Her brief encounter with Victor the cleaner can be read as a confrontation with an over-authoritative father figure.

In *Nikita* the subversive feminine is thus reintegrated into patriarchal ideologies of gender through an insistence upon her identity as child and a consequent denial of agency and independence. *The Assassin* employs a different strategy to recuperate this threat, as throughout the film both narrative and film language combine to reaffirm gradually the central female character's status as sexual object. This is achieved through the greater prominence given to the romance subplot (notably a series of flashforwards, which serve to overwrite the heroine's sexual assertiveness with images of a conventionally passive 'feminine' role within a romantic relationship) and through the film language employed to encourage the identification of the spectator's gaze with that of the central male characters.

The two strategies, infantasy and sexual objectification, find vivid illustration in a comparison of a pivotal sequence in *Nikita* and *The*

Assassin in which the heroine's two worlds (represented by the two men) meet face to face. The potential tension caused by the juxtaposition of her two roles and relationships is transcended by the sequences' main narrative drive, which asserts the role of the two central male protagonists in constructing feminine identity and emphasises the consequent confirmation of her rehabilitated status in relation to patriarchal gender norms. In both films state agent and mentor Bob, masquerading as the heroine's uncle, is invited to meet her partner, Marco/JP, at their home. In both films, in response to Marco/JP's frustration at having no information about her past, Bob constructs a fabricated image of her childhood. The scene is, however, treated very differently in the two films. In *Nikita* Marco asks specifically for details of her childhood and Bob depicts Nikita as a child in terms of her innocence, capriciousness, popularity and comical behaviour. In his established role as surrogate father and (albeit ambiguous) protector he creates a childhood for Marie (as Nikita is known to the outside world). Bob's fantasy is presented as doubly benevolent in that it assuages Marco's desire for background knowledge and, as emphasised by close-ups of Marie's tender expression, provides her with an image which is far removed from the reality of her early years. However, Bob's creation serves primarily to reinforce his status as patriarchal guardian both to his female protégée and to conventional feminine identity.

In *Nikita* there is no evident rivalry between the two men, the story passes between them and they enter into complicit agreement on the success of such images in defining Marie, as solution to an identity which they both wish to resolve and control. This construction of femininity is clearly also fundamental to their own identities, a dependence emphasised in the final sequences of the film when, in her absence, their roles and identities are evidently destabilised. The remake's treatment of the same sequence reveals the consistency of its different mechanism of rehabilitation, that of sexual objectification. In this sequence Bob and JP conduct an aggressive and hard-hitting verbal contest over Claudia (Maggie's constructed persona) as sexual property, as they evaluate each other in terms of age and (implicitly sexual) experience. Bob's fabrication of her childhood continues the emphasis on the value of conventional feminine beauty remarked upon earlier, and evidence of Claudia's courage evoked in the tale remains overshadowed by Bob's insistence upon her physical appearance and the construction of her as sexual being. The men's status as sexual rivals is thus confirmed and the heroine is consequently fixed in her role as definitively 'feminine' sexual object. The sexual objectification assigned to her through the verbal imagery of Bob's construction is reinforced by the film language employed in the sequence, as framing, camera position and editing combine to isolate Claudia as spectacle whilst encouraging the spectator to identify with the competing gazes of Bob and JP.

The different final missions presented in the two films demonstrate the strategies identified above and affirm the employment of the paradigm of dressing up, not as subversive masquerade but as reductive and limiting pantomime. Both films present the heroine's final mission as a test of professional skill and moral fortitude. In this (following the violent intervention of Victor the cleaner), Nikita must successfully impersonate the male Chinese ambassador in order to retrieve crucial industrial data. The disruptive potential of cross-dressing is radically undermined by the persistent infantasy, as she resembles not a man, but a child in an oversized suit, glasses and comically false moustache. The narrative tension of this episode centres not on the possible discovery of her femininity, but on her failure to become the agent of her own identity remake. Her dressing up is revealed as an unsuccessful and inappropriate substitute for the professional remodelling of her identity undertaken by the state.

The final mission presented in the remake is radically revised to maintain the mechanism of rehabilitation outlined earlier. In order to access and retrieve stolen data Claudia does not attempt cross-dressing but must impersonate the girlfriend of a foreign industrialist – a girlfriend who constitutes the formulaic epitome of an exaggerated 'femininity': long blonde hair, tight clothing, bitchy comments and superficial interests (indeed the agents gain access to her by posing as her hairdresser and manicurist). However, the success of this mission is dependent not solely upon a masquerade of exaggerated gender, but on the assertion of moral rehabilitation (the refusal of a bribe) and its close association with her successful remoulding into patriarchal gender norms. Having rejected corruption, Claudia, her red satin shorts and thigh-high boots reminiscent of a potential Superwoman, defeats her opponents in an Emma Peel-style display of high kicks. Her exaggerated costume, and the use of conventional devices of film language in reinforcing her status as spectacle, remove any subversive agency from her violence. Indeed the 'unfeminine' skills she displays in order to survive are ultimately effaced as the removal of agency continues in the final sequences of the remake. A tracking shot establishes her departure, but this movement and sense of liberation are countered by a series of stills, portrait photographs taken by JP, which return us to the romance subplot, her conventional 'feminine' beauty and her position as framed object of male desire.[7]

Having identified the two different strategies of rehabilitation at work within the films, I would resist the assertion of any wider patterns that relate such mechanisms to the respective different cinemas and national cultures. Vincendeau's work on the dominance of the narrative trope of the father–daughter romance in French cinema (Vincendeau 1992b) could be considered relevant to the infantasy of *Nikita*, yet in this specific context, such an approach may generate reductive implications for discussions of both national cinemas and the remake. The two films display varying degrees of narrative closure and thematic clarity, yet both narratives maintain a focus on the recuperation of the subversive feminine and its reinscription within patriarchal norms of gender. *Nikita* achieves this through the containment of the feminine within familial structures, whilst the dominant discourse of *The Assassin* equates the adoption of conventional gender roles with successful social integration and moral fortitude. The different narrative mechanisms employed to maintain gender norms in *Nikita* and *The Assassin* can thus be figured as modes of rehabilitation.

There is not space here to attempt detailed discussion of other recent remakes. However, a brief examination of a second pair of films reveals a similar pattern, as the dominant ideology is articulated through different narrative modes of rehabilitation. In contrast to the success of *The Assassin* and despite a star-studded cast and sexy marketing, Chechik's remake of Clouzot's tense thriller *Les Diaboliques* was spectacularly unsuccessful with both critics and box office. In this case the subversive feminine, contained within the discourse of Clouzot's class critique and moral censure, is emphasised in the remake in order to be rehabilitated through victimhood.

In *Les Diaboliques* a complex plot and inherent moral ambiguities combine to complicate audience identification. The narrative initially supports a crudely oppositional characterisation of the two central female characters; the submissive wife is defined by her Catholicism, affinity with children, suffering and innocence, whilst the mistress and science teacher (played so memorably by Simone Signoret) is sexually assertive, scientifically knowledgeable, glamorous and pragmatic. However, this classic binary is neither maintained nor consistently foregrounded, and the spectator is drawn into complex realignments of identification as the power relationship between the two women shifts throughout the narrative. The disruptive agency of both women is revealed as ultimately submissive to the manipulative and corrupted headmaster who decides their fates. The potential gender disruption represented by the assertive mistress is doubly contained, first within the parameters of patriarchal romance (she kills to maintain a love relationship with a man) and second through the moral censure involved in the discovery of her crime. The potential threat of the subversive 'feminine' is further rehabilitated in the film through a narrative which persistently presents its resolution in terms of an explicit class critique rather than one of sexual politics or gender oppositions. In *Les Diaboliques* it is the victory of the populist hero, the retired working-class detective, and his revelation of the adulterous, murderous and amoral behaviour rife in the bourgeois milieu of the private school which constitute the main drive of the narrative closure.

The remake achieves a similar containment of the two central female characters, not through their inclusion in a wider class critique (which remains entirely absent from the remake) but through the insistence upon their ultimate status as victims. The narrative is dominated by the sexual relationship between the three characters, as demonstrated in its promotional slogan: 'One man, two women – the combination can be murder.' The classic binary of whore/virgin is asserted: the wife is styled as pious, gothic angel and the mistress, played by Sharon Stone,[8] is an aggressive sexual animal (her persistent wearing of leopard and tiger prints provides heavy-handed visual notation of her predatory nature). Her introduction, via a slow vertical pan from the ankles up, and fetishistic framing of her body, clearly demarcate her as clichéd sexual object. The sexual characterisation is also obviously reliant upon intertextual references to Stone's other roles, specifically that of the bisexual killer Catherine Trammell in *Basic Instinct*,[9] and serves to overplay the motif of suggested erotic attraction between the two women. In the remake the perceived threat to patriarchal definitions of femininity is dissipated not by romance, or even by moral censure, but by an exaggerated construction of corrupted masculinity (achieved through additional scenes which establish the husband as habitually adulterous, violent and drunk) and the subsequent rehabilitation of both wife and mistress as victims. The radical changes to the ending could be interpreted as a search to provide further narrative twists whilst avoiding what contemporary Hollywood may perceive as an unacceptable ending, the wife's death, yet they serve ultimately to reposition both women as victims. The mistress returns to the school to enact her moral rehabilitation, prevents the wife's murder and, through her allegiance in the ensuing violence, decides who is to survive. Thus the two women unite in the murder of the husband, but this agency and sisterly solidarity are undermined as the detective's final comments and actions assign the status of victim to both women. The female detective who, crudely and superficially 'defeminised' through the revelation of her double mastectomy, performs the role of pragmatic survivor, enables the narrative closure to avoid any direct implication in the sex wars of the main narrative. The threat posed by the subversive 'feminine', ultimately of *both* central female characters in *Diabolique*, is recuperated through their rehabilitation as victims.

The films discussed here represent only a small sample of the number of recent Hollywood remakes of French films, yet, as case studies, they demonstrate that whilst the tropes employed in these films and their remakes in the service of the tenets of the dominant ideology (here patriarchal definitions of 'femininity') may vary, the narrative drive for rehabilitation of the subversive 'feminine' remains central. This brief examination of the model of the remake (mirrored in the devices of remaking and rehabilitation present in the films discussed) warns against the acceptance of superficial judgements which posit fundamentally oppositional and generalised ideological codes of production in the cinematic industries of France and Hollywood. Ideology is not added during these transatlantic crossings. As Zavarzadeh remarks: 'Ideology critique violates the principle of uniqueness by demonstrating that the logic of patriarchal (Eurocentric) capitalism underlies seemingly different heterogeneous, nomadic texts' (Zavarzadeh 1991: 3). Rather than identifying Hollywood as the primordial locus of both ideology and entertainment, we should approach the remake with a clear awareness of the different ways in which a dominant ideology can be entertained whilst being perpetually remade.

Notes

1 There is clearly a large and varied body of work which explores this argument. See Christian Metz, 'The Imaginary Signifier', and the work of Jean-Louis Baudry, 'Ideological Effects of the Basic Cinematographic Apparatus', both collected in Rosen 1986: 244–80 and 286–98 respectively.

2 It should be noted that many of these 'originals' are considered mainstream by both producers and audiences in France. It is only on making the transition to anglophone culture that they become associated with non-mainstream cinema.

3 The remake has an alternative title *The Point of No Return*.

4 After the sale of the film rights to Warner Bros, Besson was closely involved in the re-writing of the script; indeed he claims to prefer his rescripted ending of the film to that of *Nikita* (Besson 1992: 15); but he declined the offer to direct the Hollywood remake.

5 I would strongly contest Brown's approach (1996: 63), which conflates *Nikita* and remake and so removes the roles of both narrative construction and film language from his analysis.

6 In *Nikita* this is apparent in the clothes she chooses for a rare meeting with Bob: an excessive hat which has holes in the brim serves as both a parody of her supposed congruity and a humorous reference to bullet holes.

7 The ending of *Nikita* maintains a certain degree of ambiguity around her identity. She has ostensibly escaped the mould set for her by the government, yet the spectator is prevented, through the lack of complete narrative closure and her visual absence, from forming an unproblematic identification with the character.

8 It is interesting to note the odd coding of Stone in 1950s' clothes, hair and make-up, which recall Signoret, despite the setting of the remake in the 1990s. The costumes form a cliché of 1950s' images rather than a copy of Signoret's wardrobe for the film.

9 Tasker (1993: 134) discusses this character in the context of 'action heroines' and a development of the figure of the *femme fatale*.

References

Austin, G. (1996), *Contemporary French Cinema: An Introduction*, Manchester, Manchester University Press.

Belsey, C. (1980), *Critical Practice*, London, Methuen.

Besson, L. (1992), *L'Histoire de Nikita*, Paris, Bordas et fils.

Brown, J. (1996), 'Gender and the Action Heroine: *Hard Bodies* and *The Point of No Return*', *Cinema Journal*, 35, 3: 52–71.

Durham, C. (1992), 'Taking the Baby out of the Basket and/or Robbing the Cradle: "Remaking" Gender and Culture in Franco-American Film', *French Review*, 65, 5: 774–84.

Dyer, R. (1992), *Only Entertainment*, London and New York, Routledge.

Hayward, S. (1998), *Luc Besson*, Manchester, Manchester University Press.

Mazdon, L. (1996), 'Rewriting and Remakes. Questions of Originality and Authenticity', in G. T. Harris (ed.), *On Translating French Literature and Film*, Amsterdam, Rodopi, 47–63.

Rosen, P. (ed.) (1986), *Narrative, Apparatus, Ideology*, New York, Columbia University Press.

Tasker, Y. (1993), *Spectacular Bodies: Gender, Genre and the Action Movie*, London: Routledge.

Vincendeau, G. (1992a), 'France 1945–65 and Hollywood: The Policier and International text', *Screen*, 33: 50–80.

Vincendeau, G. (1992b), 'Family Plots: The Fathers and Daughters of French Cinema', *Sight and Sound*, 1: 14–17.

Vincendeau, G. (1993), 'Hijacked', *Sight and Sound*, 3: 22–5

Vincendeau, G. (1996), *Companion to French Cinema*, London, British Film Institute.

Zavarzadeh, M. (1991), *Seeing Films Politically*, New York, University of New York Press.

PETER KRÄMER

'Faith in relations between people': Audrey Hepburn, *Roman Holiday* and European integration

16

At first sight, *Roman Holiday* would seem to be a particularly inappropriate choice of topic for a chapter in a book on the relationship between ideology and entertainment in European cinema. The film was made in the early 1950s for that most powerful of Hollywood studios, Paramount, by America's most celebrated director, William Wyler, as a star vehicle for Gregory Peck, one of Hollywood's most popular leading men at the time. What could be more American and, by implication, less European than this film? Furthermore, *Roman Holiday* started out as a project for director Frank Capra and is a kind of remake of his 1934 film *It Happened One Night*, one of the greatest of all Hollywood classics, which was a big hit on its initial release, won all the major Academy Awards, and cast its shadow over much of Hollywood's output of romantic comedies from the 1930s onwards. Just like *It Happened One Night*, *Roman Holiday* tells the story of a streetwise and down-to-earth reporter who accidentally meets a young upper-class woman, who is as pampered and helpless as she is beautiful and famous. She has escaped from her familiar protected surroundings and needs help in coping with the 'real' world. The reporter befriends her because he wants to exploit his insight into her experiences for a sensational newspaper story, but the story never gets published because he falls in love with her instead. Unlike the Depression-era setting, the snappy dialogue and happy ending of *It Happened One Night*, in which the reporter marries the heiress and they, presumably, live happily ever after, *Roman Holiday* initially has more of a fairy-tale feel, featuring as it does a princess and a commoner, but it concludes with a melodramatic twist. In the end, the lovers separate because the gulf between the different social worlds they inhabit cannot be bridged, although they will always cherish the memory of their brief time together. All of this is certainly very entertaining, but does it warrant any sustained ideological analysis?

In this chapter, I want to suggest that, irrespective of first impressions, *Roman Holiday* is part of European film history, and, furthermore, it is intimately linked to cultural and political developments in 1950s Europe. Running parallel to its romance, comedy and melodrama, *Roman Holiday* contains a complex and explicit meditation on European politics and culture, in particular the debates about the integration of European nation states, as well as a self-reflexive examination of Hollywood's role in this process of European integration. In the first section, I am going to establish the film's European credentials with particular reference to its production team, most notably director William Wyler and the female lead Audrey Hepburn, and to its target audiences. In the second section, I will then take a closer look at the film's story, themes and featured attractions, and at its marketing and reception in Europe (based on the examination of press books and press clippings files in various American and European archives).

Made in Europe, made for Europe

When in 1951 William Wyler got involved in the production of *Roman Holiday*, a script that Paramount had originally tried to film with director Frank Capra, he had long established himself as one of Hollywood's top directors (Herman 1997). His most recent film was the police drama *Detective Story* (1951), a box-office hit for which he received his eighth Oscar nomination for Best Director, an award he had already won twice, for *Mrs Miniver* (1942) and *The Best Years of Our Lives* (1946) (Harkness 1994). Apart from being critically acclaimed, these two films, like many other Wyler films, were also huge box-office hits, with *The Best Years of Our Lives* distinguishing itself as the highest-grossing film of the 1940s and, after *Gone With the Wind*, the second highest-grossing film of all time up to this point (Steinberg 1980).

Despite these impeccable Hollywood credentials Wyler, like many other leading film directors in the United States such as Billy Wilder and Fred Zinneman, had been born and raised in Europe, in Mülhausen/ Mulhouse in Alsace-Lorraine in 1902, to be more precise. Wyler spent his formative years in a region that at the time belonged to Germany, before going to the United States in 1920 to join the film company of his 'uncle' Carl Laemmle (who was in fact a cousin of his grandmother). During the war Wyler returned to Europe for an extended period of time as an officer in the air force making documentaries (including the celebrated *The Memphis Belle*, 1944) about bombing missions over Germany and Italy. Having always maintained and recently strengthened his emotional ties to Europe, Wyler saw *Roman Holiday*, a story set in Rome, as a great opportunity to work again on European soil, which would also allow him to get away from the Hollywood investigations of the House Committee on Un-American Activities and to make huge tax savings (Herman 1997). Consequently, Wyler used his enormous clout within Hollywood to insist on shooting the film on location in Rome, rather than following the usual practice of reconstructing the Roman settings on a Hollywood sound stage. To complement the realism of the film's Roman locations, Wyler also insisted on casting a European actress in the role of the princess.

While Wyler's demands were motivated by his personal situation and his desire to give the film an authentic European look, they also made good business sense for Paramount. Until the 1948 Supreme Court ruling in the anti-trust case against the major Hollywood companies, which forced them to split their film production and distribution activities from their American cinema chains, Paramount had undoubtedly been one of the most powerful media corporations in the world. In December 1949, however, Paramount was divided into two separate companies, United Paramount Theatres (a chain of 1,400 cinemas in the United States) and Paramount Pictures Corporation, which comprised a Los Angeles-based film production company and an international film distribution network as well as a chain of about 380 cinemas in foreign countries (Conant 1978). Without guaranteed access to the biggest US cinema chain, which had previously constituted a secure and lucrative market for its films, Paramount Pictures now had to reconsider its production and marketing strategies.

Foreign markets, where the company still had massive theatre holdings and thus ready-made outlets for its films, became crucial in this reorientation. But it was not just foreign cinema ownership which influenced Paramount at this point. In the late 1940s and early 1950s the world market for cinema film exhibition was undergoing dramatic changes. The US market, which had always been by far the largest in the world, was shrinking rapidly. Weekly attendance figures declined from their peak of 82–4 million in the years 1943–6 to 49 million in 1951, when Wyler took over *Roman Holiday*; there was further decline ahead, with only 42 million weekly admissions, about half the wartime peak, in 1953, the year of *Roman Holiday*'s release (Finler 1988: 288). At the same time, the British market, which had traditionally been Hollywood's most important export arena, also shrank, losing almost a quarter of all paid admissions between 1946 and 1953, going down from 32 million per week to 25 million (Vincendeau 1995: 466). Other major European markets, however, were either fairly stable, such as France, or they were growing. Cinema attendances in Germany and Italy increased dramatically in the early 1950s, and continued to do so until reaching their peak in 1955/6. At this point the combined cinema admissions in France, Italy and Germany (almost 40 million per week) were not far behind the slightly recovered US figure of 50 million, whereas in 1946 combined admissions in these three markets had been less than a third of those in the US. If the British market is added, which despite its steady decline was still by far the largest in Europe, it becomes clear that in the face of a shrinking US market, Hollywood was well advised to pay close attention to the 60 million or so people who went to the cinema each week in the four major European markets in the early to mid-1950s.

What did these people want to see? In the immediate post-war years, domestic film production in most of continental Europe was recovering only slowly from the devastation of the war, and at the same time a backlog of American films, which had not been released on the continent due to the hostilities, flooded the market (Guback 1969). Therefore, Hollywood's market share was initially very high. Yet, when domestic film production recovered, it became clear that European audiences largely preferred home-made films to those imported from the United States. In the late 1940s, for example, only about one-tenth of all films shown in Italy were domestic products; yet the share of overall box-office receipts earned by Italian films grew rapidly, from 10 per cent in 1947 to 29 per cent in 1950 and 38 per cent in 1953, while the box-office share of American films, which made up the vast majority in the Italian market, was declining (Wagstaff 1991). The situation in France was similar. In 1947, domestic production accounted for only 27 per cent of all films in the French market, yet this quarter of films earned 38 per cent of all box-office revenues (Crisp 1993: 82–3). By 1955/6, the French film industry produced 30 per cent of all films in the domestic market and earned 50 per cent of the receipts. Thus, on average a French film attracted far more viewers than a foreign film. This is reflected in the list of the most successful films in French cinemas in the 1950s: of the sixty top box-office hits, more than half were French (or French–Italian coproductions with a French majority interest) and less than a third were American. The market in Germany was even more dramatically skewed in favour of domestic product. While throughout the 1950s far more American films than German films were released in Germany, out of the 100 top box-office hits of the decade, only sixteen were American, while seventy-four were German or Austrian (Garncarz 1994). Even in Great Britain, which had traditionally been quite vulnerable to American imports due to the absence of a language barrier, the top box-office attractions between 1946 and 1951 were largely domestic products (51 British films as opposed to 43 American ones) (Thumim 1991).

What all this amounts to is the preference of European audiences for domestic product, and their relative resistance or indifference to the large number of American films in their cinemas. At the time of the production of *Roman Holiday*, then, Paramount, like the rest of Hollywood, was confronted with the fact that the four major European markets were becoming increasingly important, surpassing the size of the rapidly declining American market (in terms of the number of paid admissions), yet Hollywood's share of these European markets was shrinking due to the preference of European audiences for domestic product, which was manufactured in increasing numbers by revived national film industries.

In this situation, Paramount and the other Hollywood majors began to tailor their films very precisely to European markets. This could be done, for example, by choosing European subject matter and source material for many of Hollywood's high-profile releases. This strategy is in evidence in the cycle of big-budget biblical epics starting with Paramount's *Samson and Delilah* in 1949; in the cycle of big-budget European themed musicals such as *An American in Paris* (1951); and in adaptations of classic European stories such as *Cinderella* and *King Solomon's Mines* (both 1950). It could be assumed that these European themes and sources would help to overcome the resistance of European audiences to American films, as would the presence of European stars, such as the French actress Leslie Caron in *An American in Paris*, the Austrian Hedy Lamarr in *Samson and Delilah*, and the English Deborah Kerr in *Quo Vadis?* (1951). A look at the list of the most popular female stars in Germany in the early 1950s does indeed reveal that Hollywood stars could be very popular, as long as they originally came from Europe. The most popular foreign stars were English actress Jean Simmons and Ingrid Bergman, who despite her status as a major Hollywood star was always referred to in the German press as a Swede (Garncarz 1995). Furthermore, a look at the top box-office attractions in the UK reveals not only that some of Hollywood's Europeanised productions were very successful, but also that Hollywood films made in the UK regularly became massive hits. These included *Pandora and the Flying Dutchman* (1950), Disney's *Treasure Island* (1950) and *Captain Horatio Hornblower* (1951) (Thumim 1991).

Apart from increasing the acceptability of their products in European markets, there were numerous other reasons for the major Hollywood companies to make films in Europe. The divorcement of the leading producer-distributors from their American cinema chains after 1948 initiated the dismantling of the factory-like studio system, characterised by the mass production of films carried out by technical and creative personnel on long-term contracts working in Los Angeles-based studios. The majors soon began to release staff from their long-term contracts and worked increasingly on a picture-by-picture basis, putting together production teams by hiring people only for specific films. These teams often operated as independent companies, which were financed and supervised by the major studios (Bordwell et al. 1985: 330–4). Rather than working in-house on the studios' sound stages in Hollywood, production teams could now operate anywhere in the world.

The advantages of working in Europe were manifold. First, compared to American salaries, labour costs in Europe were very low. Therefore, in so-called 'run-away' productions, key Hollywood personnel such as directors and stars would be brought to Europe to work with highly qualified but cheap European technicians and support staff. Second, due to problems with the balance of payments, European governments prevented Hollywood companies from transferring the money they earned in European cinemas back to the US. This encouraged the majors to invest frozen funds in film production in those countries. In doing so, Hollywood companies might even qualify for financial support, such as tax relief, from European governments aiming to support their domestic film industries (Guback 1969). Making European-themed films with European personnel in Europe, then, allowed the Hollywood majors both to reduce production costs and to increase the acceptability of their films in Europe.

Thus, Wyler's demands for location shooting in Rome and a European actress in the lead role for *Roman Holiday* fitted in with general industrial trends. Indeed, Italy was an excellent base for Paramount's European operations. It had the fastest-growing theatrical market in Europe, with weekly attendances increasing from 8 million in 1946 to 15 million in 1953 (Vincendeau 1995: 466). Italy also was renowned for the high quality of its technical personnel and for the massive studio complex Cinecittà in Rome. The Hollywood majors had already started producing films in Italy in 1950 with MGM's biblical epic *Quo Vadis?*. So Paramount's decision to accommodate Wyler's wishes and produce *Roman Holiday* in Italy, using both actual Roman locations and the studio facilities in Cinecittà and employing large numbers of Italian technical personnel, made perfect economic sense, as did the choice of Audrey Hepburn. In 1951 Wyler selected this relatively inexperienced and unknown actress, who had never before appeared in a Hollywood film and had never even had a major part in a successful European movie (Walker 1994, Paris 1997). Paramount agreed to Wyler's choice and immediately made her the focus of a major international publicity campaign, partly because, just like the Roman setting of the film, Hepburn was perfectly suited for Europe-wide marketing.

As we have seen, what Paramount and the other Hollywood majors were looking for in the early 1950s was a filmic product that would sell all over Europe, overcoming the resistance of European audiences to American films by offering them stories, themes and stars with which they felt a strong affinity. Despite a shared cultural heritage and shared historical experiences, audiences in different European countries had different, nationally specific preferences, and it was quite difficult to accommodate these differences in any one film. Yet there were certain stories such as 'Cinderella', certain themes such as the recent war, and certain stars such as Ingrid Bergman that transcended national boundaries, and by doing so constituted a shared and, as it were, 'integrated' European culture.

Audrey Hepburn was clearly such a border-crossing personality. As Paramount's publicity never ceased to emphasise, she was a trans-European performer, not bound by any nationality but embracing many nationalities. The daughter of a Dutch mother and an Anglo-Irish father, Hepburn had been born in Brussels in 1929, growing up in Belgium, England and the Netherlands, spending the war years under German occupation in Arnhem and starting her career in classical ballet, modelling and acting in Amsterdam, before moving on to London in 1948, where she worked on the stage in musical revues and, from 1950 onwards, as a starlet in a wide range of films. According to Paramount's publicity, during the shooting of an Anglo-French coproduction in Monte Carlo in June 1951, she was discovered by legendary French author Colette, who chose her for the lead role in the Broadway adaptation of her novel *Gigi*. What could be more European than this life and career?

Indeed, in response to Paramount's publicity campaign, which followed the signing of Hepburn for the role of Princess Ann in July 1951 and was then fuelled by the tremendous success of her Broadway debut as Gigi in November 1951, Dutch papers proudly declared in 1952 that this latest Broadway and Hollywood discovery was in fact a Dutch girl. At the same time, the British press, for whom Hepburn's nationality was clearly English, lamented the fact that the British film industry had let its most promising starlet go to Hollywood, where she would no doubt become an international superstar. Thus, Hepburn was seen to come from more than one country, and while the press in England and the Netherlands may have tried to claim original ownership of her, journalists always acknowledged that she now belonged to the world. Hepburn thus exemplified the transcendence of national boundaries in post-war Europe; she had both multiple nationalities and a transnational identity, which was perfect for Paramount's marketing of her films in Europe and helped to make her promotion a huge success. By the time the shooting of *Roman Holiday* began in June 1952, Hepburn was an international celebrity who was mobbed by the press upon her arrival in Rome. Not coincidentally, both Hepburn's transnational identity and the shared European culture which Paramount was trying to appeal to are self-consciously addressed in the iconography and story of *Roman Holiday*.

Reflections of Europe, reflections on Europe

The film's opening immediately establishes its Europeanness. The credits include an abundance of Italian names as well as the statement 'This film was photographed and recorded in its entirety in Rome, Italy.' The words are superimposed on spectacular Roman sights of monuments, ruins, squares, fountains and sculptures, which are presented to the cinema audience in the form of a mini-travelogue (a feature which was high-lighted in the accompanying publicity and in most reviews). This is followed by a mock documentary, copying the visual style and voiceover narration of the newsreels that formed an important part of cinema programmes at the time. The 'Paramount News Flash' concerns Princess Ann, 'a member of one of the oldest ruling families in Europe', who, the voiceover explains, is on a 'good-will tour of European capitals' aiming to 'cement trade relations between her country and the Western European nations'. A strong effort is made here to blur the boundary between the fictional princess and real-life royalty, to link her story to the political realities of post-war Europe, and also to show her appeal to people across Europe. The newsreel intercuts shots of Ann with documentary footage of cheering crowds in London, Paris and Rome, thus covering three of Hollywood's four major European markets, while carefully referencing the particular details of Hepburn's biography through the inclusion of Amsterdam. The newsreel begins to suggest a parallel between the actress and the character she plays, both being extraordinary and universally known and adored women, performing on the stage of a trans-European public sphere. Princess Ann's relationship with the crowds that gather everywhere she goes is offered as a model for the future relationship between Hepburn, the film star, and her fans all over Europe. In its opening sequence, then, the film announces that it will deal with the reality of European locations, political relations and royalty, while also implying that Hollywood's fictions and stars have a role to play within this reality.

The ensuing story about Princess Ann's official duties and her temporary escape from them repeatedly refers to the necessity of a move towards closer economic and political co-operation, even integration, of European nation states, a matter of intense public debate in the early 1950s. This integration, it is implied, is the best way to avoid the kind of conflict which had recently devastated the continent. The film's concern for European integration is represented most explicitly by Princess Ann's cultural mission, which she is seen to carry out at the beginning of the film and which she returns to at its end. She is on a tour across Europe to promote trade relations, a political federation and friendship between the peoples of Europe. The warm and enthusiastic welcome she receives from crowds all over Europe and also from members of the European aristocracy and from the international press corps in Rome (all played by real-life aristocrats and journalists, as the film's publicity pointed out) indicate that Princess Ann has achieved a transnational status (just like the actress who was playing her). Her very person already represents the integrated Europe that her goodwill tour promotes. And her ability to mingle and connect with common folk in Rome (after her escape from the palace) underlines her symbolic status as an integrative force, while her aborted romance with the American journalist indicates the important, yet restricted role that the US was meant to play in European relations: supportive, but ultimately detached.

The film's emphasis on the symbolic role that royalty such as Princess Ann might play in the post-war European order was highly topical. *Roman Holiday* was released in Europe in the autumn of 1953, only a short time after the coronation of Queen Elizabeth in June. The coronation had been a major news event all over Europe, the subject of widely circulated newsreels that must have looked very much like the London sequence in *Roman Holiday*'s 'News Flash'. It would seem that royalty constituted a common cultural currency in 1950s Europe which also provided an archaic bond between nation states. With European royal families closely connected through blood relations or marriage, European royalty was effectively a widespread familial network which, symbolically at least, was able to transcend national boundaries by representing a shared historical experience of past alliances and exchanges, and by offering a point of reference for imagining an integrated Europe in the future. This point of reference was represented in the film by Princess Ann.

Yet there is more to the film's engagement with the real-life symbolic role of European royalty. During the coronation of Queen Elizabeth on 2 June 1953 a tender gesture by her sister Margaret towards Group Captain Peter Townsend, which was captured by press photographers and then circulated all over Europe, revealed her scandalous affections for this commoner, who, to make matters worse, was also a divorcee (Aronson 1997). In the weeks and months following this revelation, a heated debate took place both in the UK and in the rest of Europe about the pros and cons of this romance, while the lovers themselves were forcibly separated, with Townsend being posted to Brussels. This was not the first time that Princess Margaret had made the headlines all over Europe. During an official visit to France and Italy in the spring of 1949, she had been hunted down by press photographers, who took revealing pictures of her in a swimsuit. Paramount's publicity department made the most of the connection between Princess Ann's 'Roman holiday' and the previous scandal surrounding Princess Margaret's Italian holiday, and also of the striking parallel between the doomed romance in the film and Princess Margaret's equally doomed romance in real life. Paramount publicists issued denials that the film was in any way based on the escapades of Princess Margaret, and by doing so they alerted everyone to the parallels, which resulted in reviews and articles all over Europe proclaiming that the film was, in fact, loosely based on Princess Margaret, to whom, as many commentators observed, Audrey Hepburn bore a striking semblance. In the film, of course, Princess Ann's country is never named, and judging by the costumes and behaviour of its officials and agents it would appear to be one of those 'Ruritanian' central European kingdoms which exist only in operettas. Nevertheless, the publicity for *Roman Holiday* ingeniously inserted the film's fiction into pre-existing scenarios and debates concerning real-life royalty.

The film managed to absorb the public's fascination with European royals into its reception, and also to usurp the symbolic role of royalty, by offering its female star, Audrey Hepburn, and the filmic spectacle itself as a modern version of royalty. Matching the dignity, refinement and elevated status of royals and the momentousness and glory of their public receptions and processions, in a spectacular filmic display *Roman Holiday* presented European audiences with a new and thoroughly modern princess – the film star Audrey Hepburn (who just happened to be descended from Dutch aristocracy, a fact that could always be highlighted if people were not already convinced of Hepburn's elevated status). By implication, then, the film declared that from now on it was Hollywood's role to identify and present the new European royalty and to carry out the largely symbolic duties that old royalty had had: transcending national boundaries, circulating as a common cultural currency, helping to imagine and to bring about a culturally, economically and politically integrated future Europe.

If this project succeeded, Paramount and the other Hollywood majors would reap enormous financial rewards from the successful marketing of their films in an integrated Europe. When Princess Ann, during the press reception at the end of *Roman Holiday*, expresses her 'faith in relations between people', she equates the intimate connection between her and her lover, which is also the connection between the star and her fan, with the relationship between European nation states, thus merging love, cultural consumption and European politics into one. This, I think, is a pretty good summary of what Hollywood was trying to do in its key European markets in the post-war period.

To conclude, let me admit that my argument is quite perverse, positing as it does the commercial imperatives of major American media corporations looking for integrated markets as a major contributing factor to the process of European integration. In fact, I would want to relativise this argument. First of all, like Princess Ann, Hollywood was aware of the limitations of its symbolic role in, and influence on, the economic and political developments in Europe, but, again like Princess Ann, it set its hopes in youth and the future. Princess Ann's escapades in Rome present an image of a young generation shaking off traditions and developing its own consumerist and hedonistic lifestyle, revolving around fancy hair-cuts (like Hepburn's much-imitated short hair) and fancy food such as ice cream, around mini-cars and motor-scooters, midnight dances and international travel. In the years to come, it was indeed the young generation who, through exchanges, travel and a shared popular culture, established the foundations for successful economic and political integration in Europe. Already in the 1950s Hollywood (as well as the American music industry) participated in this development by success-fully tapping into the emerging youth market in Europe, offering its films and stars as an alternative to, rather than as an extension of, traditional European culture. Second, like Gregory Peck's reporter in *Roman Holiday*, Hollywood had to come to terms with its exclusion from established European culture. The integrated European market that Hollywood envisioned in the early 1950s did soon come into existence, but not so much through the successful circulation of Hollywood films as through intra-European film trade and European coproductions, which made Toto, James Bond, spaghetti cowboys, Louis de Funes and Old Shatter-hand popular heroes over much of Europe in the 1950s and 1960s.

References

Aronson, T. (1997), *Princess Margaret: A Biography*, London, Michael O'Mara.

Bordwell, D., J. Staiger and K. Thompson (1985), *The Classical Hollywood Cinema: Film Style and Mode of Production to 1960*, London, Routledge and Kegan Paul.

Conant, M. (1978), *Antitrust in the Motion Picture Industry*, New York, Arno.

Crisp, C. (1993), *The Classic French Cinema, 1930–1960*, Bloomington, Indiana University Press.

Finler, J. (1988), *The Hollywood Story*, London, Octopus.

Garncarz, J. (1994), 'Hollywood in Germany: The role of American films in Germany', in D. W. Ellwood and R. Kroes (eds), *Hollywood in Europe: Experiences of a Cultural Hegemony*, Amsterdam, VU University Press.

Garncarz, J. (1995), 'Populäres Kino in Deutschland: Internationalisierung einer Filmkultur, 1925–1990', post-doctoral dissertation, University of Cologne (FRG).

Guback, T. H. (1969), *The International Film Industry: Western Europe and America since 1945*, Bloomington, Indiana University Press.

Harkness, J. (1994), *The Academy Awards Handbook*, New York, Pinnacle.

Herman, J. (1997), *A Talent for Trouble: The Life of Hollywood's Most Acclaimed Director*, New York, Da Capo.

Paris, B. (1997), *Audrey Hepburn*, London, Weidenfeld and Nicolson.

Steinberg, C. (1980), *Film Facts*, New York, Facts on File.

Thumim, J. (1991), 'The "popular", cash and culture in the postwar British cinema industry', *Screen*, 32, 3: 245–71.

Vincendeau, G. (ed.) (1995), *Encyclopedia of European Cinema*, London: Cassell/British Film Institute.

Wagstaff, C. (1991), 'Italian cinema in an international market', paper presented at the BFI Summer School.

Walker, A. (1994), *Audrey: Her Real Story*, London, Weidenfeld and Nicolson.

Index

(*Editors' note:* film titles are given in the form in which they appear predominantly in the text i.e. in the original *or* in translation)